Decolonizing Economics

Decolonizing the Curriculum

Anna Bernard, *Decolonizing Literature*
Devika Dutt, Carolina Alves, Surbhi Kesar & Ingrid Harvold Kvangraven, *Decolonizing Economics*
Ali Meghji, *Decolonizing Sociology*
Sarah A. Radcliffe, *Decolonizing Geography*
Robbie Shilliam, *Decolonizing Politics*
Soumhya Venkatesan, *Decolonizing Anthropology*

Decolonizing Economics

An Introduction

Devika Dutt
Carolina Alves
Surbhi Kesar
Ingrid Harvold Kvangraven

polity

The author order is randomized. All authors contributed equally to the book.

Copyright © Devika Dutt, Carolina Alves, Surbhi Kesar and Ingrid Harvold Kvangraven 2025

The right of Devika Dutt, Carolina Alves, Surbhi Kesar and Ingrid Harvold Kvangraven to be identified as Authors of this Work has been asserted in accordance with the UK Copyright, Designs and Patents Act 1988.

First published in 2025 by Polity Press

Polity Press
65 Bridge Street
Cambridge CB2 1UR, UK

Polity Press
111 River Street
Hoboken, NJ 07030, USA

ISBN-13: 978-1-5095-4547-6
ISBN-13: 978-1-5095-4548-3(pb)

A catalogue record for this book is available from the British Library.

Library of Congress Control Number: 2023939906

Typeset in 10.5 on 12.5pt Sabon
by Fakenham Prepress Solutions, Fakenham, Norfolk NR21 8NL
Printed and bound in Great Britain by Ashford Colour Ltd

The publisher has used its best endeavours to ensure that the URLs for external websites referred to in this book are correct and active at the time of going to press. However, the publisher has no responsibility for the websites and can make no guarantee that a site will remain live or that the content is or will remain appropriate.

Every effort has been made to trace all copyright holders, but if any have been overlooked the publisher will be pleased to include any necessary credits in any subsequent reprint or edition.

For further information on Polity, visit our website:
politybooks.com

To all those who came before us and paved the way. And to those who will come after.

To my mum, for helping me to be resilient. To my friends Farwa, Angus, Camila, and Carol, whose support has lifted me time and again. To my loved ones lost during the pandemic. To all the women who have crossed the age of forty. To Mark, whose boundless love has been a guiding light in my life, and to Cahal, for bringing hope and brightness into my days.
— Carol

To my dear mother, Neeru Dutt, who taught me unknowingly to never give up and be a giant pain in the neck.
— Devika

To my chosen family for unwavering sisterhood; to my mom and brothers for unconditional support; to Tom for love, patience, and nourishment; and last but not least, to my dad and grandmother who remain sources of light and inspiration.
— Ingrid

To my mumma Brij Bala, my mamu Kapil, my mentor Snehashish Bhattacharya, and my partner Ihsaan, who provided the most crucial objective conditions.
— Surbhi

Contents

Prologue: Why this book? Why now?

This project has been a long time coming. We got together to write this book back in 2019 – just as "decolonization" was about to become a buzzword. Some of us had just founded a new organization – *Diversifying and Decolonizing Economics (D-Econ)* – but our history of organizing and exchanging ideas with each other stretches further back.

We all did PhDs in Economics in self-labelled heterodox institutions: South Asian University in India, SOAS University of London in the United Kingdom, and the University of Massachusetts, Amherst and The New School in the United States. We were all interested in understanding the realities of the Global South and examining how the global economy is shaped by unequal power relations where the capitalist center is dominant. But international academic spaces, both mainstream and heterodox, were mostly oblivious to scholarship about and from the Global South and often considered it obscure or niche. We, like many other critical scholars, were faced with what felt like an overwhelming resistance to both our ideas and our identities. Even though the spaces we belonged to situated themselves as progressive, given that they specialize in radical and heterodox ideas and scholarship, many of the spaces were quite intensely sexist, racist, and elitist, and generally hostile towards South-centered scholarship. We were doing our PhDs and Post-docs during the period of #MeToo, and the #MeToo moment of Economics that was spurred on by Alice Wu's undergraduate thesis (2017) confirmed that these lived experiences were based on a broader structural problem. This book project is a step towards investigating this problem.

We were angry about the state of affairs and found ourselves raising our voices and organizing for a better community with peers across heterodox institutions, whom we met through PhD programs, summer schools, workshops, and conferences. The community we found was empowering, but also resistant to change. Nonetheless, we at least found each other and like-minded comrades and friends with whom we eventually came to form the network D-Econ.

This book is informed by our experience and research. We wish we had a book like this when we were studying economics ourselves. It lays bare how mainstream economics is Eurocentric and the implications this has for the field, including the role, the potential, and the limits of heterodox economics. We recognize that we are only scratching the surface of the relevant problems. We are all relatively early in our careers with limited experience and exposure, and so writing a book like this is probably risky. However, we also recognize that writing a definitive account of what decolonizing economics means is impossible; our perspective will necessarily be partial. This is why this book does not aim to be an exhaustive overview of scholarship on decolonization, Eurocentrism, colonialism, or imperialism in economics. It also certainly does not aim to be an encyclopedia of scholarship from the periphery or even anti-colonial or non-Eurocentric scholarship. Instead, our aim with this book is to provide our account of, and some productive ways to think about, what we believe the decolonization of economics entails, putting forward a political and scholarly argument based on our own theoretical and political training, readings, and convictions, which of course rests on an immense amount of existing scholarship. We hope readers will see it as an invitation to engage critically with our ideas, to take them further, to interrogate them, debate them, to provide alternative analyses, and to fill in the inevitable gaps. If we manage to at least push the door a bit further to open a conversation about Eurocentrism and decolonization in economics, we will be happy.

A lot has changed since we first started working on this book. One important development is that "decolonization" has now become a full-blown buzzword across the world. In the capitalist center, this has often meant liberal co-optation, reducing decolonization to issues of identity and diversity. In some parts of the periphery, decolonization has been put to nativist ends by right-wing governments. As such, calls for decolonization have become increasingly difficult to navigate conceptually and politically. We are sticking to our guns and linking decolonization to the concept of Eurocentrism, inspired by radical scholars who sought to decolonize universities in the 1970s and challenged Eurocentrism from a radical perspective in the 1980s. Because the term has now come to mean many different things, we spend more time in the book explaining what we mean by it and what we *do not* mean by it than we had initially intended.

What is striking is that earlier scholars challenging Eurocentrism in economics have been so severely marginalized by the mainstream of the discipline that most conventionally trained economists will not have heard of these arguments. We know our arguments, similarly, will be insufficient to tilt the power balance towards theorization that challenges Eurocentrism and ultimately the material conditions of capitalism, shaped by imperialism, patriarchy, and white supremacy. We hope the book will reach beyond academia and that it can be a companion to the growing dissatisfaction with economics bubbling across the globe. As we insist in the book, structural power shapes our lives and our political economy, and only a serious challenge to this power will be sufficient to fundamentally shift the status quo. As Karl Marx long ago suggested, there may be limited hope for a scientific political economy after the rise of the bourgeoisie, which means calls for the decolonization of economics will need to be accompanied by radical change in society more broadly.

We also recognize that large parts of this book are responsive and critical. We only lay the seeds for what an alternative economics would look like, both by illuminating some important anti-colonial and non-Eurocentric work from across the world and by putting forward what we believe a decolonization agenda could look like. We hope readers will take this foundation as an invitation to build more.

We are writing as a decolonization movement against occupation and apartheid in Palestine is being brutally repressed on the ground. In the midst of the unfolding genocide and Palestinians' resolute struggle against colonization, we acknowledge the inherent limitations of academic discourse, which can never compare to on-the-ground struggles. Nonetheless, we also position our intervention, with all its limits, as a call for greater awareness of the need for decolonization in both material and discursive terms, and as a support for resistance against all manifestations of oppression and power in every sphere of society.

Since we first started shaping this project, we have benefited greatly from the generosity and support of many friends and scholars. Perhaps most important is the network of like-minded and critical scholar-activists in D-Econ, including steering group members Ariane Agunsoye, Alexandra Arntsen, Bridget Diana, Aditi Dixit, Paul Gilbert, Michelle Meixieira Groenewald, Danielle Guizzo, Deepak Kumar, Cecilia Lanata-Briones, Amir Lebdioui, Farwa Sial, Narayani Sritharan, and Hanna Szymborska. We are particularly grateful to Paul Gilbert, Ndongo Samba Sylla, Matías Vernengo and two anonymous reviewers for providing very detailed and helpful comments on drafts of our manuscript and to Ihsaan Bassier and Snehashish Bhattacharya for comments on specific aspects of the book. We are indebted to the many students, friends, and colleagues who have patiently and curiously engaged with our ideas over the years and especially to the student groups across the world that continue to support and engage with our work.

We are also grateful to our editors at Polity who have been incredibly supportive and understanding, as we struggled to make the deadlines we had set ourselves as we all moved workplaces, some moved countries, dealt with the challenges of the pandemic, faced personal losses, and some finished their PhDs all during the writing of this book.

–PART I–

Eurocentrism in Economics

–1–

Introduction

While there have been repeated calls to *decolonize* the social sciences over the past half century, remarkably decolonization has only recently made its way onto the agendas of many economics associations and university committees in institutions of the capitalist center.[1] In stark contrast to the anti-colonial calls for change that originally spurred the decolonization agenda, the approach of the top echelon of the discipline has been severely limited.

By "top" we mean the institutions – departments and journals – that lead in mainstream rankings, which are ultimately defined by power hierarchies, not by any broader measures of quality or relevance (Amsler and Bolsmann, 2012; Shahjahan et al., 2017; Heckman and Moktan, 2020; Zacchia, 2021). What gets accepted as legitimate and mainstream knowledge in economics is largely decided in the top echelons of the discipline, given the power, funding, and prestige that they possess. Unsurprisingly, the way this hierarchy is produced is one of the major barriers to the decolonization of economics.

A recent intervention by the economist Dani Rodrik exemplifies well how the problem is perceived at the top of the discipline. In 2021, Rodrik wrote a short article in *Project Syndicate* reflecting on the lack of diversity within the ranks of economists, elaborated further in a research article in 2024 (Aigner et al., 2024). His concern is that power within economics is based overwhelmingly in a few departments in North America and Western Europe. He cites studies that show nearly 90 percent of authors in the top 8 economics journals are based in the United States and Western Europe (Fontana et al., 2019), while the editorial boards of the 50 highest-ranked journals are dominated by researchers based in just a few universities in the United States (Angus et al., 2021). This, Rodrik writes, demonstrates a worrying lack of representation of views of scholars based in periphery countries. In particular, he argues that insights from regions outside the United States and Western Europe are extremely important and have historically been crucial for the development of Nobel Prize-winning ideas in economics.[2]

Rodrik explains how observing sharecropping relationships in Kenya was pivotal for the Nobel-winning economist Joseph Stiglitz in developing his influential theory on asymmetric information (Stiglitz, 2001). Similarly, Albert Hirschman's time in Nigeria studying rail companies helped him develop the ideas presented in *Exit, Voice, and Loyalty* (1970). Rodrik emphasizes that when conventional wisdom in economics is confronted by "anomalous" behavior in "unfamiliar" contexts, economic theory is greatly enriched. While Rodrik's (2021) categorization of much of the world outside of the United States and Western Europe as "anomalous" and "unfamiliar" is not meant with malintent, it reveals that the conventional wisdom in economics is founded primarily on how economies of the capitalist center are thought to function – though they encompass only the minority of the world's population. What counts as the dominant thinking and scholarship in economics today developed on the canvas of the capitalist center's economies, as if they were the global norm. Further, the canvas seems to have been painted in isolation, to which the history of global capitalism, colonialism, or the Transatlantic Slave Trade was just an additional, primitive, or incidental backdrop.

Rodrik's observations are welcome, but they are symptomatic of the limits of mainstream economics. Specifically,

economics has been and continues to be fundamentally
challenged from many angles and corners of the world.
Scholarship centered on the periphery presents crucial alternatives to the dominant economics paradigm, but it tends to
be ignored and even suppressed. The dominant economics
framework only considers how economies in the periphery
are aberrant vis-à-vis the center; and alternate theoriza-
tions from the vantage point of the periphery are summarily
discarded. This reflects a deep-seated ideological bias against,
and systematic exclusion of, alternative ways of making sense
of the world. Rodrik's observations are also symptomatic of
self-reflection within the field, which only focuses on certain
unequal outcomes instead of digging deeper into structural
processes of exclusion, of which the lack of diversity is
merely a symptom.

The power and powerlessness of economics

Two distinct definitions can be employed to describe
economics. One is a broad definition, referring to research
on how economic processes are structured, how they interact
with various social and natural processes, and what they
reveal about our social systems (e.g., H.-J. Chang, 2014). This
understanding includes research from across the globe and
from all theoretical traditions that deal with questions related
to the economy. The other is a narrower definition, characterizing economics as primarily concerned with allocation
of resources for the most efficient production in the face of
scarce resources and the need to optimize human behavior to
achieve efficient outcomes – or, as Robbins (1932, p. 15) puts
it, economics is "the science which studies human behavior
as a relationship between ends and scarce means which have
alternative uses." Typically, this second definition is consistent
with the theories and practices that guide dominant research
and teaching. Even when non-economic dimensions, such as
social identity or natural interactions, are explored within
the economics discipline, they are only explored within this
framing. When we refer to today's mainstream or dominant

economics, we are referring to approaches consistent with this definition.

This dominant school of thought is called "neoclassical economics" and its more contemporary variation is "late neoclassical economics" (Madra, 2017).[3] This framework has been the most powerful in shaping how economists, as well as people, generally think about the world. Its dominance reflects how the economics discipline has changed over time from being more consistent with the broader definition to a more exclusive focus on this narrow definition. This development involved writing off all ways of approaching economic questions that are inconsistent with late neoclassical economics. The narrowing has obscured contestations surrounding economic thinking and concealed competing theoretical frameworks that often provide different answers to economic questions, such as Marxist or Keynesian theories. Furthermore, the rise to dominance of (late) neoclassical economics is related to ideological and political developments (Resnick and Wolff, 2006). Late neoclassical economics imposes constraints on what economic analysis can ask and achieve, relegating debates about a society's values, goals, and aspirations to a realm beyond economic theory.

The power of economic thinking in shaping conventional wisdom and policymaking

It is presented as natural and intuitive in mainstream economics that competing ends and scarce means guide our lives and economies. The idea is that there are constraints on human behavior when, through a constrained optimization approach, we make choices by weighing their costs and benefits. Businesses and governments are also seen to operate in this way. In her recent book, Elizabeth Popp Berman highlights how the "economic way of reasoning" pervaded economic policymaking in the United States between 1965 and 1985 (Berman, 2022, p. 3). She argues that this style of policymaking is centered around two main features: a deep attachment to markets as efficient allocators of resources and an emphasis on efficiency as the measure of a good policy.

And why shouldn't it be? Isn't achieving a particular policy goal in the most cost-effective manner an unequivocal good? It is likely that most people would agree with this sentiment, reflecting the power of economics. It shows that economic thinking does not only impact how economists themselves think but has also come to pervade what is considered conventional wisdom (Galbraith, 1998).

Although economic ways of thinking have been fundamentally normalized, they are not natural, obvious, or politically neutral (Berman, 2022). The value of efficiency is a political notion that displaces other values, such as equity (Knafo et al., 2019). In economics, efficiency in the context of production means producing the most profitable goods or services at the minimum possible cost. In general, an efficient allocation of resources across competing ends or competing interest is one that cannot be changed without making someone worse off. The value of efficiency in economic thinking obfuscates the political nature of the process behind identifying what the goals of an economic policy should be and the parameters on which efficiency is measured. This way of thinking has been institutionalized in governments and international policy organizations (Charusheela, 2005; Fourcade, 2009).

For example, policymakers shifted from thinking of pollution as a menace to the natural environment to considering it an externality that is simply not properly priced by the market (Işıkara, 2023), or from thinking of healthcare as a universal right to concentrating on its most efficient and cost-effective delivery, which meant the introduction of means-testing and cost-sharing (Berman, 2022). This economic reasoning not only valorizes efficiency, but also delegitimizes competing ways of thinking about economic policy (Marglin, 1974). While there are many different approaches to public service provision (e.g., universal access) and many ways to govern such institutions (e.g., democratic collective action), the way economics frames the problem rules out these alternatives from the get-go (Auerbach and Skott, 2022).

While economic thinking affects policymaking, policy institutions also create a demand for a particular kind of economics, thus creating a mutually reinforcing relationship (Bayliss et al., 2011). There is ample evidence of the dominance of mainstream economists and mainstream economic ways of thinking in policymaking institutions across the globe both in international institutions (Rao and Woolcock, 2007; Mueller, 2011) and in governments across the periphery (e.g., Babb, 2001; Mkandawire, 2014; Cohn, 2021). Given that mainstream economics emphasizes competitive markets and the freedom of exchange, the high concentration of one way of thinking and structural exclusion of critical scholars and scholarship from positions of influence is revealing. In fact, there has been a "high and rising" concentration of Nobel Prize winners in a handful of top US universities; more than half their combined career time has been spent at just eight economics departments (Freeman et al., 2024, p. 1). This is while concentration in other disciplines, from natural sciences to the humanities, is going the other way. As Rao and Woolcock (2007, p. 480) put it, referring to the monopoly of economists in the World Bank's research think tank, this "is deeply ironic, since a core tenet of economic policy is to point out the collective benefits that accrue from the absence of monopolies."

The power of economics in shaping the world

Economists do not simply observe the world but help shape how we understand and approach it (Mitchell, 2007). This is not to say that economics constructs the world or that the global economy is not underpinned by material political economy forces. Instead, it suggests that economics helps to shape institutions, policies, and state priorities. Often, it legitimizes the hierarchies embedded in the economic system by providing us with a particular worldview that naturalizes inequalities or, at times, even prefers them (Christophers, 2014).[4]

A striking example is the debate over caste-based affirmative action in India. Historically, the Indian population was divided into various socioeconomic groups or *jatis*, with certain population groups kept from accessing resources and subjected to social marginalization by the dominant ones (Ambedkar, 2014). For administrative purposes, *jatis* were categorized into four caste categories based on their degree of economic and social marginalization, comprising Dalits that were the most economically and socially marginalized; scheduled tribes, comprising the indigenous population groups; other Backward castes; and the forward or the socioeconomically most privileged castes. Caste-based affirmative action has been instituted in the Indian constitution in an effort to undo the historical and ongoing structural oppression and marginalization of the marginalized castes. Yet, concerns of efficiency have become so ingrained in public thinking that social and policy debates in India have been tilted *against* affirmative action, citing concerns about the inefficient allocation of resources stemming from such policies (Chandrachud, 2023). Even studies that examine caste and equity concerns are limited to identifying the outcome and opportunity gaps between different caste groups, addressing efficiency concerns, and/or examining the role of caste networks in facilitating upward mobility (Deshpande, 2011; Asher at al., 2024). Structural forces and power dynamics that perpetuate and shape caste-based inequities (Teltumbde, 2010b; 2018; De Neve, 2012; Jodhka, 2017; S. Bhattacharya and Kesar, 2024) are largely absent in mainstream accounts, as are concerns about equity if there is a tradeoff with efficiency.

Consider another example: the World Bank program between 1992 and 1994 in Peru which provided formal property titles to hundreds of thousands of households in informal settlements, assuming this would increase households' access to formal credit (Mitchell, 2005). While the World Bank's own study found no evidence of its original hypothesis, the authors observed that the adults in households with formal titles to their homes were now spending more hours outside the home in paid employment as compared to those without formal titles. They supposed this must have been a result of private property rights. Consequently, the authors argued that the provision of private property rights allowed adults to spend more hours working as they no longer had to defend their property from theft. While the hypothesis was not backed up by any credible evidence, and several scholars have pointed out catastrophic flaws even on the narrow technical terms of the research design, the World Bank study is popular and widely cited. It confirmed one of the tenets of mainstream economic theory, namely that securing private property rights drives efficiency, growth, and development (Fine and Milonakis, 2009).

It is not that the authors of the World Bank study discovered an unintended consequence of the property titling program. Rather the new hypothesis was already sought after within the development economics field in that period, despite scant evidence to support it (Mitchell, 2005). The study did not consider alternative theories or methods to find an explanation, which might have led them to consider the role of structural factors or macroeconomic conditions that impact why people may increase their working hours. Furthermore, the study contributed to solidifying the use of natural experiments for studying problems of development, to the detriment of other quantitative or qualitative methods.

This understanding of private property rights as a key condition for development gained prominence in the 1980s and 1990s – when it became increasingly clear that free market policies associated with the Structural Adjustment Programs (SAPs) promoted by international financial institutions (IFIs) had not stimulated growth and reduced poverty in the periphery. Within IFIs, scholars and policymakers determined that it is institutions that are indispensable for market reforms (Krueger, 2004). A theoretical tradition within mainstream economics that emphasizes property rights and transaction costs in market economies, known as New Institutional Economics, became prominent. Notably, within this theoretical tradition, the failings of market economies are pinned on imperfect institutional arrangements that do not adequately support capital accumulation (North, 1991; de Soto, 2000). This shift in theoretical and political orientation buttressed market-oriented policy prescriptions accompanied by policies to develop secure private property rights, as the assumption was that strengthening private property rights would help existing markets work more efficiently. Policies associated with New Institutional Economics were then rolled out across the periphery as a part of International Monetary Fund (IMF) and World Bank programs (KS and Fine, 2006). This development is part of the paradigm known as the post-Washington Consensus (Fine, 2006).

However, studies from outside mainstream economics have shown that strengthening private property rights does not facilitate market transactions in a neutral manner and that private property rights may not even be the best means to support growth-enhancing reforms, even if that may be a worthwhile goal. Property arrangements impact the power balance between social groups where these reforms are implemented, rather than simply facilitating market transactions. For example, the institution of private property in agriculture in India through the British colonial government's land title system allowed dominant caste groups to maneuver the new formal written ownership to their benefit at the expense of marginalized caste groups, who lost ownership claims to the land on which they were dependent (Ilaiah, 1990). Furthermore, awarding property titles to tribal populations for the common land on which they depend for their liveli-hoods – which brings this land within the ambit of market exchange – opens the land to private takeovers given the lower power that the tribal population can wield in such exchanges (R. Bhattacharya et al., 2017). Supporting the development of private property rights without considering the political economy of production and land distribution can thus have devastating consequences for vulnerable popula-tions (Nyamu-Musembi, 2007; Joireman, 2008).

The assumption within New Institutional Economics that strong private property rights are needed for economic development is often supported by the observation that industrialized countries today have strong property rights (H.-J. Chang, 2001). However, countries that are industri-alized today did not have strong property rights when they were industrializing but acquired them after or at a later stage of industrialization (H.-J. Chang, 2001; M. H. Khan, 2012). Property rights were also, ironically, created all over the world through large-scale dispossession and enclosure of common or indigenous land. Therefore, there are arguably better ways to uncover the historical character of institutional forms of capitalist development and provide better empirical explanations of uneven capitalist development (Ankarloo, 2002; Grinberg, 2018; Ince, 2022a). IFI policy prescriptions continue to be founded on strong property rights despite evidence that suggests that property rights do not in themselves explain uneven development. Furthermore, even when property rights are a top priority, equitable ownership of land resources and massive land redistributions are not on the radar, even if these can enhance access to productive resources for marginalized populations.

Not only does economics shape how we understand and approach the world through its theories and practices, but its hegemonic position also displaces other ways of reasoning. Alternative ways of imagining and organizing the global economy have always existed, although they do not get recognition at the top of the discipline. For example, in the 1970s, anti-colonial leaders across the periphery responded to an intensified post-colonial predicament with their most ambitious project of worldmaking – the New International Economic Order (NIEO), which was adopted by the United Nations General Assembly in May 1974. NIEO laid out ambitious proposals to end colonialism and dependency and to implement global redistribution and global welfarism (Nyerere, 1977; Amin, 1982). The NIEO's policy proposals recognized the immense inequalities produced by colonialism and imperialism and laid out principles that challenged the dominance of global capital. While these may seem like completely reasonable demands given these countries' experience with colonialism and desire for control over their development, they are difficult to fit into the theoretical frames of mainstream economics as they are premised on challenging structural power. However, not only was the NIEO incompatible with the dominant economics paradigm, it was, crucially, also not in line with the prevailing global power dynamics and global class structures supporting the status quo at the time, and therefore did not achieve its stated aims of redistributing power and resources (Amin, 1984; Ogle, 2014; Styve and Gilbert, 2023). Such drastic challenges to the status quo are hardly taught or studied within the mainstream of the discipline, despite their importance for understanding uneven power structures.

The power of economics in shaping social sciences: the imperialism of economics

Economics spreads its methods and theoretical frameworks to other disciplines as well. Boulding (1969) called this economics *imperialism* (see also Lazear, 2000; Fine and Milonakis, 2009). Edward Lazear (2000) argued that the spread reflects the superiority of economics, given that its rigorous and generalizable toolbox can be used to address a wide variety of questions both inside and outside economics. He argued that by using a particular mathematical language, researchers can strip away complexity to see what is essential in a rigorous and precise manner. As such, economics has allegedly experienced resounding success in explaining everything from consumer theory, discrimination in the labor market, and the household division of labor, to religion, the firm, law, and political economy. Despite the spread of economic ideas to other disciplines through economics imperialism, other disciplines have not had the same impact on economics (Fourcade et al., 2015; Angrist et al., 2020).

From an economist's perspective, other social sciences, like sociology, anthropology, and political science, are great at identifying interesting questions and problems through rich descriptions but are unable to provide satisfactory answers due to the absence of rigorous cost–benefit analysis in their arsenal. According to Lazear (2000), the answers economists provide to these questions are the most scientific:

Economics has been successful because, above all, economics is a science. The discipline emphasizes rational behavior, maximization, trade-offs, and substitution, and insists on models that result in equilibrium. Economists are pushed to further inquiry because they understand the concept of efficiency. Inefficient equilibria beg for explanation and suggest that there may be gaps in the underlying models that created them. (Lazear, 2000, p. 142)

However, the answers that economics provides are only satisfying within the parameters of a specific form of economic reasoning, and within values normalized by economics. At the beginning of their education, students of economics are told to distinguish between positive statements in economics, that is, the description and quantification of the world as it is, and normative statements, that is, value judgments of the world as it should be. This completely misses that the theoretical frame through which economics approaches the world is normative and itself underpinned by ideology. Each framework constructs its own perspective of the world and understands realities accordingly. Economics thus obscures or is oblivious to the politics embedded in theorization itself. According to Lerner (1972, p. 259), "economics gained the title of Queen of the Social Sciences by choosing solved political problems as its domain." In this book we return political questions to the heart of economic theorizing.

The powerlessness of economics

Lazear (2000) argues that stripping away complexity to put questions into mathematically precise and analytically rigorous frameworks is the strength of economics. It is how economics generates core theoretical insights that are testable and falsifiable. However, this obsession has come at a cost. These frameworks may be mathematically precise, but are they always the most relevant for understanding reality (Mayer, 1992)? This is questionable, as the frameworks do not recognize the power dynamics underpinning the economic structures and social processes in which interactions take place.

By ignoring the dynamics of social structures that do not easily fit into a cost–benefit or optimization framework, economics provides limited and often wrong answers. A stark example is how economics deals with – or does not adequately deal with – power. It is not that neoclassical economists ignore all kinds of power. Rather, they tend only to think about market power (Palermo, 2007) – the sway one individual or firm holds over another, and that can (and ideally should) be done away with to ensure more competitive markets. While this is better than not considering power at all, it ignores structural power. That is, it does not deal with ways in which society is organized to *structurally* shape the economy.

Neoclassical economists understand power as one individual, firm, or group exerting influence over another due to imperfections or incompleteness in markets, or due to institutions not functioning smoothly. They take for granted the deep structure of economic production and how society is organized. For example, they take the differential endowments – capital versus labor – as given. However, the way production is organized, such that the ownership of the product and profit lies with the capitalist and not the wage work, is a key source of structural power (Resnick and Wolff, 2006). The discipline similarly ignores how class structures the economy and society and downplays the processes that created social arrangements to begin with, including capitalism, racialization, patriarchy, and imperialism.

Given its privileged status as the go-to profession for providing policy solutions for social, political, and economic problems (D. Hirschman and Berman, 2014), ignoring structural power means that economics is helping to maintain it. It legitimizes a belief system where structural power is not important or perhaps not scientifically measurable. This is a serious problem given how structural power permeates and governs the conditions of lives and livelihoods that we normalize, the ideologies we internalize, and what we can even dare to question. The field's neglect of structural power, or inability or unwillingness to properly theorize it is also, simply put, bad for economics in its quest to be a rigorous social science (Harding, 1995; Hartsock, 2006; Kvangraven and Kesar, 2023).

Eurocentrism, colonization, and decolonization of economics

The discussion about the political nature of the discipline and its colonial foundations allows us to consider a specific characteristic of the discipline: Eurocentrism. Although Eurocentrism is deeply embedded in the economics discipline, it largely remains ignored. Discussions of it are relegated to the discipline's margins.

Eurocentrism and the colonization of economics

Eurocentrism is a view of the world that positions a partial and mythical experience of the development of capitalism in Western European as central, interpreting all other phenomena only in relation to it. The myth is that capitalism developed endogenously in Western Europe through improvements in technologies, hard-work, and rationality associated with the Enlightenment (Amin, 2009 [1988]). This myth distracts from the violent processes of exploitation, expropriation, and change in social relations that underpinned the development of capitalism (Brenner, 1976; U. Patnaik, 1990; Chatterjee, 1993; E. M. Wood, 2000; Wynter, 2003). It also distracts from the role of imperialism, racialization, caste, and patriarchy, which sustained, and continue to sustain, capitalism (Gibson-Graham, 2006; Teltumbde, 2010a, 2010b; Inikori, 2020). It neglects the concrete historical role that colonialism and the Transatlantic Slave Trade played in shaping capitalism and the enrichment of the capitalist center at the expense of the periphery (Du Bois, 1935; Williams, 1944; Rodney, 1972).

In Eurocentric theory, this distorted understanding of capitalist development comes to represent an idealized essence (Lazarus, 2011). Eurocentric social and economic theory universalized the view by expecting capitalism everywhere to evolve in this same manner – endogenously through improved rationalities, efficiencies, and technologies (Meek, 1976). This means that the wealth of nations is thought to arise from a rational process of expanding free markets, free trade, and capitalist institutions. This is a *teleological* view of history, where an idealized view of the capitalist center represents the end of history, while the countries of the periphery are at an earlier stage. History, it is assumed, will push them steadily ahead to eventually reach the same stage as the center (A. Sen, 1983; Zein-Elabdin, 2011). This Eurocentric universalization leads to epistemological errors with crucial political implications.

Our understanding of Eurocentrism is intrinsically linked with the development of capitalism, and not with a geographical location. The Europe in Eurocentrism is really about the elevation of the capitalist center more generally – a metaphorical Europe – as the essence of capitalism, while everywhere else is perceived as an aberration ("anomaly," as per Rodrik) that is expected to transform along the lines of this metaphorical Europe with growth and development. Thus, economics as a discipline was born Eurocentric because its theories implicitly or explicitly assumed this teleology. On this Eurocentric, depoliticized foundation, economics puts forward a set of principles, laws, and theoretical assumptions about human and firm behavior, macroeconomic dynamics, and institutions. Economic theory forms the ideological basis for a global material project that has also shaped capitalism itself (Amin, 2009 [1988]).

This understanding of Eurocentrism helps us examine how economics creates categorical hierarchies, often presented in the form of binaries, where deviations from the norm are consistently evaluated in relation to an idealized Eurocentric expectation of how capitalism, capitalist institutions, and rational actors operate. In this approach, the capitalist center is understood as the idealized embodiment of capitalism rather than a specific world region. Peripheries, often shaped by dispossession to facilitate capitalist growth in the center, are perceived as aberrations to be fixed by imitating the center (Sanyal, 2007; Kesar and Bhattacharya, 2020). The periphery is understood only in contrast to the center, characterized by what it lacks or how it deviates from the capitalist norm – reflected, for example, in its cultures, traditions, institutions, and failure to be adequately capitalist (Hobson, 2012; Pierre, 2012; Inayatullah and Blaney, 2015). This dichotomy extends to identities as well. Identities in economics, when considered, are also understood only in relation to the idealized rational economic agent who is assumed to be male, white, ahistorical, and autonomous from social structures (Nelson, 1995; Kaul, 2007). By limiting itself to such a Eurocentric understanding of reality, economic theory fails not only to provide good explanations for uneven development, but also to provide good explanations for economic and social phenomena *within* the capitalist center itself, including issues of capitalist exploitation, racialization and patriarchy that shape economic processes.

While these Eurocentric features were foundational even in much of classical political economy in the eighteenth and nineteenth centuries, scientific enquiry was then more open for debate, including about turbulent dynamics of the capitalist system and class struggle (Blaney, 2020). However, as capitalism became globally dominant, the space for debates that did not take capitalism to be the optimal system were increasingly marginalized. Simultaneously, the formation of strict disciplinary boundaries in social sciences also contributed to the narrowing of economics. The contours of inquiry, then, came to be shaped not by the issue, but by the discipline's tools and frameworks. This led to the formal creation of the economics discipline, in which Eurocentric frameworks became dominant,[5] squeezing out non-Eurocentric, anti-colonial, anti-imperialist, and what would eventually become known as heterodox scholarship in the 1960s (Blaug, 2003; F. S. Lee, 2009) – the latter being used to refer to economics that is not based on the theoretical and methodological foundations of today's hegemonic mainstream. In this way, economics became a *colonizing discipline*.[6]

Eurocentric ideas not only become the dominant form of reasoning in the discipline, but Eurocentric theorization and methodologies are increasingly presented as neutral. As we shall see in this book, this Eurocentric style of economic reasoning has been used to legitimize colonial interventions as well as to legitimize support for military coups against left-wing socialist or social democratic governments in economies of the newly independent periphery, to ensure that the newly independent governments rather served the economic interests of the capitalist class, including the US – the dominant capitalist superpower. This often-violent political process was also accompanied by a parallel discursive process in higher education, which involved purging Marxist, institutional and Keynesian economists from economics departments in the 1950s, 1960s, and 1970s. Today, economics is hierarchically structured to exclude alternative economic thought, often making the reproduction of Eurocentric thinking and colonial structures more covert.

Many mainstream economists may take issue with our characterization, arguing that economics has grown beyond the consensus that free markets, free trade, and capitalist institutions are the be-all and end-all of economic theory. And they are not entirely wrong: mainstream economic theory has come a long way from the neoclassical economics of the 1970s. Nonetheless, it has retained its core Eurocentric features that only allow for studying limited deviations from it. One important development, for example, is that the field has taken an *empirical turn*, which has led many economists to see their work as atheoretical, neutral, or simply empirical (Angrist and Pischke, 2010; Kvangraven, 2020). Much of the recent change in economics has in fact emerged from decades of empirical research backed by extensive resources put toward refuting some aspects of dominant economic theory. However, the search for more and better data may serve to distract from problems with the underlying theoretical framework and rather reinforce it (McGoey, 2017).

Another development is that there have been important extensions, deviations, and developments within neoclassical economics itself (Colander et al., 2004; Dequech, 2007–8; Madra, 2017). However, despite many studies convincingly challenging many orthodox neoclassical assumptions from the inside, a lot of the core has remained intact, and variants of neoclassical orthodoxy still dominate economics teaching and research globally, especially at the undergraduate level, which has the widest audience. Even in the most innovative corners of the top of the discipline, the framework has remained quite resistant to fundamental changes. As Colander et al. put it back in 2004,

> modern mainstream economics is open to new approaches, as long as they are done with a careful understanding of the strengths of the recent orthodox approach and with a modelling methodology acceptable to the mainstream. (Colander et al., 2004, p. 492)

To publish in economics journals and contribute to knowledge within its disciplinary boundaries, one must do it in mainstream terms. We must keep answering the questions and puzzles of mainstream theory, which are necessarily limiting. This is compounded by the exclusionary dynamics and structural hierarchies within the discipline, which keep it a predominantly white, male, and elitist profession of scholars from the capitalist center. If mainstream economics was willing to consider alternative theoretical frameworks as legitimate alternatives, take seriously values outside of the parameters of mainstream economic theory, and take critiques of Eurocentrism seriously, perhaps not so much time, resources, and energy would have been spent trying to fix or explain the shortcomings of the dominant theoretical framework.

For or against decolonization?

At the time of writing, *decolonization* has become a buzzword in academia, which some see as a trope used to perform "morality" or "authenticity" (Táíwò, 2022, p. 4). Many scholars are in the business of decolonizing curricula, teaching, research, seminars, or even themselves (Shringarpure, 2020). However, in many instances, there does not appear to be careful thought behind what it means to decolonize this or that (Larsen, 2022). At the very least, the thought process in many spaces is not evident.

Movements to decolonize social theory, universities, and economics

The call to decolonize the social sciences or the university is around half a century old (Bhambra et al., 2018; Ndlovu-Gatsheni, 2023). It can be traced back at least to the period immediately after African countries gained independence, when a range of institutions were set up across the continent in the spirit of decolonizing the university and creating alternate narratives to Eurocentrism (Olukoshi, 2006; Mamdani, 2016). Shortly after, in the 1970s and 1980s, Latin American and Asian, as well as African, intellectuals made explicit efforts toward decolonizing the social sciences and challenging Eurocentrism in social theory (e.g., Stavenhagen, 1971; Oteiza, 1978; Ake, 1979; C. Kay, 1989; P. Patnaik, 1997; Amin, 2009 [1988]). At the same time, the post-colonial tradition was being developed, largely in Europe and North America, as social scientists examined how European modernity had formed part of a larger hegemonic colonial discourse and how this had impacted knowledge production (Said, 1979; Bhabha, 1983; Spivak, 1988). This led to a period of significant intellectual transformation in the social sciences and humanities, with scholars in disciplines such as history, philosophy, literature, and politics scrutinizing how their disciplines have been informed by worldviews and assumptions that justified colonial rule (Sabaratnam, 2017; Bhambra et al., 2018).

While calls to decolonize the university, along with many anti-colonial movements, have never fully faded, they gained renewed widespread attention with the Rhodes Must Fall student movement in 2015, which was originally directed against a statue of Cecil Rhodes on the University of Cape Town campus, and which ended up reverberating across the world, including in Britain (Ndlovu-Gatsheni, 2018). Since then, there have been protests internationally against how social sciences and universities address legacies of colonialism, structural inequalities, and white supremacy, including campaigns against caste prejudice in India (Economic and Political Weekly, 2021), student debates on the curriculum in South Africa (Bassier, 2016), and the "Why is My Curriculum White?" student campaign in Britain (Gopal, 2021).

However, it was only when the public protests in the US escalated following the murder of George Floyd in 2020 – and the violence of structural racism reached mainstream news channels in the capitalist center – that a greater number of economists started to raise concerns publicly about the discipline's lack of attention to racial inequities. This led to a Black Lives Matter (BLM) moment for economics, although the debates so far have been narrowly focused on incorporating questions about race into existing frameworks that do not have the capacity to deal with structural power and racism. Unsurprisingly, without many satisfactory answers to questions about enduring processes of racialization and violence, many Black economists have denounced how poorly economics has dealt with racialization and systemic racism (Spriggs, 2020). While BLM for economics is an important development, it is telling that it was only after the issue of structural racism reached the mainstream news in the capitalist center that it became a conversation in the top of the profession.

Decolonizing economics: our view

The decolonization of economics, as we envision it, departs from any framework that considers as its starting point an idealized experience of endogenous capitalist development in the capitalist center and makes sense of realities only in relation to it. It challenges a teleological view of capitalist development and unravels the apparatus of power through which the center–periphery dichotomies are constructed and legitimized. Capitalist and colonial exploitation created these hierarchies, which were then legitimized through colonial and racist discourses that can be identified in the conceptual categories and frameworks of the economics discipline. The categories and frameworks reinforce such hierarchies

(Charusheela, 2013). We understand a *decolonization agenda* to be one that opens space for exposing the categories, studying them, and challenging them to put forward alternative explanations for existing hierarchies and unequal economic outcomes.

More concretely, decolonizing economics means dismantling the dominance of Eurocentric theories, methodologies, and approaches in the discipline and challenging the structural exclusions that support and legitimize Eurocentrism, and in turn, capitalism and imperialism. This necessarily entails shaking the pedestal of neutrality that economists claim to speak from, while deconstructing the hierarchies of the field and the world that have allowed Eurocentrism to remain hegemonic. Our goal is to topple this pedestal entirely.

This is not simply a project geared toward understanding the periphery better, but one geared toward understanding global realities. As has long been recognized by anti-colonial scholars, exploitative conditions established through colonialism boomerang back to the former colonizers, as they bring practices of repression home and as their violence ultimately has global implications (Césaire, 1950).[7] Colonization is simply not something that was done to countries of the periphery long ago. It has had implications for people everywhere and is crucial for understanding global processes. Moreover, capitalism as an economic system is global in nature – both in its origins and its dynamics. For example, the availability of cheap labor in peripheral economies impacts the decision of capital to relocate to these economies, which in turn impacts the jobs available in the center and labor's bargaining power. We cannot understand any part of the world in isolation, given the interconnectedness of social, political, and economic processes. An economics that does not consider the dynamics in the periphery in their understanding of global capitalism, and rather relegates them to aberrations, is incomplete.

In making the dynamics of capitalism and structural oppression central to our discussion of the colonization and decolonization of economics, our agenda also contends with hierarchies of gender, class, caste, and race, both within and between the economies of the center and periphery, and the role global capitalist dynamics plays in sustaining and legitimizing these hierarchies. This means going beyond both methodological individualism and methodological nationalism – the notions that individuals and nation-states, respectively, are the most relevant units of analysis – when trying to understand the world. A decolonization agenda focuses rather on structural power, and it must fundamentally depart from nationalist thought, given that the nation-state category is based on a Eurocentric understanding of the world (Chatterjee, 1986).

The decolonization of economics is both a discursive and a materialist project. The first involves opening space for theoretical starting points that include non-Eurocentric frameworks and a vantage point that includes the periphery (Harding, 1995; Amin, 2010), exposing the biases necessarily involved in devising research questions, centering relations of power and domination that allow for understanding structural processes of oppression, and exposing and challenging Eurocentric theory.

The materialist project requires dismantling the concentration of power in economics localized in the capitalist center and addressing the widespread structural discrimination in the discipline. This entails challenging existing structures related to teaching, research evaluation, rankings, citation practices, hiring practices, journals, funding practices, and more. However, we must acknowledge that the project of decolonizing economics cannot be achieved without also shifting the balance of power in the world more generally, as knowledge production is supported by and supports society's existing power hierarchies. The decolonization of economics, then, ultimately becomes an anti-imperialist project along with a radical critique of and challenge to power in all its forms and manifestations.

Since many of us work at universities, which play an important role in shaping our understanding of the world, we consider the importance of *decolonizing the university*. While some scholars see such efforts as a domestication of the concept of decolonization, as decolonization is fundamentally a violent process that entails repatriation of land (Tuck and Yang, 2012), we take a different view. Movements for the repatriation of land and dismantling the global imperialist infrastructure are certainly crucial for any decolonization agenda, but universities were also historically important sites through which colonialism and dispossession were institutionalized and naturalized (Pietsch, 2013; Steinmetz, 2014). Universities continue to shape conventional wisdom, training young minds, and legitimizing certain ideas. Therefore, the process of decolonization involves universities too. Indeed, the economics discipline can itself be considered a "child of imperialism," given that the economic interests of the capitalist class shaped the theories of political economy that developed in the elite universities of the capitalist center, which were eventually exported to the whole world (U. Patnaik, 2022, p. 334).

The decolonization of a university is not only about challenging Eurocentrism in the curriculum or research, or about reclaiming space for critical thinking (Eagleton, 2015). Universities must also be held accountable as political actors. Decolonization involves repatriation of profits from colonialism and the Transatlantic Slave Trade that many universities built their wealth on. It involves challenging ways in which universities support imperialism and colonialism today, through contracts with the military, consultancies, and government institutions. The ongoing Boycott-Divest-Sanction (BDS) movement in support of Palestine against the State of Israel is an important effort in this direction. It calls for universities to divest from Israeli businesses and sanction Israeli universities that support the occupation, as ways to put pressure to end the apartheid regime and universities' complicity in supporting it.

Faced with the neoliberal universities of today, it may be difficult to imagine that universities have historically also been spaces where students and scholars organized to resist oppressive and colonial structures, both in the capitalist center and the periphery (Gilmore, 2022). One example is the Casa dos Estudantes do Império (House of Students from the

Empire) in Lisbon, Portugal, which the Bissau-Guinean and Cape Verdean anti-colonial leader Amílcar Cabral attended, and which brought together Black students to read, think, and organize collectively about Empire and resistance (Castelo and Jerónimo, 2017). Various colleges of Delhi universities in India were also important sites of student organization against the British colonial state. Even today, student movements in universities in India, including Jawaharlal Nehru University and Jamia Milia Islamia university, posed a strong opposition to the current political regime's anti-Muslim policies (Yassir, 2024). To decolonize the university entails working to make it possible for universities to be liberatory public spaces for resistance.

What decolonization is not

Decolonization cannot be reduced to a box-checking exercise or to efforts to improve diversity (although such efforts are important in their own right). We agree with Olúfẹ́mi Táíwò in his *Against Decolonisation* book (2022) on that point – we do not refer to increasing diversity as a process of decolonization. Scholars from marginalized backgrounds or the periphery may be equally Eurocentric as a white man from the capitalist center, so improving diversity will not necessarily lead to decolonization.

Decolonization also does not mean simply celebrating pre-modern or pre-colonial institutions, or any institutions, ideas, or scholarship simply because they are from outside the capitalist center. Privileging scholarship simply because of its location can easily work against decolonization, as it may be (and has been) co-opted by nativist forces interested in upholding rather than dismantling hierarchies (A. Lewis and Lall, 2024).[8] While decolonization necessarily requires critical reflexivity in teaching and research, which includes attentiveness to the researcher's own location within structures of power and to the politics of knowledge production (Charusheela, 2013), it does not mean uncritically judging research based on the researcher's identity. Nonetheless, a decolonization agenda involves exposing how economics legitimizes the oppression and marginalization of researchers from certain groups and the adoption of certain frameworks.

The vantage point of theorization is also critical for a decolonization agenda. Certain vantage points are more amenable to revealing certain realities and understandings. This is not to be confused with relativism (i.e., all vantage points are not equal): a decolonization agenda is anti-relativist (Charusheela, 2004), since it prioritizes entry points that allow us to uncover and expose oppressive structures and relations, wherever they occur, be it on a global scale or within the periphery. In line with this, decolonization means working toward a universalism that allows us to see capitalism as a global, albeit uneven, system shaped by structural power, and that can replace the Eurocentric faux universalism that characterizes economics today. We need theoretical frameworks that are amenable to capturing dynamics of the periphery as a part of the general dynamics of a totality, instead of being treated as aberrations that do not align with the center.

Reflections of structural exclusions in economics: Identifying the missing link

Economics has only recently started seriously grappling with its lack of diversity and discrimination, despite this problem being well known for decades (Bayer and Rouse, 2016). Initiatives to improve diversity and discrimination are important, but these alone fall short of addressing the depth of our current challenge. While conversations about diversity have opened space to deal with the dominance of ideas that are governed by rationalities and institutions of the idealized capitalist center, and the dominance of white heterosexual men in the field, they have largely failed to acknowledge the root cause of the problem. The blind pursuit of diversity to solve the complex problems of the economics field can even be counterproductive: academia can add black and brown people to their panels, departments, and syllabi, pretending that the problem is resolved, making it even harder to identify the elephants in the room: Eurocentrism and structural discrimination. Nonetheless, it is worth highlighting the studies and initiatives that have contributed to making space for these conversations, a few of which have indeed recognized the structural root of the problem.

Particularly since 2017, there has been an explosion of studies, initiatives, and groups that have proposed solutions for increasing diversity in Economics. The most recent impetus for the Economics #MeToo moment was triggered by the research conducted by Alice Wu (2020) regarding sexism and misogyny rampant in the economics community in the United States as evidenced by comments and posts made on the anonymous job market forum, Economics Job Market Rumors (EJMR). Wu finds that comments made about women economists, especially those on the job market, were likely to be of a personal nature and based on physical appearance. She shows that the words "hotter," "hot," "attractive," "pregnant," "gorgeous," "beautiful," "tits," "lesbian," "bang," and "horny" were the 10 most common words used to describe women economists, while "homosexual," "homo," "philosopher," "keen," "motivated," "fieckers," "slides," "Nordic," "filling," and "textbook" were the 10 most common words used to describe men. Furthermore, she shows that discussions about women were more likely to devolve into discussion about personal information and appearance than research. These findings found resonance with many women in the profession who shared the experience of casual sexism and structural discrimination. While several initiatives and studies attempted to spur the discipline into action to improve representation of women in the economics profession long before 2017, it was Wu's paper, perhaps because it coincided with the #MeToo movement in the film industry that spread virally in 2017, that fueled the demands for action and research. Challenging the economics profession on its male dominance now appears to have become relatively uncontroversial.

Similarly, ethnic, racial, and caste-based exclusions have long been a problem in the profession. When these came to light in the United States and Britain with the revival of the BLM protests in 2020, Black economists shared on social media their experiences of discrimination, which was met with a new awareness and willingness to root out racist attitudes in the discipline. Once again, it seems that economics has at least recognized that it has a problem of structural exclusion (Ouma, 2021). Since then, economics has also been exposed for the lack of scholarship on race-related issues in its journals (Advani et al., 2024). Unfortunately, studies that expose such gaps themselves often suffer from the deep-seated theoretical and methodological narrowness in the field, given that what counts as economics scholarship to begin with is extremely selective. For example, Advani et al.'s (2024) study of race-related scholarship in economics does not consider non-mainstream journals such as *The Review of Black Political Economy*, where heterodox economists publish on important race-related topics such as racial stratification, racialized economic discrimination, and racial capitalism.

Similarly, long-entrenched geographical biases in economics have also recently been illuminated, including by Rodrik, as mentioned above. It remains much more likely that academic work focused on the United States will be published in a top-five economics journal than research on other countries, a bias that cannot be explained by data or researcher quality (Das et al., 2013; The Economist, 2018). Even when publications engage with areas outside of the United States, the authors of the journals tend to be based in the US. For example, on average, only 25 per cent of the journal articles published on Africa in leading economics journals had at least one Africa-based author in the period 2005–15 (Chelwa, 2021).

Within development economics, scholars based in the periphery rarely publish in top economics journals – for example, only around 10% of papers in development economics had such an author or co-author in 2018 (Naritomi et al., 2020), which indicates a familiar pattern of scholars in the capitalist center setting the research agenda and researching issues in the periphery, while excluding scholars based there (Hountondji, 1997). Furthermore, economists considered part of the mainstream, even those in the periphery, are less likely to teach about racial inequalities and colonialism, compared with heterodox economists and economists based in non-economics departments (Kvangraven and Kesar, 2023).

The increased attention to these patterns has led to the dramatic expansion of initiatives that seek to improve the representation of women and racial, ethnic, and caste minorities in economics, not only in increasing their number, but also in improving representation at seminars and conferences, and in edited volumes, reading lists, journals, and in citation practices. For instance, Diversifying Economic Quality or Div.E.Q. is a wiki that was created by Amanda Bayer in 2011 (2021) to present data on gender- and race-based participation and share resources on teaching and mentoring practices that encourage "women, students of color, and members of other underrepresented groups to continue their study of economics" (Bayer, 2021). Similarly, the Sadie Collective, started in 2018, seeks to improve the representation of Black women in economics and related fields in the United States. The Black Economists Network seeks to challenge the lack of diversity by "bringing together and raising the profile of Black people in economics by working alongside other organizations on their diversity strategies," primarily in Britain.

These new initiatives for greater diversity have not been limited to the United States and Western Europe. For example, the Bahujan Economists Network in India seeks to break the stranglehold of upper caste economists in the discipline in India and elsewhere (Tagat et al., 2021). The Nawi – Afrifem Macroeconomics Collective (Nawi Collective), a Pan-African Feminist initiative launched in 2020, is building a community in Africa of individuals and organizations working on influencing, analyzing, deconstructing, and reconstructing macroeconomic policies, narratives and understanding them through an intersectional Pan-African feminist lens. Rethinking Economics for Africa (REFA) is an organization of students based in South Africa with local chapters across the country, perhaps best known for their annual

Rethinking Economics for Africa Festival. Ecofeminita is a Latin American critical feminist organization that works to make gender inequality visible and raises awareness about feminist economics.

However, the more pressing issue remains that the most common approach to diversity within economics largely overlooks the significance of structural barriers that contribute to the exclusion of certain groups. This approach mirrors the tendency of mainstream economics to overlook structural factors in its theories. For mainstream economists, diversity is primarily a problem of adding bodies and changing incentives, without necessarily dismantling the structures that produced exclusion in the first place. How could mainstream economics even identify these structures, without having a theoretical framework that grapples with structural power and its interaction with other social processes? This approach of adding bodies and changing incentives suggests that the problem can be resolved by mentoring students from minority groups or providing them strong role models from minority groups, as if the problem lies in the training and background of the economists, rather than deeper structures within the world and the discipline.

While economics has begun to scratch the surface of its diversity issue, it is secure in its Eurocentric theoretical and methodological foundations. Economics textbooks, when they touch on the history of economic thought, often assume that all progress in theory and practice has been an objective and linear process of refinement (Mearman et al., 2018b). Economists often assume that prevailing ideas are those that are superior in the marketplace of ideas (Straussman, 1993). Therefore, we do not need to be familiar with older, allegedly discredited ideas. It is no surprise then that the history of economic thought is typically marginalized within the discipline. As a result, the historically contingent nature of its own development, the marginalization or expulsion of alternative schools of thought, and the political nature of economic theory are not typically part of the training to become an economist (Tavasci and Ventimiglia, 2018).

Just as current events forced the economics community to confront its demographic homogeneity, the Global Financial Crisis of 2007 spurred demands for reform to address economists' unsatisfactory performance in understanding the dynamics of the crisis, its causes, and its consequences, which also led to older demands for reform finally being taken more seriously. Student groups such as Rethinking Economics, Post-Crash Economics Society, and Young Scholars Initiative emerged as communities of young students and scholars demanding teaching and research on non-mainstream approaches to economics, such as post-Keynesian economics, feminist economics, modern monetary theory, Marxist critiques of political economy, structuralist macroeconomics, and institutional economics.

Those movements acted in the long tradition of heterodox economics. Some of these traditions were more accepted in the hegemonic center before the Cold War, whereas others – especially those of the more radical variety or those from the periphery – were never widely accepted in elite universities of the center. In any case, insights from heterodox economics are not considered part of the discipline anymore, despite their capacity to provide equally, if not more valuable, explanations of economic phenomena. This is often made clear when mainstream economists discover key insights from heterodox economics and attempt to integrate them into their own frameworks, often by diluting the concepts and not providing acknowledgment. For example, despite being a key insight of post-Keynesian economics for decades, Stansbury and Summers (2020) seem to have "discovered" the macroeconomic impacts of declining worker power. Similarly, Acemoglu and Johnson (2023) "discover" that technical change is often driven by the need to exert power on workers, peasants, and slaves, even though the concept of power-biased technical change is decades-old news in heterodox macroeconomics.

Nonetheless, the vigor of these movements indicates that that much remains wanting in the discipline, both in who studies, teaches, and conducts research, and in the theoretical frameworks in use. We see these as symptoms of the same problem: a discipline that studies the world through a narrow Eurocentric lens and is unwilling to contend with alternative frameworks that study the dynamics of the peripheries in their own terms and address broader structural issues of power. It is one that is unwilling to center capitalist exploitation, the history of colonialism, the enduring structures of imperialism and consequent dependencies and inequalities, and the impact of those on constructing the edifice of structural oppression today. Therefore, we can identify patterns of geographical exclusion among economists (Rodrik, 2021), but no rigorous analysis or structural solution is offered by the discipline. Given that there is a general consensus in the top of the discipline regarding its capacity to provide rigorous theoretical and methodological research (Kvangraven and Kesar, 2023), then the problem of diversity becomes one of charity and not one that challenges the conceptual foundation of economics itself.

Although diversity without decolonization is insufficient, increased diversity can certainly bring benefits, given that marginalized groups are more likely to contribute viewpoints that may be absent. For example, women have historically been more likely to recognize problems associated with excluding care work from gross domestic product (GDP) and more likely to recognize discrimination in the labor market (May et al., 2018). This is probably not surprising given that many feminist economists also happen to be women. Nonetheless, it is important to keep in mind that many individuals from marginalized groups will not, simply because of their position, be better able to understand the world. On the contrary, many have historically adapted to the dominant paradigm and continue to reproduce the status quo of economic theory (Christensen, 2001; Bonilla-Silva and Zuberi, 2008).

Intellectuals across the world, including many in the periphery, are trained in Eurocentric thinking, either through their own institutions, which increasingly use American textbooks, or because many – especially those in the elite – tend to obtain training in institutions of the center (Ndlovu-Gatsheni, 2023). Indeed, it reflects the dominance of Eurocentrism that even students and scholars from marginalized groups and across the periphery are taught to "think epistemically like the ones in the dominant positions" (Grosfoguel, 2007, p. 213). For this reason, decolonization is equally important in the capitalist center as elsewhere. The Indian Marxist economist Utsa Patnaik put it succinctly in the 10th anniversary lecture she gave for the *Agrarian South: Journal of Political Economy*: "it struck me that the problem was really of knowledge production in the global North, for the educated in the Southern countries read the textbooks and study the theories emanating from Universities in the North" (U. Patnaik, 2022, p. 334).

The dominance of English serves to cement the dominance of thinking from the capitalist center, marginalizing work done in other languages and that has not yet been translated, such as the pioneering work on superexploitation by Vânia Bambirra (1978), financial dependency by Maria da Conceição Tavares (1985), or African subordinate monetary systems by Joseph Tchundjang Pouemi (2000 [1980]) – to name only a few. This creates structural exclusion too – if you do not write in English your work will not be acknowledged at the top of the disciplinary hierarchy. Worse, reviewers of mainstream journals often critique authors who cite too many articles in languages other than English or that are published in regional journals.

Once we discuss these Eurocentric theoretical, methodological, and practical issues, unfortunately, the observations Rodrik made about the discipline seem rather superficial. While it is an advancement that a development economist at the top of the field recognizes that the periphery can be a space for the discovery of theory, Rodrik ignores alternative theoretical frameworks. He simply aims to use the anomalies of the periphery to correct some blind spots in a fundamentally Eurocentric framework. This is unlikely to improve economic theorization fundamentally or to serve a decolonization agenda. Unfortunately, Rodrik's intervention also shows that longstanding critiques of Eurocentrism in social theory have still not seriously penetrated the pinnacle of economics (Zein-Elabdin and Charusheela, 2004). Kayatekin

(2009, p. 1113) puts it aptly: this "intransigence" is related to "the history of the discipline, its place in the evolution and spread of capitalism through colonialism and imperialism, and, without a doubt, its self-perception as a 'science'."

A roadmap of the book

The book is organized into two parts. The first part explores Eurocentrism in economics: how it originated, how it became an inherent part of the discipline, and its influence on current mainstream frameworks. We also discuss how the most obvious potential source of decolonization of economics – the subfield of development economics that took shape in the context of political decolonization in many countries of the periphery – did not deliver. The second part focuses on the process of decolonizing economics: examining the potential and limitations of critical frameworks for decolonization, identifying theoretical and methodological features of a decolonization agenda, introducing perspectives on contemporary economic topics that can contribute toward a decolonization agenda, and discussing strategies for fostering decolonization within various academic and non-academic spaces.

In chapter 2, following this introduction, we explain what we mean by Eurocentrism in economics and how economics became a colonizing discipline, tracing it back to the official story of the development of capitalism within economics. In this story, capitalism evolved endogenously in Europe, because of high labor costs, low energy costs, the politics and culture of the English, and an abundance of coal. The story also goes that Enlightenment values permeated even the sphere of production, with rationality dictating that activity be guided not by custom or tradition, but the pursuit of profit. This mainstream narrative suggests that capitalist development followed organically from market exchange, and that this was not only natural, but universal. The parts of the world that do not appear to follow this dynamic are seen as deviations that need to conform. We present an alternative narrative of the development of capitalism in Europe – one of violent dispossession to transform social relations and create a mass working class in England; one shaped by colonialism and the Transatlantic Slave Trade; one of racialization, patriarchy, and other forms of structural transformation. It is no accident that this history is marginalized by mainstream economic theory. Even when topics of colonialism or racial differentiation are studied, they are necessarily approached from a limiting theoretical framework that does not allow us to understand structural oppression as a macro-historical and ongoing phenomenon.

In chapter 3 we trace how the seeds of a Eurocentric political economy grew into what we know as economics today. We discuss how the principles of equilibrium, rationality, scarcity, and choice become universal in content and application. With the increasing mathematization, the search for scientificity took hold, and economic laws came to be devised with the view of creating a field more like physics. Economics, then, became increasingly narrow during the Cold War. At a point when the global world order was centered on competition between two world systems – capitalism versus socialism – neoclassical economic theory provided precisely the anti-revolutionary ammunition that was in high demand in the capitalist center. This narrowing supported marginalization of scholars and scholarship that took more radical approaches, pushing critical and radical theoretical strands to the margins. This process cemented Eurocentrism in economics, including through the establishment of economic laws, through the establishment of equilibrium as an analytical anchor, and by establishing objectivity and neutrality as the basis for empirical research.

It may be reasonable to expect that significant insights for constructing a non-Eurocentric economics would stem from the subfield of development economics, particularly because it originated as an exploration of regions beyond the capitalist center. Development economics played a pivotal role in the aftermath of national independence movements, drawing inspiration from the decolonization endeavors of newly liberated nations. However, even though direct colonial control had ended in many parts of the world, the hegemony of Eurocentric thought permeated the new development project – both in how economic development was conceptualized and in how it was supposed to be brought about. That even development economics became a colonizing discipline is a good illustration of the challenges we face in decolonizing economics, and we discuss these in chapter 4.

Next, in chapter 5, we evaluate to what extent heterodox economics could lend itself to a decolonization agenda. We argue that the marginalized, yet vibrant heterodox traditions provide a productive starting point for decolonizing economics. This is because heterodox economics offers an alternative set of frameworks that have a theoretical focus on social relations and structural power, which is more amenable to a decolonization agenda. In heterodox economics, what is understood as political is not limited to studying political parties or political processes, but rather, it is about the uneven distribution of economic, social, and political power. This has important implications for our understanding of production, inequalities, histories of colonialism, and much more. That said, heterodox economics is not immune to Eurocentrism either, both in its theorization and knowledge production, and it also needs to confront its own biases that tend to exclude scholarship that centers dynamics associated with the peripheries, such as those of imperialism, race, and patriarchy. This is laid out in chapter 5, where we identify heterodox economic theorization as a necessary but insufficient condition for decolonization.

In chapter 6, we broaden the discussion to outline key features of a decolonization agenda for economics. Such an agenda seeks to unravel the apparatus of power through which the dichotomies of center and the periphery are constructed, naturalized, and maintained. Drawing on a range of radical theories, such as anti-colonial Third World Marxism, post-colonialism, dependency theory, feminist theory, and the Black Radical Tradition, we expose how different dichotomies have been produced and reproduced, and how they have become uncritically and universally accepted. The dichotomy is between those that align with a Eurocentric vision of capitalism and those that do not.

We show how these traditions provide building blocks for both challenging Eurocentrism and promoting radical, non-Eurocentric, anti-colonial, and/or anti-imperialist scholarship. This exploration aims not to prescribe a singular path for decolonizing economics, but rather to provide avenues for critical examination, laying the groundwork for a decolonization agenda.

Non-Eurocentric work in economics is not new. There is a rich and enduring scholarship to draw on. This is the topic of chapter 7, where we put forth some insights from non-Eurocentric frameworks, mainly based on scholarship that emerged in the peripheries or that centers the periphery in theorization. While numerous themes across all branches of economics could be examined, we start by examining three to show how non-Eurocentric approaches can bring different understandings of key economic processes. These are growth and structural transformation in the periphery, labor and informality, and rationality and institutions. In our engagement with these themes, we present the non-Eurocentric scholarship on its own terms and demonstrate how it could contribute to a decolonization agenda and show how it offers an entirely different understanding to standard economic thinking. We selected these themes to underscore that decolonizing economics is not solely crucial for studying the periphery but also for comprehensively theorizing and understanding economic dynamics across the world.

In chapter 8, we outline several efforts to contribute to a decolonization agenda, both within universities and beyond. As the call to decolonize is not detached from wider social struggles, the gains from decolonization of universities can have significant political and social implications outside the academy, given its importance in shaping policy priorities. Our optimistic attempt is to locate this contribution in a much bigger transformative global decolonization movement, of which economics and, more generally, academia, are just small, albeit crucial, links. Our pragmatic attempt, on the other hand, is to push economics to be grounded in a serious critical enquiry and to contend with the values it upholds and the utopias it chases. Toward that, we start with the discussion on decolonizing the university. First, we ask what students and staff can do to work toward decolonizing the classroom, before discussing how to approach decolonizing universities more broadly. We then move on to exploring what can be done beyond the classroom, including how to think about evaluating policymaking.

We cannot tell you about all the ways in which economics is deficient or propose a complete roadmap for reform. Each of the authors of this book has their own independent research agenda that focuses on a specific research theme that aims to take a non-Eurocentric perspective. But since this book is targeted at the general reader, we do not dwell further on the need for decolonization in all these various streams of economic research. In more general terms, to decolonize economics, we must depart from current sanitized discourse, prancing about in neat lemmas and mathematical models. Economics needs to be re-politicized so that the stakes of the debates are made clear and so that it can be more suited to understanding complex and unequal realities.

–2–
The Foundations of a Eurocentric Discipline

How is economics Eurocentric? How does this relate to its views on the development of capitalism and the field's understanding of its own history? These are the questions that concern us in this chapter. We argue that the official story of the development of capitalism within the economics discipline lays the foundation for a Eurocentric understanding of the economy. However, there is an alternative story of capitalism's development and an alternative way of approaching economic processes, which centers structural relations and forces of oppression, and can, ultimately, better allow us to grasp how exploitation and subordination have supported and shaped the dynamics of global capitalism.

The official story of the development of capitalism and the discipline of economics

The birth of economics as a separate discipline is often linked to Adam Smith's publication, in 1776, of *An Inquiry into the Nature and Causes of the Wealth of Nations*, and Smith is often regarded as the father of the discipline. At the beginning of the *Wealth of Nations*, the division of labor is said to contribute to "general plenty," which "diffuses itself through all the different ranks of the society" (p. 18). A simplified and small selection of Smith's theories became the building blocks of classical political economy and then modern mainstream economics (Blaug, 2020). Notably, the concept of the *invisible hand*, though mentioned only once in the book, has served as a foundational pillar for the field's portrayal of the rationality inherent in competitive market economies. It illustrates the unintended yet beneficial outcomes that arise when individuals pursue their own self-interests, thereby contributing to the greater social good and public welfare (Carroll and Manne, 1992; Gates and Steane, 2007). This interpretation supports the view of a global market comprising numerous equal and independent nations capable of prospering alongside each other within a competitive system. The marketplace creates efficiency through gains from specialization and exchange, but also stimulates technological advancement through competition among capitalists, and humans' natural "propensity to truck, barter and exchange one thing for another" (Smith, 1776, p. 77). Such an interpretation of Smith suggests that capitalism evolved naturally, logically, and progressively through market processes and specific behavior, depoliticizing and dehistoricizing our understanding of its development (Fraser, 2016a).

Smith viewed colonial societies as primitive and assumed that they would evolve linearly into superior, European-type capitalist societies (Meek, 1976; Pradella, 2017). This teleological perspective is seen throughout economics, where it is assumed that economic processes inherently lead to a specific state serving a specific purpose – for example, processes leading to the development of a well-functioning capitalist system of wealth across the world, or the invisible hand leading to equilibrium economic outcomes. Within the official story, Enlightenment values were also often seen to be foundational to the development of capitalism, as they are perceived to having provided a rational basis for morality, rights such as equality before the law, and progress through scientific and technological advances. Property law, in fact, occupies a distinctive place in Enlightenment thought and subsequent discussions of capitalist modernity (Bhandar, 2018). Thus, as Wood rightly puts it, "liberalism, capitalism, and the intellectual project of the Enlightenment together represent a single cultural formation whose constitutive principle is rationalism" (E. M. Wood, 2000, p. 405).

The Enlightenment introduced capitalist modernity and rationality, and was thought to permeate all social spheres, including markets and production methods (Gates and Steane, 2007). Weber (1971 [1904]), for example, used rationalism as a term to describe an economic system based not on custom or tradition, but on deliberate and systematic adjustment of economic means to the attainment of profit. It's not simply any rationality, but a very specific kind – one aimed at maximization via self-interest, i.e., *capitalist rationality*. This concept of capitalist rationality has since become a widespread foundation for contemporary economics, where it has become widely believed that "the greatest efficiency occurs when open competition in a free market determines outcomes" (Carroll and Manne, 1992, p. 9).[1] Such views create and perpetuate the idea that associates constraints on development in the periphery with tradition and culture, while the capitalist institutions and rationality in the economies of the center are associated with modernity and progress.

In this narrative, capitalism comes about by intensifying existing commercial processes, such as market exchange, a division of labor, and technological improvements (E. M. Wood, 2000). Self-interested, rational individuals and scientific advances gradually remove obstacles to the development of capitalism, such as political and cultural constraints. The development of capitalism is seen as a matter of *quantitative* change in existing processes (technological improvements, increasing division of labor, and changes in costs), rather than a qualitative break, whereby new structures, production and labor processes, and institutions were actively, often violently, created (E. M. Wood, 2002). The mainstream narrative, thus, sees capitalist development following directly from market exchange, where history becomes a solid line showing continuity between non-capitalist and capitalist societies. Along this line, markets are mainly defined as places to buy and sell, with no coercion but freedom, opportunity, and choice. Moreover, beyond being natural, the principles and laws of capitalism are also seen as universal (E. M. Wood, 2000).

What we see in this official history is the acceptance that capitalism, as it developed in Europe, is the triumph of rationality and scientific progress. In this story, European Enlightenment values and ideas are considered universal and objective, allegedly allied with liberty, fraternity, tolerance, and human wellbeing. This view of capitalism as idealized, natural, and universal, with Europe as its highest stage, remains the dominant paradigm in economics today.

It has become dominant in textbooks across the world, even recent ones like *The Economy* by CORE, which was developed in response to critiques of the field in the wake of the financial crisis of 2008. These textbooks characterize capitalism by the existence of private property, markets, and firms (see CORE, 2017, 2023). The development of capitalism, then, is presented as the emergence of these characteristics, specifically in England during the Industrial Revolution. CORE (2017) attributes this emergence to relatively high labor costs coupled with low costs of local energy sources (Pomeranz, 2000; Allen, 2011), Europe's scientific revolution associated with the Enlightenment the century before (Mokyr, 2004), and the political and cultural characteristics of the English at the time (Landes, 2006). Even when colonialism is introduced as one of the explanations for capitalism's development in Europe in the later version of CORE (2023), it is presented as an add-on explanation, not as crucial to all these other dimensions. Moreover, it is presented as something to be studied as a historical occurrence that supported capitalism's development in Europe without considering its impact on creating capitalist underdevelopment in the peripheries.

To make it even harder for economics students to spot any problems with this naturalized view of capitalism, the discipline's own history also tends to be told in a way that excludes alternative ways of theorizing capitalism. Economists typically adopt a Whiggish view of history, assuming that past errors in economic theorizing have been rectified, leading to the current state of economics. This progression is traced through influential scholars such Adam Smith to David Ricardo, Thomas Malthus, John Stuart Mill, Stanley Jevons, and Alfred Marshall (D'Ippoliti and Roncaglia, 2015). Accounts exploring the political landscape that favored certain ideas have been overlooked, while the focus on technical training reinforces the idea of continuous progress in the discipline.

Despite attempts after the financial crisis of 2008 to address the lack of attention to the politics shaping the history of economic thought and ideas, most efforts remain Whiggish in perspective. The CORE textbook's dismissal of past economic ideas as "defunct bodies of theory" and its lack of meaningful engagement with their contributions or critiques is characteristic of how modern economics deals with the history of economic thought (Guizzo, 2020, p. 122; see also Mearman et al., 2018a). This limited view has also been exported to the rest of the world (Keita, 2020).

An alternative story of the development of capitalism and the discipline of economics

The official story of the birth of economics is appealing and intuitive but distorts reality, misrepresenting both how capitalism evolved and, relatedly, how the discipline developed. Many scholars, often outside economics, have continuously provided a fertile ground to debate alternative accounts of capitalism's development by studying the history of colonialism and contemporary forms of imperialism (see Césaire, 1950; Frank, 1967; Marini, 1978; U. Patnaik, 2018). We highlight two key aspects that are neglected in the dominant account, namely the change in social relations and the role of other forms of structural oppression – like colonialism, patriarchy, and racialization – in shaping capitalist development.

Transforming social relations

Marxist scholars have explored the radical transformations of social relations that underpinned the development of capitalism, which is an important explanation for industrial capitalism's emergence in England and not elsewhere (Brenner, 1976; U. Patnaik, 1990; Perelman, 2000; E. M. Wood, 2002; Gibson-Graham, 2006; Bonefeld, 2014). Despite differences within this literature, this view starkly contrasts with the standard belief that increased trade during the Industrial Revolution was a natural process.

The shift in social relations created a mass proletariat – a working class reliant on wage earnings – through a process known as primitive accumulation (Marx, 1977 [1867]; E. M. Wood, 2002). This process entails, on the one hand, the expropriation of common resources, upon which a significant portion of the population depended, for private use. This was often achieved through the enclosure of large tracts of land and resources. On the other hand, this same process created a vast population dispossessed of these common resources, compelled to look elsewhere for work by means of selling their labour power given the now absence of alternative livelihood means. Consequently, this process gave rise to both private ownership of capital and a propertyless majority susceptible to wage exploitation by the owners of resources and means of production. Before wage labor was normalized, these individuals were forced into work through direct coercion, facilitated by political and judicial intervention.

As vividly described by E. P. Thompson (1963) in *The Making of the English Working Class*, the process of proletarianization was violent and far from the natural process described in economics textbooks. Even if truck and barter might be a natural propensity, the selling of labor power was institutionalized through a long history of coercion and violence (Denning, 2010; U. Patnaik and Moyo, 2011). And there is increasing evidence that human beings' propensity to barter is perhaps not as natural as assumed by economists (Graeber, 2011).

Primitive accumulation, or even pre-capitalist modes of production, such as feudalism and chattel slavery, were the historical prerequisite and the basis of capital – the very premise on which capitalist social relations were built (Bonefeld, 2014). Some of these historical forces continue to shape how capitalism operates, such as processes of dispossession through primitive accumulation continuing to support capital accumulation and extraction and providing political stability to the capitalist social formation across the globe today (Harvey, 2003; Sanyal, 2007).

This brings us to what we see as the first flaw in the mainstream account: there were high levels of commercialization outside of England, such as in Florence and the Netherlands (Banaji, 2020), and important technological advances outside of Europe, for example in China (Hobson, 2004). However, these increases in market exchange and productivity elsewhere did not lead to the imperatives of capitalist development. As the mainstream account misses the qualitative change in social relations, it is unable to explain the emergence of capitalism in Europe.

Capitalism's encounter with colonialism, racialization, and patriarchy

Understanding the emergence of capitalism requires more than just examining class conflict and violence in England. This brings us to the second key flaw in the mainstream account: it does not adequately consider the ways in which capitalism's development was shaped by a global system of oppression, including colonialism, racialization, imperialism, and patriarchy (see Du Bois, 1935; Robinson 2000 [1983]; Federici, 2004, Leech, 2012; Anievas and Nisancioglu, 2015; Sen and Marcuzzo, 2017; U. Patnaik, 2018). It is important to note here that we are focusing on the structural forms of oppression that shaped the development of *capitalism* as it emerged in England, not forms of oppression that have existed in other spaces and times, such as other forms of slavery, oppression, or even other empires that existed before the British and before the development of capitalism.

From 1492, over three centuries of the Transatlantic Slave Trade and European conquest and colonization unfolded across the globe, profoundly shaping the world in crucial ways (Williams, 1944; Inikori, 2020; Berg and Hudson, 2023). The Transatlantic Slave Trade shaped capitalism's development in England, as merchants and planters – dominating the West Indies but living as absentee landlords in England – relied on profits from the slave trade to play a pivotal role in England's economic and financial affairs.[2] Additionally, the Transatlantic Slave Trade boosted industries like shipbuilding, contributing significantly to England's supremacy in overseas trade. Liverpool's shipping industry, in particular, catalyzed Manchester manufacturing. The increase in trade created wealth and stimulated investments, and, while mercantilism initially fueled industrial capitalism, the latter "outgrew mercantilism and destroyed it" (Williams, 1944, p. 19).

The Transatlantic Slave Trade was also responsible for constructing a racial hierarchy which served to legitimize the exploitation of Black slaves (Williams, 1944; Du Bois, 1999 [1920]; Cooper, 2017 [1892]). Racialization was used as a tool to enslave Black labor, expropriate their land and other resources, and forcefully deploy them as cheap labor in mines, plantations, and other industries that produced cheap raw materials and other inputs that supported wealth accumulation, and eventually the development of industry in Europe and North America, laying the foundation for the emergence of capitalism (Padmore, 1936; Nkrumah, 1963; Fraser, 2016b).

Colonies conquered by the British and other colonial powers also provided crucial raw materials, including agricultural produce, cotton, silver, gold, diamonds, and other precious minerals, fueling and expanding the colonial power's economies. Additionally, they provided cheap, often enslaved, labor, which both facilitated the spread of capitalism to the colonized economies and the development of industry in the colonizing economies (Beckert, 2014; Habib, 2017; P. Patnaik and Patnaik, 2021). In total, the colonies contributed 6 per cent of Britain's GDP in 1801 (Habib, 2017, p. 12). With time, the institution of wage relations in the countries of the center – allowing white workers to have freedom and rights, albeit very limited, to choose their employer – was aided by a violent process of instituting racialized and enslaved labor relations and destruction of the social and cultural fabric in the periphery (Rodney, 1972; Galeano, 1973; Robinson, 2000 [1983]).

Colonies served as markets for finished goods as well, frequently leading to the displacement of indigenous industries, as seen in the cotton industry in India (Beckert, 2014). As such, colonialism not only supported industrial development in the center economies but hindered the potential for indigenous industrial capitalist development in the peripheries (Rodney, 1972). This historical account suggests that capitalism by its very nature unfolded unevenly across the globe (Furtado, 1964; Amin, 1974; Das Gupta, 2016). The support for development in one part of the world accompanied by underdevelopment elsewhere is written off in the official story but is brought to light with alternative accounts.

Differentiation along racial and gendered lines was central to the Enlightenment project of human reason, which was built upon the oppression and dehumanization of the vast segments of humanity which colonizers thought needed instruction in civilizational progress (Wynter, 2003). Even modern property laws, based on Enlightenment values such as equality before the law, emerged along with and through colonial modes of appropriation.

> [The] justifications for private property ownership were articulated through the attribution of value to the lives of those defined as having the capacity, will, and technology to appropriate, which in turn was contingent on prevailing concepts of race and racial difference. (Bhandar, 2018, p. 4)

For example, the establishment of private property rights in agricultural land in India, by the colonial British government and by the Indian State, was based on large-scale displacements of marginalized caste groups. These groups, who traditionally cultivated the land and relied on it for their livelihood, frequently lost their ownership claims when these were formalized through written documentation (Ilaiah, 1990).

Capital accumulation was also shaped by patriarchal systems that restricted women's autonomy. The years before the European Enlightenment were marked by increased witch hunts aimed at controlling women's bodies and sexuality, thereby confining them to domestic roles (Federici, 2004). This became an essential precondition for introducing the breadwinner–housewife model, enabling a sexual division of labor where men engaged in capitalist wage relations while women provided the social and reproductive work in the household. The *housewification* of women's work – a social construction of women as housewives and non-workers – not only kept women relegated to the household, but also aided in keeping them unorganized while still available to work as cheap wage labor, often at home (Mies, 1982, 1986).[3] The ways in which the sphere of social reproduction and the ensuing gender relations are structured have undergone several changes and restructurings under different phases of capitalism, often in response to the needs of capitalism (Fraser, 2016a; Ghosh, 2009; Cantillon et al., 2023).

The great gap in the fatherhood of economics

The discussion so far highlights significant gaps in the official story of capitalism's development, including oversight of colonialism, the slave trade, patriarchy, racialization, and other forms of structural oppression. It is unsurprising, then, that the mainstream history of economics also exhibits biases and omissions. In addition to distorted explanations of capitalism's development, the official history of economics also focuses almost exclusively on European – and almost always white male – thinkers (Boring and Zignago, 2018; Gomez Betancourt and Orozco Espinel, 2018; Madden and Dimand, 2018). The discipline not only marginalized scholars studying issues such as colonialism and race, but also overlooked those who developed economic ideas as vital as Adam Smith's but who originated from non-European contexts.

Before Smith, Asian and Middle Eastern thinkers had already developed similar ideas about the economy. For example, Chinese scholars such as Liu An and Kuo Hsiang influenced many of Smith's ideas (Hobson, 2004). This happened as Smith drew much inspiration from the French physiocrat François Quesnay, who at the time was often called the "French Confucius" because of the strong influence of Confucian ideas on his thinking. This included foundational critiques of mercantilism and state intervention in agriculture. Chinese scholars had romanticized the natural laws of the markets as early as 300 AD through their concept *wu-wei*, later translated into French as *laissez-faire*. Other concepts that are often attributed to Smith, such as the importance of the division of labor for the increase in productivity, were first conceptualized by the Arab scholar Ibn Khaldun in the fourteenth century (Irwin, 2018), albeit not without racial undertones. Moreover, there is a burgeoning literature in political economy and history that shows the multi-directionality of economic ideas, making it difficult to establish their origins by nationality, and showing how many ideas we often think of as Western actually emerged from countries in the periphery (Mkandawire, 2010; Helleiner, 2021; McClure, 2021; Fajardo, 2022; Thornton, 2023). The standard lineage of Smith – Malthus – Mill – Ricardo – Marshall – Keynes does not even represent the economists that were most popular when they were writing, but it is a lineage that has been created in retrospect (Reinert and Reinert, 2018).

Also, although the naturalization view of capitalism is associated with Smith, a closer reading shows that his elaboration of the labor theory of value, for example, can serve as a basis for understanding accumulation as a global process, encompassing colonialism and imperialism as constitutive components (Pradella, 2017). Thus, mainstream economics and its interpretation of Smith's ideas are more Eurocentric than Smith himself, reflecting the discipline's selectivity and bias.

Scholars worldwide have studied and proposed many ideas about economic processes that directly contradict the mainstream naturalization view of capitalism. For example, in the nineteenth century there was a significant scholarship on mechanisms of colonial drain in India (Naroji, 1901). The African scholarship on *ubuntu* offers an alternative way of conceptualizing human behavior to the dominant view of humans as primarily self-interested (Menkiti, 1984; Mbiti, 1990). Marxist perspectives highlight how capitalism's development was underpinned by violent processes of dispossession and exploitation. Overall, there is scholarship across the world on issues ranging from dependencies in the periphery, post-colonial capitalism, and various forms of anti-colonial Marxism, to alternative ways of understanding institutions and rationality. It is this rich but neglected history that led Schumpeter (1954) to argue that there is a "great gap" in the history of economic thought, with whole periods and traditions completely neglected.

The strands of thought that center processes of structural power in their understanding of capitalism do not feature in mainstream history. Marginalized is scholarship theorizing from the vantage point that includes the periphery as well as scholarship critical of a Eurocentric narrative, such as dependency theorists, scholars of the Black Radical Tradition, scholars of post-colonial capitalist development, and post-development theorists. It is also not surprising that the official history of economic thought also excludes the substantial contributions made by women and feminists to economic ideas (Madden and Dimand, 2018; Kuiper, 2022), as well as approaches that focus on how patriarchy shapes production and social reproduction in particular ways (Waring, 1990; Fernandez, 2018; Becchio, 2020).

Exposing Eurocentrism in economics

The official narrative of capitalism's development idealizes an endogenous economic process within Europe, stemming naturally from Enlightenment rationalities. It is a story of triumphs of rationality and scientific progress, that portrays capitalism as a natural system and economics as a science governed by generalized laws that can explain the principles governing the system. However, this history is highly distorted and partial, as it ignores and obfuscates the role of structural power relations, exploitation, oppression, dispossession, and qualitative changes in social relations that characterized both the inception and the development of capitalism.

This partial, distorted, and idealized view of capitalist development is then imposed on the rest of the world, which is then expected to undergo the same development trajectory; that is, a transition to fully fledged capitalism through the establishment of rational capitalist institutions and incentives for endogenous technological and scientific advancements and unbridled capitalist expansion (Meek, 1976; Amin, 2009 [1988]; Hobson, 2012; Ndlovu-Gatsheni, 2018). Capitalism is expected to unfold to the rest of the world – as if Europe represents the predetermined trajectory for all countries (Chatterjee, 1993; Sanyal, 2007; Hostettler, 2012). This idealized version also serves as the norm against which other societies are evaluated, positioning economies in the peripheries as deviations needing correction (Zein-Elabdin and Charusheela, 2004; Pierre, 2012), without considering how many of these so-called deviations are precisely an outcome of the process of capitalist expansion.

When a framework places this flawed view of the development of capitalism in Europe at its core, with all else viewed in relation to it, we classify it as *Eurocentric* (Amin, 2009 [1988]). In this context, "Europe" symbolizes not merely a geographical location but rather an idealized essence of capitalism (Lazarus, 2011). This is the essence of a Eurocentric theory. Such theory, in turn, forms the ideological basis for a global polarizing project that has shaped capitalism, reinforced imperialism, and profoundly influenced economists' view of capitalism (Amin, 2009 [1988]).

Economic theories, methods, and history are informed by worldviews and assumptions that work with this Eurocentric narrative, without considering – in fact, actively excluding – the critical role of colonialism, racism, slavery, exploitation, and expropriation (Blaut, 1993). As a consequence, the field is characterized by a set of principles and methods, developing in a linear fashion since the work of Adam Smith, rather than being a contested field riddled with contradicting and competing theories and methods.

It is worth noting, then, that science does not necessarily move forward based on an objective measure of how to best explain social phenomena (Kuhn, 1962), although that may be the mainstream self-perception. Different or new research programs do not necessarily provide better answers to the same questions posed by previous programs but address different questions altogether (Lakatos, 1978). Even when the same issues, such as welfare and justice, are considered, they are approached from different theoretical and political starting points.

Narratives stemming from the Enlightenment and capitalism's triumph have shaped perceptions of humanity and economic progress, often justifying and rationalizing racial hierarchies, colonialism, and slavery. These narratives have silenced the histories, experiences, and acts of resistance of those exploited, oppressed, racialized, and marginalized, impacting how society remembers the past (Trouillot, 1995). The silence gets weaved into, and operates in, our very framework of knowledge, influencing what economists choose to remember and which aspects of the dynamics of capitalism are studied.

The mainstream accounts of capitalism's development and the history of economic thought limit our worldview due to these silences. This omission restricts inquiry and overlooks alternative approaches, transforming the violence of mercantile trade, conquest, colonialism, and the development of capitalism into stories of universal progress, modernization and freedom (Chatterjee, 1993). This is used to justify – and whitewash – the imperialist and capitalist interests (U. Patnaik, 2022), portraying post-colonial economies as less advanced capitalist societies struggling to emulate their betters (Hostettler, 2012). The aim thus becomes to liberalize these economies so capitalist forces can take control and usher in progress and modernization.

The implications of a Eurocentric economics

To illustrate how Eurocentrism shapes the study of capitalism, let us consider capitalism's relationship with the Transatlantic Slave Trade. Anna Julia Cooper's (2017 [1892]) essay argued that America's domestic racial formation was tied to international colonialism and that the exploitation and oppression experienced by Asian, Black, and Indigenous peoples in the US were an integral part of the imperialist ideology of racial hierarchies. In 1900, W. E. B. Du Bois (1995 [1900], p. 639) famously argued at the Pan-African congress that "the problem of the twentieth century is the problem of the color line." Cooper, Du Bois, and others formed the foundation for what has come to be known as the Black Radical Tradition.[4] This scholarship tended to see race and class as being co-constituted, evolving together in historical and contemporary capitalism.[5] As such, race and class could not easily be disentangled but were part and parcel of the infrastructure that makes up the global political economy (see also Edwards, 2020). This scholarship stood strong in the first half of the twentieth century and emphasized the role of the Transatlantic Slave Trade in shaping capitalism globally.

However, by the 1970s, revisionist accounts of the role of the Transatlantic Slave Trade in capitalism's development started to emerge. Economic historian Stanley Engerman (1972) is responsible for the most widely cited revisionist account of this history and is well known for his quantitative historical work. Co-authored with Robert Fogel, his book *Time on the Cross: The Economics of American Negro Slavery* (1974) narrowly focuses on investigating the extent to which slavery was an economically viable institution and slave ownership a profitable investment, using solely cliometrics – the technique for the interpretation of economic history, based on the statistical analysis of large-scale numerical data. Engerman's work diverges from conclusions of mercantilists and scholars of the Black Radical Tradition.

[The] importance of the Engerman article in subverting the conventional wisdom on the slave trade cannot be overemphasized ... [Engerman] deliberately chose to utilize a neo-classical model which denied the reality of "multiplier effects" which would have included, for example, the impact of the slave trade in stimulating shipbuilding and related industries. Though he acknowledges that this will yield vastly different results from the model used in *Capitalism and Slavery* and other works, he never asked if his model reflected the real world of a slave-trade based economy as described by the mercantilists. (Bailey, 2014, p. 264)

The Engerman thesis also ignored crucial historical elements that would render his estimates irrelevant, such as the high degree of centralization in the slave trade. For example, the top ten (of forty) firms in the 1790 Liverpool slave trade controlled almost 65 percent of the trade (with London and Bristol being even more monopolized), undermining Engerman's assumption of high competition (Inikori, 1981). His estimates of average profits from the slave trade relative to British national income are less relevant given the high concentration of profit among few firms. That is why the work of critical scholars like Eric Williams was not centrally about counting profits from slavery, but the role that the slave trade and colonialism played in supporting mercantilism, which in turn supported the development of the American colonies and industrial capitalism (Darity, 1975a). Despite historians challenging Engerman through detailed studies of the slave trade's impact on British capital formation and the transformation of economic and social relations (e.g., Inikori, 1976; Bailey, 1986), his thesis remains largely accepted in economics today.

The Engerman thesis is a famous example of how cliometrics led to a radical overturning of doctrines about the place of slavery in history (Haupert, 2017). The focus of the discipline's analysis of African American slavery in the US shifted with this rise of cliometrics, moving toward a greater focus on slavery's efficiency and productivity (Sutch,

2018). The Engerman thesis exemplifies how the ascendence of a certain approach is not merely the result of an impartial, objective, and neutral evolution of economic theory and methodology. Instead, this development has often privileged specific types of research questions, methodologies, and entry points, while silencing others.

The neoclassical theoretical framework that underlies the use of cliometrics in economics and economic history has also been extended to other disciplines and subfields, as the tools of economics are increasingly being taken up by other social sciences. In this way, the narrow theoretical apparatus and methodological framework of economics closes the door for investigating how capitalism's development in Western Europe was founded on structures of oppression. The history of the conceptualization of the Transatlantic Slave Trade's role in capitalist development

> is arguably one of the best examples that all of "history" is terribly socially constructed, and will reflect the ideas and ideals and, most importantly, the perceived interests of the races, nationalities, classes, and genders which construct it. (Bailey, 2014, p. 263)

Racialization of capitalism did not end with the Transatlantic Slave Trade. We still see the role of racialization in the US South in the reluctance of white plantation owners, hoping to extract more surplus, to yield economic power over the black plantation workers (Keeanga-Yamahtta, 2016). The system of apartheid instituted in South Africa by the settler colonial government is another stark example. It provided a mechanism of domination and control over the racialized Black African and Cape colored workers for providing cheap labor power for production processes controlled by Whites (Wolpe, 1972). Even since the official end of apartheid in 1994, racialized structures have remained in various forms (Visser and Ferrer, 2015; Meagher, 2019; Chari, 2024). Similarly, Israel's development is subsidized by its access to racialized Palestinian labor. Palestinians are often paid less, segregated into occupations with insufficient

Israeli workers, and considered disposable when production slows (Locker-Biletzki, 2018). Moreover, Palestinian territories provide access to land and other resources that aid in capital accumulation (Locker-Biletzki, 2018) – a control that is maintained via a process of settler colonialism and genocide (Pappé, 2006).

Capitalism kept evolving in the capitalist center when racialized workers were brought within the ambit of wage labor relations. Modern forms of expropriation and land grabs take place worldwide often in a highly racialized manner (Fraser, 2019). Wage and wealth differentials between workers from different racial groups point to the continued role played by these identity-based processes in subsidizing capitalist accumulation. Expropriation can take different forms in different spaces and phases of capitalism but includes outcomes like lower wages for racialized workers, sorting them into low paid jobs, or charging them a higher rate of interest for loans. For example, the 2007–8 crisis showed that predatory loans and debt markets in the US were heavily racialized, with interest rates being much higher for marginalized groups (Chakravarty and Ferreira da Silva, 2012).

Challenging Eurocentrism in economics entails exposing the ways in which such structural oppression, exploitation, and unevenness underpins capitalism's development and continued functioning, as well as exposing how these questions have been silenced in the discipline's own history of thought. Centering the role of social relations and structural oppression allows us to see different aspects of the system and that capitalism is variegated, heterogeneous, and contradiction-ridden, and does not, by its very nature, smoothly unfold in a similar way universally. Capitalism rather integrates and reproduces forms of exploitation across the world in institutionally specific ways (Frank, 1967; Banaji, 2010).

-3-
Colonization of the Discipline: From Political Economy to Contemporary Economics

Economics students and researchers today may not recognize the field as portrayed in chapter 2, given that the development of capitalism and the field's evolution are rarely explained explicitly in the curriculum. Rather, students tend to start with discussions of supply and demand, the rational economic agent, and how competitive and imperfectly competitive markets operate. Economists might tell you that economics is primarily about establishing credible econometric research designs (Angrist and Pischke, 2010) or finding ways of fixing concrete policy problems (Duflo, 2017).

By paying attention to the history of economic thought, we can see how the broader field of political economy developed into contemporary economics, which has allowed economists to understand and portray themselves as neutral problem-solvers or as empiricists removed from ideological battles. In the process of the field's development, Lionel Robbins' (1932, p. 15) definition of economics as the study of "human behavior as a relationship between ends and scarce means" became solidified. This is evident in the definition of economics on the American Economic Association (2024) website:

Economics can be defined in a few different ways. It's the study of scarcity, the study of how people use resources and respond to incentives, or the study of decision-making.[1]

The development of economics into its current form followed efforts to make the discipline more scientific. For example, Léon Walras, whose scholarly contributions significantly influenced the discipline in the nineteenth century, was convinced that economics would progressively evolve into a scientific discipline akin to the hard sciences, envisioning economic laws as rational, precise, and as incontrovertible as the laws of astronomy (Walras, 1954; Jaffé, 1965). Similarly, Stanley Jevons and Alfred Marshall, at the beginning of the twentieth century, were key players working to establish a science of economics along the pattern of physics (Mirowski, 1984), although their analysis of trade was informed by colonial ways of thinking about civilization and race (Blaney, 2020). By the end of World War II, economics became increasingly focused on mathematical formalization and econometric estimation, which further cemented its reputation as neutral and value-free (Alves and Kvangraven, 2020). Economics went from being rather pluralist in the first half of the twentieth century to becoming composed of a relatively monolithic mainstream during the Cold War, which has endured to this day. While this transformation is often presented as a path of refinement and improvement, as we shall see, it involved a political process of separating the economic from the social, centering on individuals rather than structures and processes, and excluding alternative ways of theorizing. This process strengthened the Eurocentric characteristics of economics that emerged during the heyday of political economy.

From political economy to economics: An overview

During the eighteenth and nineteenth centuries, economic questions were addressed by scholars of political economy.[2] Despite critical differences among political economists of that time, scholars associated with the paradigm explained the capitalist economy by drawing on political and social characteristics relevant to their historical moment and using a range of methods and methodologies. For example, Adam Smith combined deductive and inductive reasoning. Inductive reasoning involves observing the world to derive general principles or theories, making broad generalizations based on concrete observations. This contrasts with deductive reasoning, where conclusions are derived logically from given premises. David Ricardo pioneered the use of deductive reasoning in economics, which later became fully embraced by the discipline, despite Schumpeter's (1954) criticism of his tendency to approach complex problems through simplistic mathematical models with unrealistic assumptions, known as the Ricardian Vice (Kurz, 2009, 2017). In comparison, Karl Marx employed a combination of abstract, social, systemic, and historically dynamic reasoning. All political economists, despite their differences, paid attention to class dynamics in their analysis of capitalist economies, albeit in radically different ways.

Political economy debates were common before the establishment of social science disciplines as separate fields. In Europe, it was only after 1870 that the economics discipline began to take shape, as scientific inquiry started to be divided into distinct disciplines (Parrish, 1967; Easton, 1991). In the late nineteenth and early twentieth centuries, new categories of knowledge emerged more generally, eventually leading to their solidification across various disciplines (Easton, 1991).

In the late nineteenth century, the rise of *marginalism* laid the foundation for the establishment of economics as a distinct discipline (Fine and Milonakis, 2009). Marginalists introduced a subjective theory of value, asserting that a product's value was determined by the utility it provided to an individual, which became an "all-embracing theory of purposive conduct" (Stigler, 1972, p. 572), rather than by labor theories of value, as favored by political economists. Economic analysis increasingly focused on the concept of utility. While utility theory was not new (Howey, 1989), William Stanley Jevons, Léon Walras, and Carl Menger provided a much deeper and more systematic discussion.

They introduced marginal utility as the core concept of the so-called marginal revolution. Marginal utility refers to the satisfaction or benefit an individual gains from consuming one additional unit of a product or service. Utility is the product's ability to satisfy wants, but this power is not inherent in the products themselves; it is tied to individual subjectivity (Jevons, 2012). Therefore, the value in use decreases as the quantity consumed increases. In contrast to the social and historical specificity and attention to inequalities produced through class relations that characterized political economy, Jevons, Walras, and Menger adopted deductive reasoning centered on principles of utility maximization, rationality, and equilibrium. This shift effectively abandoned the political economy approaches that favored inductive historical reasoning.

Underlying marginalism is the paradigm of *methodological individualism* – the notion that individual humans and firms are the most relevant units of analysis. In this framework, markets are assumed to reach equilibrium based on individuals and firms acting rationally by maximizing utility and profits. Consequently, economics came to be understood in "extremely narrow and specific terms" (Milonakis and Fine, 2009, p. 2). As Barbara Wootton (1938) observed, it became about defining economic theory as the study of the market process in a specific sense – focusing on the mutual interactions of demand, supply, and price – with equilibrium and competitive markets being central. This approach sidelined the importance of human actions and interactions within and between groups, reducing the complexity of economic and social phenomena to the behavior of isolated individuals and firms.

Robbins' widely accepted view of economics as the study of behavior in the context of scarcity reflects the methodological changes seen in the twentieth century. In the early twentieth century, Alfred Marshall played a crucial role in institutionalizing what came to be known as the neoclassical school of economics, based on marginalist principles (Aspromourgos, 1986; Fine and Milonakis, 2009).[3] Then, equilibrium analysis – with equilibrium being a situation where quantities and prices do not change, as there is no incentive on anyone's part to change (Arrow, 2007) – was further developed and refined, most famously by Arrow and Debreu in the 1950s. This paved the way for what we know as general equilibrium theory.[4] It also set the tone for economics to become more focused on choices that households, firms, and workers make, given their preferences, budget constraints, and relative prices. This centrality of choice gives the impression of both consumer and firm autonomy in a market economy (Friedman, 1962).

It is crucial to highlight that the marginalist revolution didn't immediately put an end to big debates in economics. Economic theorizing and methods remained pluralist until the 1950s (Blaug, 2003). During this period, various schools of thought, such as the German historical school, old institutional economics, Keynesian economics, structuralism,[5] and neo-Marxism,[6] co-existed alongside neoclassical economics in the dominant institutions of the capitalist center. It was only from the 1950s onwards, with the onset of the Cold War, that "global uniformity in the analytical style of the economics profession" became more evident (Blaug, 2003, p. 145). In the middle of the twentieth century, conceptual principles such as equilibrium, rationality, scarcity, and choice became increasingly universal in content and application. While the scope of application of marginalist principles was initially limited to market relations, it gradually expanded further as these principles gained general acceptance. Thus, even though marginalism was initially intended to describe only parts of human behavior in particular circumstances, it evolved into an analysis that was perceived to be "unlimited in scope" (Blaug, 2003, p. 151).

Both the Walrasian and Marshallian equilibrium economic models take perfectly competitive markets as their point of reference.[7] An economic model in this context is essentially a mathematical representation of the world, and often contains multiple equations that try to simplify our complex reality into its relevant elements. The model of perfect competition takes as a starting point that consumers are rational (they allocate their incomes to maximize their satisfaction from the goods and serves they consume), producers are rational (they allocate resources in order to maximize their profits), and economic agents make decisions in the light of perfect knowledge (e.g., buyers and sellers know all the prices of all the goods in the market, know everything they need to know about the quality of goods and the character of the other economic agents). There is also the assumption that markets consist of many participants who are price-takers, meaning that an individual participant has no influence on market prices, that there are no barriers to market entry or exit, and that commodities are broadly homogenous (e.g., you cannot distinguish one apple on the market from another).

As it became evident that markets do not operate perfectly, the economics discipline evolved and incorporated market imperfections attributed to informational asymmetries, transaction costs, or other institutional or behavioral deviations. This evolution gave rise to a tradition known as *late neoclassical economics*, as described by Madra (2017), which builds upon neoclassical economics but relaxes some of its most untenable assumptions. According to Madra (2017), contemporary mainstream economics exhibits heterogeneity characterized by a patchwork of attempts to restore, rehabilitate, and reconstitute the theoretical humanist presuppositions of neoclassical economics. These humanist presuppositions require a centered, unified, and autonomous conceptualization of the human subject, who is presumed to know what would improve their welfare, form preferences reflecting their welfare, and make choices accordingly.

With the incorporation of imperfections in economics, its engagement with the social sphere increased, stretching beyond its original terrain of market production and consumption, understanding social phenomena as responses to imperfect workings of the market (Fine and Milonakis, 2009). Within this late neoclassical framework, economic and social structures, including institutions, culture, habits, and seemingly non-rational behavior, can be explained as rational or strategic responses to market imperfections. For example, discrimination by employers – a seemingly irrational practice – is often explained as a rational response to information asymmetries, where employers don't have full information about an applicant, but they know how the applicant's identity group might on average differ from other groups.

The rational economic agent has also been modified within mainstream economic theory by introducing influences from altruistic and endogenous preferences; by external institutions, norms, and society (e.g., Bowles, 2003), by imposing bounds on rationalities by incorporating bounds as an additional cost for optimization (e.g., Simon, 1957; Klaes and Sent, 2005; Madra, 2017), and by introducing behavioral imperfections (e.g., Thaler and Sunstein, 2008). Institutions, which were viewed as existing outside the economic system in much of neoclassical theory, are now introduced as integral to it. This is done through behavioral game theoretic modeling, which allows individual interactions and strategies to be influenced by social and cultural institutions; through experimental economics, which simulates social interaction of individuals in a laboratory setting; and through agent-based modeling, which allows the system to evolve naturally based on how individuals with different social characteristics interact.[8] These important developments broaden the notion of rationality beyond self-interest and introduce institutions central for understanding economic interactions.

How did the theoretical narrowing of economics happen?

Examining the political, institutional, and economic forces that shape particular worldviews is essential to understanding the political economy of knowledge production. For instance, political economy was dominant during capitalism's development, seeking to understand the tumultuous and often violent changes accompanying economic and social shifts. By the twentieth century, John Maynard Keynes' ideas gained institutional traction in countries like the United Kingdom and the United States amid high unemployment during the Great Depression and in the context of War Socialism, fostering skepticism toward prevailing paradigms.

Consequently, significant parts of the political and economic establishment were receptive to Keynesian concepts of demand management (A. O. Hirschman, 1981). Similarly, the context of the Cold War is essential to understanding how economics evolved into what we know today. In this period, the idea that the economic system is based on dynamics that are compatible with equilibrium came to be favored over the idea that the system is disruptive, exploitative, and not necessarily providing full employment. Ironically, at a point when the key dispute of the global world order was centered on the competition between two world systems – capitalism versus socialism – the marginalist revolution had provided precisely the anti-revolutionary ammunition that was in high demand in the capitalist center, given that it lent itself to demonstrating how the competitive price mechanism present in capitalism led to efficient outcomes.

The Cold War accelerated the dominance of institutions that increasingly "embraced the formal method's promise of efficiency, accuracy and mastery of the social and economic world" (Fourcade, 2009 p. 90) and it involved attacks on educational institutions, artists, and public figures suspected to be associated with radical politics (Schrecker, 2002). With McCarthyism on the rise, institutions such as the RAND Corporation – which provides research for the US Armed Forces among other things – played a significant role in supporting, for example, research within game theory in economics (Weintraub, 2017, p. 576). Between 1968 and 1979, the funding patterns of the National Science Foundation were heavily biased toward "quantitative research and econometrics" (Fourcade, 2009, p. 90).

As a part of this broader trend, there was discrimination against radical scholars across universities in the United States and United Kingdom (Solberg and Tomilson, 1997; F. S. Lee, 2009) and economics textbooks and academic economists that supported radical ideas were undermined (Buckley, 1951; Backhouse, 2010; Giraud, 2014). Investigations were often followed by denial of tenure (Weintraub, 2014) and there was a widespread hesitation within departments related to appointing or promoting economists likely to cause discomfort among the universities' governing bodies, donors, and alumni (Goodwin, 1998). This was the context when the so-called measures of excellence were also erected to control the production of knowledge about economics (F. S. Lee, 2009).

With the fall of the USSR in 1989, real-world alternatives to capitalism became more difficult to come by and imagine, which contributed to the further marginalization of radical, anti-capitalist, and non-Eurocentric scholarship. The persecution of scholars not committed to neoclassical and late neoclassical economics continued. In the early 2000s, one of the leading institutions for providing teaching and research outside neoclassical thinking in the United States was thwarted: there was a removal of the so-called heterodox faculty members in the economics PhD program at the University of Notre Dame (Ancochea, 2004). The official reason was that these economists did "not meet minimum standards of quality" (Ancochea, 2004, p. 9). Something similar happened at the University of California Riverside (Klamer, 2007, p. 133). This trend was not limited to universities in the United States and was exported to the rest of the world during the Cold War through campaigns carried out overtly and covertly by the CIA as well as structural adjustment programs of the World Bank and the IMF, including across African universities (Stein, 2021). We discuss this in greater detail in the next chapter.

Where does this leave the discipline today?

Economics teaching and research has increasingly become standardized globally within the late neoclassical tradition, which we term *mainstream economics*. Like late neoclassical economics, mainstream economics is no longer just based on neoclassical and marginalist principles, but includes new theoretical developments such as behavioral, experimental, New Institutional Economics, and evolutionary game theory (Colander et al., 2004; Coyle, 2007; Dequech, 2007; Colander, 2009). Lively research agendas within the mainstream are now based on studying incompleteness of markets, evolving social behavior, and bargaining in labor markets – a sharp break from Marshallian and Walrasian equilibrium economics.

Nonetheless, now, more than ever before, rigor in economics is fundamentally associated with quantitative deductive methods (Lawson, 2013). Mainstream economics is a "complex system of evolving ideas," but new approaches are only welcomed if "they are done with a careful understanding of the recent orthodox approach and within a modeling methodology acceptable to the mainstream" (Colander et al., 2004, pp. 489, 492). But most importantly, all these changes in mainstream economics do not in any way mark a fundamental break from the emphasis of neoclassical economics on the possibility of a harmonious reconciliation of diverse interests of selfish, autonomous, rational agents in the presence of competitive markets and private property rights (Madra, 2017). Individuals are still seen as having predetermined interests that can be incorporated into a model of stable equilibrium or evolutionary stability. The dominance of this framework is based on squeezing out alternative theoretical and methodological frameworks. Consequently, many economists today do not engage in broader theoretical and methodological debates and see economics as a discipline based on a set of tools and techniques rather than a subject matter.

Despite recent developments, extensions, and deviations from neoclassical theory at the level of research, the undergraduate economics curriculum, which is the first (and only) formal introduction to economics for most students, continues to be taught as a set of principles based on neoclassical economics.[9] How economics is taught is incredibly important as it lays the foundation for how economists think about theory and methods, which leads them to see the world in particular (limited) ways when they go out into policy, research, or academia. Textbooks hold enormous power, given the many students who obtain their foundational understanding from them. As Paul Samuelson, a leading economist and textbook author once argued: "Let those who will – write the nation's laws – if I can write its textbooks" (Samuelson and Barnett, 2007, p. xxii). Textbooks are a politically powerful tool, perhaps even more powerful than lawmaking, given their capacity to shape the minds of generations of students.

Even when there is a push for a shift away from these orthodoxies in economics teaching, what seems to be taking its place are curricula like CORE, mentioned in the previous chapter (CORE, 2017, 2023). CORE introduces students to various tools of economics intended to help them analyze the world around them "as it exists." However, students are not introduced to the plurality of models from different schools of thought. It is obscured from students that different models have different starting points (e.g., class process in Marxist frameworks versus preferences and endowments in neoclassical/late neoclassical theories) and these starting points have implications in terms of the processes they readily reveal and conceal (e.g., class conflict). Like standard economics textbooks, CORE does not provide students with an understanding of which models become canonical and why, and the political factors that determine which theories are worthy of canonization and inclusion in textbooks (Toporowski, 2021). Unsurprisingly, the tools of economics (with which CORE wants students to be familiar) are often applied in haphazard ways, with multiple, often irreconcilable frameworks used in the same chapter. While efforts such as CORE are an improvement on the orthodox representation of economics as simply a set of (neoclassical) principles as in Mankiw's (2020) textbooks, they remain firmly within the late neoclassical paradigm and thus do not challenge dominant thinking. Despite trying to equip students to understand a more real world (e.g., teaching imperfect rather than perfect competition), it still uses a perfectly competitive capitalism as its first-best world – and considers ways and policies to push the economy closer to this. By not exposing students to the hidden assumptions underlying their tools and methodologies, CORE also contributes to depoliticization of knowledge and reinforcement of the idea that economics is universal, neutral, and objective (Kvangraven and Kesar, 2023).

How is mainstream economics Eurocentric?

Three fundamental features of late neoclassical economics cement the Eurocentrism that characterized the field's foundations. These are the establishment of economic laws that are abstracted from social and historical processes, the establishment of equilibrium as the attempt to reconcile individual and structural spheres, and the empirical turn in the field.

Establishing economic laws: removing social, political, and historical structures

The movement from political economy to contemporary economics left social and political factors and historical developments out of what is conceived of as *the economy* to effectively establish economic laws and principles. However, this created some tensions that economics is continuously trying to resolve. One of them is the tension between an economic and social sphere, which can be traced back to Adam Smith. As Duncan Foley (2006) explains:

> Smith consolidated ... a way of looking at modern society as made up of two spheres: an economic sphere of individual initiative and interaction, governed by impersonal laws that assure a beneficent outcome of the pursuit of self-interest; and the rest of social life, including political, religious, and moral interactions which require the conscious balancing of self-interest with social considerations. (Foley, 2006, pp. 1–2)

Since then, we have seen a separation into the economic and so-called non-economic, where the former is associated with economic rationality and the latter with social considerations. Smith, however, was never able to resolve a fundamentally irreconcilable tension in the logic of the operation between the capitalist economic and non-economic spheres. Smith believed in the individual's pursuit of private self-interests within the institutions of capitalism, which he thought would collectively lead us to better overall outcomes; but this meant individuals act differently – with distinct rationalities – in the non-market, such as the household, spheres (Foley, 2006). Economics dealt with this tension by gradually extricating itself from the domain of the social, resulting in the de-socialization and de-historicization of economic theory. The laws and principles thus developed are considered "universal," as they are applicable "without reference to time, place, or even humans and the market" (Fine and Milonakis, 2009, pp. 6–7). Social issues, when introduced, are treated as though they are only to exist within and according to market principles. This approach sustains and obfuscates the divide between the economic rational actors, associated with capitalist market principles, and the rest.

Intriguingly, after the development of a core technical apparatus based on marginalism in the first half of the twentieth century, the extension of the apparatus's application to economic and non-economic issues dominated the latter half, without taking the specificities of non-economic issues seriously (Fine and Milonakis, 2009). This tendency was widely acknowledged among economists. As the Economics Nobel laureate Ronald Coase (1978) wrote:

> There are, at present, two tendencies in operation in economics which seem to be inconsistent but which, in fact, are not. The first consists of the enlargement of the scope of economists' interests so far as subject matter is concerned. The second is a narrowing of professional interest to formal, technical, commonly mathematical, analysis. This more formal analysis tends to have greater generality. It may say less, or leave much unsaid, about the economic system, but, because of its generality, the analysis becomes applicable to all social systems. It is this generality of their analytical systems which, I believe, has facilitated the movement of economists into other social sciences, where they will presumably repeat the successes (and failures) which they have had within economics itself. (Coase, 1978, p. 207)

A parallel implication of the separation of individual behavior from their broader social fabric is evident in the way countries are analyzed. For example, in efforts to understand trade through theories of comparative advantage, marginalists such as Jevons and Marshall, building on Ricardo, suggested that countries could be treated as abstract individuals, rather than situating them within their historical and political contexts (Blaney, 2020). This is *methodological nationalism* (discussed in greater detail in chapter 6). With this, dichotomies such as developed versus underdeveloped were produced to categorize countries, with the *developed* representing societies where economic rationalities and modernity dominate and the *underdeveloped* representing those yet to be fully penetrated by capitalist modernity. However, treating countries as independent units and their realities as isolated phenomena, rather than as interconnected parts of a single historical process of Empire and colonization that created social and economic differences among countries, obscures the true nature of the underlying processes.

Context remains absent and the Eurocentric core intact when economics explores non-economic issues. This is evident in how economics considers rationality and institutions. Capitalist rationality and the institutions that align individuals with such rationality are viewed as modern, and non-capitalist rationalities and their supporting institutions as traditional and primitive. For example, ownership structures that are organized around culturally complex institutions, including communal or kinship relations, rather than strong individual property rights are deemed inefficient and inadequate because they do not enforce contracts in the manner that institutions in the capitalist center do (Stein, 1995). Institutions of the periphery are not considered on their own terms but deemed as producing high transaction costs and standing in the way of economic growth (Zein-Elabdin, 2009). These dichotomies further reinforce a colonial cultural hegemony, where the modern is associated with superior scientific rationality informed by Enlightenment principles, and the latter as irrational and degenerative, informed by primitive and backward subjectivities (Bhabha,

1994; Zein-Elabdin, 2009). Traditional institutions, then, are viewed as constraints on individuals' maximizing rational behavior (Zein-Elabdin, 2009). As a result, creating better capitalist institutions for the periphery, which can also allow individuals to behave more rationally, is viewed as a key policy intervention. The underlying assumption here is that capitalist development will lead to better outcomes if institutions of the social sphere are reshaped to better support capitalist economic behavior by individuals and firms.

Given that understanding processes of exploitation and oppression demand the social and historical not be separated from the economic, the unresolved tension between the economic and so-called non-economic has cemented Eurocentrism in economics.

Establishing equilibrium: the attempt to reconcile individual and structural spheres

The evolution from political economy to economics involved both reducing the units of analysis to the individual (from class analysis to methodological individualism) and organizing analyses of the macroeconomy through the lens of equilibrium. A key challenge associated with this development is that of reconciling individual rationality with aggregative – collective, social, market – rationality (Madra, 2017).

Individual rationality is based on understanding humans as autonomous, self-transparent, and rationally self-conscious, who know or can eventually know what their preferences are and what improves their welfare, who can translate these preferences into choices, and who recognize themselves as intentional and autonomous subjects responsible for their choices. But how do competing choices and interests interact with each other and how are these resolved? Aggregate rationality is understood as the specification of conditions of this resolution, which in neoclassical and late neoclassical economics is a contradiction-free socioeconomic order, or states of equilibrium. This means individual rational behavior is reconciled with the social via a state of equilibrium. While there are schools of thought in economics that focus on either individual rationality (e.g., feminist economics) or aggregate states of equilibria (e.g., Keynesian or Kaleckian economics), late neoclassical economics is unique in its insistence that individual rationality is consistent with and can support a stable socioeconomic system (Madra, 2017). The socioeconomic order thus becomes one that reflects and accommodates the needs of these rational agents. According to Madra, this characteristic underpins all developments and deviations in late neoclassical theory. Consequently, various deviations and developments within mainstream economics are not about a change in analytical method, but about the way the reconciliation of the individual and aggregate rationality is theorized.

There are a few different ways in which economics reconciles individual and aggregate rationality. In a Walrasian model, which for a long time remained the canonical model of economics, an equilibrium model is built from the ground up, emphasizing the role of an imaginary auctioneer using an invisible hand to adjust prices to reach an equilibrium. In these models, individuals are self-interested with exogenous preferences, and complete and costless contracts allow for a rigorous and elegant model of human behavior. Marshall developed equilibrium models further (Colander, 1995), to allow for non-selfish preferences and motives, and endogeneity, within a neoclassical model. Thereby, Marshallian models opened avenues for theorizing that did not begin with the same strict assumptions of human behavior that Walras did (Bowles and Gintis, 2000). But even within Marshallian models, a harmonious resolution of the theoretical tension between individual rationality and systemic stability is achieved. Instead of a static equilibrium approach of an invisible auctioneer, as in Walras, competition is understood as a selection process, where inefficient firms or households are driven out, and the selection mechanism plays the role of the invisible hand (Madra, 2017).

While Walrasian and Marshallian frameworks rest on the assumption of perfectly competitive markets, in late neoclassical economics, many of the assumptions associated with perfect competition are relaxed to correct for imperfections such as altruistic preferences, bounded rationality, transaction costs, incomplete contracts, and incomplete information. These departures, however, do not overcome the central tension of reconciling diverse interests of rational agents with some kind of market equilibrium (Madra, 2017).

Within these frameworks, you will find economists both defending and opposing government intervention, depending on whether they believe that reconciliation of the individual and aggregate rationality can be achieved based on competitive markets and institutions of property rights, or whether they do not and call for intervention to correct for market failures. Over time, the Walrasian frameworks centered around an auctioneer were used to propose the control of government over economic decision making, while the Marshallian framework, which later influenced the Chicago school of economics, tended to focus on leaving the market alone to produce efficient outcomes through a selection process.

From the relationship between individual and aggregate there is also a direct line to the field's Eurocentric's foundations. First, this relationship operates in a framework that rests on a neoclassical understanding of human rationality that forms the basis for a reconciliation of individual and aggregate rationality. This is a Eurocentric view of (capitalist) rationality that is unlikely to reflect or represent the behavior of large parts of humanity. Second, insisting on understanding the macroeconomy through the rationality of individual-level actors makes it easier to see the capitalist center as exceptional, and to assume pioneering agency on behalf of the capitalists in the center. This assumption has led to the widely held belief in economics that the source of wealth of the richest countries are their exceptionally productive workers. It follows that spaces of poverty, destitution, and underemployment are associated with inferiority, irrationality, inability to align with capitalist logic and even backward culture (Hobson, 2012; Inayatullah and Blaney, 2015) that are barriers to the achievement of harmonious reconciliation between individual and aggregate rationality.

Third, and crucially, various structural aspects of power relations, colonialism, dispossession that are at the center of anti-colonial frameworks find their genesis not in individual choice and decision-making but at a structural level – or as a process embedded in the very functioning of a social system – that cannot be captured by unit-level analysis. Such structural aspects, then, are not simply issues of reconciliation, but are built into the logic of economic organization itself. In late neoclassical theory, however, even when bargaining and contested exchanges are introduced, it is described against a benchmark of individual and/or structural rationality and their contradiction-free reconciliation.

Establishing neutrality and objectivity: the empirical turn

There has been an empirical turn in economics in recent years, or what Angrist and Pischke (2010) have called a *credibility revolution*. As a result, many economists think economics is merely about uncovering empirical truths through econometric methods, unmoored from the idea that all empirical work is also fundamentally shaped by theory (consider, for example, how one chooses dependent and independent variables, which hypothesis one chooses to test, which units of analysis are chosen, or which variables are considered relevant).

Even though some empirical explorations are based on revising the theoretical assumptions of some canonical, albeit Eurocentric, late-neoclassical model, for the most part, this empirical turn in economics is a further move toward positivism. Positivism implements standards of knowing that assume that objective reality exists and that anyone can discover it using scientific method, requiring a social distance and objectivity in the relationship between researcher and the research subject (McCloskey, 1985). Take, for example, the 2019 Economics Nobel laureate and proponent of experimental methods Esther Duflo (2017), who likened economists to "plumbers," suggesting that economists' work is purely technical. Similarly, as Banerjee et al. (2007, p. 115) put it when writing about the knowledge that emanates from randomized controlled trials (RCTs): "[RCTs are] simple to interpret. The beauty of randomized evaluations is that the results are what they are." Banerjee and Duflo (2011) argue that RCTs are a way to get away from ideology and let the findings speak for themselves, and empirical truths can be neutrally consumed without any theoretical bias. This is also based on the idea that one can separate economic laws, trends, and regularities from the broader social fabric – a key feature of the field we defined earlier. RCTs have become immensely popular and are often considered the gold standard in development economics research (Cartwright, 2011).

In 2021, the Economics Nobel further entrenched the celebration of empiricism, as the prize was awarded partly to Joshua D. Angrist and Guido W. Imbens for their "methodological contributions to the analysis of causal relationships" (Nobel Prize Outreach, 2021), without a discussion of how their research is placed within late neoclassical economics. Celebrating a method without situating it in its political and theoretical context entrenches the idea that empirical research is neutral, limits the kinds of questions that can be asked, and how they can be answered.

The empirical turn in economics is a deepening of Eurocentrism. First, the empirical approaches focus on small tractable issues. This focus ignores and obfuscates the broader processes through which those issues emerge. For example, processes of imperial subjugation, racialization, and dispossession, which are linked to the creation of poverty and inequality, are ignored and the attention is given to fixing small problems, often by inducing changes in human behavior, which are symptoms of these broader processes. The issue is not that we should not care about small or localized issues such as poverty, hunger, low productivity levels, or community health – and how behavior relates to them – but that when dealing with such issues it is crucial to situate the problems within broader structures that have produced these problems and will continue to produce these problems if not dealt with (Reddy, 2012). In her article, "Small development questions are important, but they require big answers," Stevano (2020) provides the following example to illustrate

this point: it is not that asking why farmers do not adopt fertilizer even if it might increase productivity (as in Duflo et al.,
2008) is illegitimate, but that methodologically searching for
answers only within the individual behavior and the temporal
bias of farmers creates a huge blind spot in the research. It
fundamentally fails to consider agroecological and political
economy factors that shape this behavior. Crucially, the
relationship between fertilizer and yields depends on the
quality of the soil, thereby affecting how farmers consider
their opportunities to obtain fertilizer. Farmers with access to
poorer quality land will be the least likely to adopt fertilizers,
regardless of their temporal bias. Patriarchal structures also
shape access to land and fertilizers, which are not considered
in the mainstream's behavioralism. Taking a non-Eurocentric
approach with attention to structures would therefore only
broaden the scope for understanding behavior.

Second, the empiricism that has come to characterize
economics suggests that economic enquiry can be neutral,
universal, and bias-free. But all approaches to economic
enquiry are founded on specific ways of viewing the world
and the choice of analysis is never neutral. This depoliticization was actively pursued as the mainstream of economics
transitioned from political economy to economics, as
economists searched for abstract theory free from "the
mundane muddles of society" (Hong, 2008, p. 128). This
led to the emergence of a professional culture that curtailed
discussions of contentious issues of power related to the
"private property system, unequal distribution, nationality,
and political ideology" (Hong, 2008, p. 129). Thinking of
economics as being ideologically neutral not only leaves
intact both the late neoclassical economics dominance and
the dynamics that suppress pluralism and radical ways of
theorizing, but also cements the assumption that Eurocentric
theory is superior and objective.

This is not an argument against using empirical tools to
understand the real world, but against expecting data to
reveal truths without a careful consideration of the underlying processes, which are only reflected in data in a very
specific way. Even the categories that we collect data on are

not neutral but informed by our biases of how we approach an issue. RCTs, once again, are a prime example of this. Most studies analyzing an intervention's impact are devoid of analysis of the structural processes that underlie the issue to be resolved.

Furthermore, the claim to neutrality combined with depoliticization of the field causes confusion among economists regarding what is normative and what is positive (Myrdal, 2017 [1932]). While economic theorization and research is presented as neutral, policy advice is often considered normative, even though it flows from this allegedly neutral – although always normative – scientific research. As such, mainstream economics suppresses debates about normative values when discussing theory. However, as Myrdal (2017 [1932]) points out, the normative values will eventually show up in the analysis, when connections are made to policy. It is precisely this kind of confusion that led Thomas Piketty (2020) to argue that while his empirical work is rational and unbiased, it is only his policy recommendations that are ideological and normative. This is symptomatic of economics as a whole.

Implications of deepening Eurocentrism in economics: Inequalities between groups

The implications of late neoclassical economics can be illustrated well by how economics analyzes inequalities between social groups. In much of late neoclassical economics, capitalism, if functioning perfectly, is seen as color blind and, hence, any race (or identity)-based inequality is an imperfection in the system, which is otherwise assumed to produce neutral outcomes. This neutral depiction of capitalism's relationship to race displaces the idea that the process of racialization is endogenous to capitalism, as we briefly noted in the last chapter.

Within mainstream economics, the historical evolution of racial differentiation and its central role in the development of capitalism is left unconsidered, and the limited focus, instead, is on its current manifestations. One of the first theories in mainstream economics to explain identity-based inequality is taste-based discrimination. This is often seen to be a result of individual behavior motivated by discriminatory tastes and preferences (Becker, 1957). Becker explored two sets of questions: how to measure discrimination and why it is that people discriminate. To the first, he answers that money can be a measure of discrimination. Discrimination can be measured as a coefficient, which is the price an individual is willing to pay to avoid being in contact with an individual from a group that they discriminate against. To the latter, he answers that people discriminate simply because they have a taste for it. Albelda and Drago (2013) characterize Becker's theory as follows: "Discrimination then is like tofu in that it is something you are willing to pay for – if you have the 'taste'."

The implication of this approach is that in competitive markets, discriminatory employers or firms will find it difficult to compete with non-discriminatory employers who will be able to secure higher profit margins since they do not pay a higher wage for the workers from their preferred group and will eventually be driven out. Decades later, however, we can still see discrimination and inequality persisting. As a response, economists directed their focus toward understanding why Becker's expectation did not bear out. Given the original hypothesis, economists were naturally drawn to explanations that argue that markets are in fact not perfect or competitive enough.

Phelps (1972), Stiglitz (1973), and Arrow (1998) argued that the impact of incomplete information and incomplete markets for rational choice were important factors. In their narrative, discrimination may persist in the labor market because employers often do not have complete information about the candidates applying for a job. In the absence of information, employers are only able to form expectations based on prior information on group-based statistics or stereotypes, such as observable attributes, which include the individuals' social group, based, for example, on gender, race, or nationality. As a result, the employers make hiring and wage decisions based on expected and not actual productivity. Discrimination, then, is rational on the part of the employer who is unable to have access to complete information about the productivity of the individual. This extended theory suggests focusing on correcting market imperfection and informational asymmetries that facilitate this statistical discrimination, for example through designing better mechanisms to access information, nudging disadvantaged identities to opt for better signaling mechanisms, providing unconscious bias trainings, or, in more centrist circles, advocating for better opportunities for these socially disadvantaged identities. This narrative "whitewashes capitalism and exonerates 'the market system'" (Koechlin, 2019, p. 562). Much of recent work in late neoclassical economics remains limited to calculating the taste-based versus statistical component of discrimination. Yet, as Nobel Prize-winning economist Kenneth Arrow (1998) noted in his review, while

> racial discrimination pervades every aspect of a society in which it is found ... its economic dimension hardly appears in general treatments of economics, outside of the specialized literature devoted to it. (Arrow, 1998, p. 91)

The tradition that follows these identity-based inequality analyses contributes to conflating racial differentiation and discrimination, having much less interest in the former. Gregory Mankiw's bestselling textbook (2008) devotes seven pages to discrimination, with no discussion of racial differentiation. This is illustrative of how canonical undergraduate teaching treats issues of race, that is, suggesting that solutions to racial differentiation can be found through the market. As Mankiw (2008, p. 409) puts it, "markets contain a natural remedy for employer discrimination." In his review of textbooks' treatment of race, Koechlin (2019) thus found:

> A student is likely to leave ECON 101 (or an economics major) with a sense that "economic science" has

"shown" that discrimination is not that big a deal, and that the history of racist plunder and exploitation in the USA (of which there likely has been no discussion) is not relevant to "economics." (Koechlin, 2019, p. 562)

Becker's work is perhaps also a great example of the attempt to extend economic principles to all social spheres. Becker treated other areas of society as if they were governed by market-like interactions. Identity is also taken as pre-given rather than being socially formed. Notably, Akerlof and Kranton (2010) and Bacharach (2006) introduced the notion of individual identity being socially informed and argue that individual decisions are not simply formed by idiosyncratic tastes (Becker) or based on statistical discrimination (Phelps), but also by internalized social norms. However, even in this intervention, identity is simply seen as a perception of the self and the role of power and structural aspects in shaping identities and norms are not recognized.

As late neoclassical economics celebrates the power of markets to eliminate discriminatory behavior, it presents markets as the solution rather than the problem (Koechlin, 2019). This perspective overlooks how markets can facilitate racial differentiation. In fact, critical scholarship that focuses on social relations and structural power inequalities is excluded from economics. Crucially, this takes the origins and evolution of structural inequalities as its starting point, rather than simply noting the contemporary outcome of wage, wealth, education, or other forms of unequal outcomes and boiling them down to a consequence of individual discrimination. Radical scholarship, rather, examines differentiation processes along racial, gender, and colonial lines, and evaluates ways in which capitalist institutions reproduce racial inequalities in a systematic manner, beyond the individual institutions responsible for the racist practices in question.

Capitalism is a racialized, gendered, and colonial system from its very inception, and differentiation along these lines remains a structural feature. These forms of oppression are systemically produced and are co-constitutive and evolve with other economic processes in contemporary capitalism (Cox, 1948; Fraser, 2016a; 2016b). For example, lower average levels of income or wealth for some groups are unnatural and have been produced by historical factors and the structural oppression of certain marginalized groups in labor processes. A stark example is segregating different identity groups into different occupations, and then devaluing the earnings – and increasing the profits – associated with those occupations where marginalized groups are overrepresented (Mies, 1982; De Neve, 2012).

The case of gender-based and caste-based inequalities is, in some ways, similar. For example, an emerging literature focuses on measures to increase women's participation in the labor force, assuming it to be the way to resolve gender-based disparity. Such work appears deeply unaware of the oppressive gendered practices and structural marginalization of women in the workplace and beyond. Folbre and Nelson (2000) show that market-based care work, where women tend to be overrepresented, is systematically devalued, both since it is carried out mainly by women and since preferences of care are undervalued by the market. In fact, in family-based enterprises when different household members engage in a productive activity, women's work, despite being equally important, tends to be categorized as unskilled and is often unpaid (De Neve, 2012). In various construction activities in India, even when women join the men for wage work, the wages are paid as a couple wage, which is 1.5 times the wages for a single person wage.[10] These are instances in which gendered social processes shape market outcomes but a simplistic focus on market engagement as the solution does not allow us to adequately grapple with them.

The co-evolving nature of identity and market-based processes is evident in how social reproduction, including care work, household work, etc., has been reshaped in different phases of capitalism to allow for different ways to stabilize the economic system, with distinct implications for gendered work (Fraser, 2017). For example, the post-World War II United States breadwinner model, in providing a family with wages, allowed the women to undertake the social reproduction work. However, to facilitate more capitalist accumulation as the real wages in the US declined, it shifted toward a two-earner wage model, with women increasingly drawn into the workforce, making social reproduction more precarious. This precarity worsened with the withdrawal of social welfare institutions, making the socioeconomic system more unstable. As a result, the burden of social reproduction shifted from the household to low-paid precarious immigrant and racialized labor. Therefore, market and non-market spheres need to be studied together when trying to understand structural inequalities, but markets do not simply provide a solution and may actually worsen inequalities.

The way late neoclassical economics dealt with identity-based inequality – drastically different from radical scholars – should not be a surprise if we consider that economics has become a field about market choices given certain constraints. As Koechlin (2018) aptly puts it:

> Economics is about choice. And, by implication, it is not about institutional racism or sexism, discrimination, inheritance, exploitation, the systematic global transfer of surplus over centuries, the legacies of racism or sexism or colonialism, or dumb luck. (Koechlin, 2018, p. 442)

While a field centered on people making choices given their endowments, preferences, and constraints within the market may be initially appealing, it keeps economics from grappling with systemic, structural, and historical forces that have shaped capitalism. Within such a narrow framework it is not easy to spot or accept how racialized and gendered hierarchies were produced by a global economic structure and how most economics now relies on Eurocentric theories, methodologies, and practices. While the toolbox of late neoclassical economics can in practice study anything, the depth and usefulness of its analyses is limited by its theoretical and methodological narrowness.

−4−

Development Economics: A Failed Attempt to Break from Colonial Roots

Deconstructing the field of development economics is a fruitful way to examine how Eurocentrism has actively and passively pervaded the economic, political, and social spheres of the world, even in this subfield, which often claims to take the particularities of the periphery seriously. While this sub-discipline is vast and encompasses many theoretical traditions, including radical, non-Eurocentric scholarship, we focus here on its mainstream. In the mainstream, the origin story of the development project – its ideas, policies, and institutions that support it – is located firmly in the capitalist center, with US President Truman's inaugural speech in 1949 as its launchpad (Meier, 1974; J. Ferguson, 1990; Sachs, 1992; Rist, 1997). From there onwards, the development project was thought to spread globally, "from western origins to global faith" (Rist, 1997). In his speech, Truman said "we must embark on a bold new program for making the benefits of our scientific advances and industrial progress available for the improvement and growth of underdeveloped areas." He went on to outline the need for capital investment and expansion of private business in the periphery to promote development. The Bretton Woods Institutions – the IMF and the World Bank – were an essential part of the apparatus meant to promote this development in the periphery.

Despite this seemingly neutral facade, the ideas of development and underdevelopment took on very specific meanings that later became the underpinning of the dominant framework for development economics. Development, here, was understood singularly as capitalist transition, presupposing a linear and rational progression devoid of historical understanding. Other development indicators were expected to improve with the transition, leading to a process of cultural and social modernization so that the periphery could become more like the capitalist center. As such, a Eurocentric frame was immediately erected. The speech also reflected a continued paternal responsibility expressed by the leadership in the capitalist center to help develop the former colonies by opening them up to global capital. In this way, ":the development programme allowed it [the US] to deploy an anti-colonial imperialism" (Rist, 1997, p.75; see also Jennings, 2005).

Why consider development economics as a special case to draw broader lessons for the challenges and opportunities associated with decolonizing economics?

First, the project of economic development, and concomitantly the sub-discipline of development economics, is often thought to be born in the wake of decolonization movements, as newly independent countries were politically and intellectually engaged in charting their own sovereign paths. Due to its focus on former colonies, it had the potential to take issues of decolonization, sovereignty, and power inequalities seriously. However, the sub-discipline was ultimately not able to transcend Eurocentrism. On the contrary, it became subsumed under the rules defined by the center and eventually lost any potential to become an anti-colonial project. This critical deconstruction thus provides us with insights into the enduring challenges the discipline faces in relation to decolonization. It shows that intellectual freedom is limited in a world with unequal distribution of power, and demonstrates that (formal) political independence is alone not sufficient to deliver this freedom (Rist, 1997).

Second, development economics has always been closely related to policymaking. Outlining the sub-discipline's evolution allows us to demonstrate how it shaped policy-making in the center and periphery, as well as the debates in international and academic institutions, and how this in turn impacted former colonies in material ways. The discipline has arguably become a vehicle for center countries to justify their attempts to impose intellectual, economic, and political dominance over other countries, often mirroring the colonial period when imperial powers promoted development in their territory to legitimate the expansion of colonial rule (Macekura and Manela, 2018). As such, the way the sub-discipline evolved provides an apt illustration of the central challenges associated with decolonization, both materially and discursively.

The colonial roots of development economics

While the formal initiation of the project of economic development is generally located in the post-war era and Truman's speech, the roots of some key ideas in contemporary development economics can be traced all the way back to the colonial era (Cowen and Shenton, 1996; Goodacre, 2018; Kothari, 2019).

We can start with imperialist ideas of a civilizing mission and the paternalistic view of the development subject. The civilizing mission allowed Europeans to justify violent intervention based on the assumption that the people of the colonies needed civilizing – meaning Westernization and obliteration of local cultures (Sud and Sánchez-Ancochea, 2022). This is also associated with the Enlightenment idea of Europeans producing modernity and logic and non-Europeans producing myth and superstition (Said, 1979; see also chapters 2 and 6). As such, colonialism was an economic and cultural project that created and maintained hierarchies between groups of people (Dirks, 1992). Dichotomies like modern and traditional used to characterize the economic structures, institutions, and rationalities of the periphery were often invoked to justify colonial interventions (Bonilla-Silva and Zuberi, 2008).

When colonialism formally came to an end, many projects that had been formerly initiated by colonial administrators continued in various ways in the name of foreign aid and development policy (Mamdani, 1996). Indeed, development management as it is practiced today owes an unacknowledged debt to indirect rule instituted during colonial administrations (Cooke, 2003). For example, IMF and the World Bank practice is supported by managerialist participatory methods to achieve alleged local ownership of programs. The conceptual foundation for these methods has its roots in John Collier's work in the US Bureau of Indian (i.e., Native American) Affairs, where he developed participation as a method of indirect rule to ensure limited autonomy and maintain power. Despite the claims that IMF and World Bank programs are participatory and rooted in local ownership, activists and scholars across the world have found compelling evidence that policy conditionalities are still being pushed from the center (Kentikelenis et al., 2016). When the international institutions do engage with local conditions, they do so from a Eurocentric worldview of how they expect an economy to work and make recommendations accordingly.

The history of economic thinking within development economics also goes back to the colonial period. For example, Goodacre (2018) traces the origins of development economics back to William Petty (1623–87), often considered a precursor to Adam Smith. Petty pioneered the division of the economy into labor, capital, and land, and analyzed the process of transition from one kind of socioeconomic formation to another – a key concern in development economics with regard to less developed economies. Petty was also a part of the British colonial administration, and he made no effort to disguise his aim to obliterate indigenous social, cultural, and intellectual traditions, which he considered a threat to colonial power. He evoked the civilizing mission metaphor often, particularly to justify the British colonization of Ireland, as he argued that the Irish are lazy because of their culture, and that it was therefore in their interest to let British govern them. He also wrote about the idea of turning Ireland into a factory that would produce goods for Britain. Although these are central ideas that can still be found in development theory and practice today, their colonial origins are rarely acknowledged. As Kothari (2019) argues, the development field's concealment of its colonial past creates a dichotomy between a colonialism of the past that is bad, that we reject, and an idealized development that is good. In this way, the alleged virtues of the development field go unquestioned (Rist, 1997).

Finally, the roots of what has become development economics was introduced at universities during colonialism. For example, the School of Oriental and African Studies in London, now one of the few institutions upholding the tradition of radical political economy, was founded by the British state in 1916 to strengthen Britain's political, commercial, and military presence in Asia and Africa. Similarly, in the 1940s, the University of Oxford introduced Colonial Studies for those wanting to train for service in the colonial empire (Goodacre, 2018). Counterparts were also created in the colonies as the colonizers set up or restructured the existing universities in the colonies to serve the colonizer (Pietsch, 2013; Carvalho and Flórez-Flórez, 2014).

The anti-colonial development project: A prelude to the Truman origin story

During the colonial period and in its immediate wake, there were contrasting currents within development economics. While the dominant current was steeped in Eurocentric thinking and imperialist motivations, there were countercurrents too, mostly from the colonies, notably from recently independent countries in Latin America, as well as from scholars and politicians in China, India, and Ethiopia. While the countercurrents' conceptions of economic development were powerful both in their ideas and their influence, they are usually relegated to footnotes, if acknowledged at all, in mainstream accounts.

The late development economist Thandika Mkandawire (2011, pp. 10–11) differentiated between two versions of the origin story of development: the first, which he calls the "Truman version," tells the conventional, US-centered story. The second, which he calls the "Bandung version," locates the source of the development project in a global, South-centered, emancipatory project. The Truman version and the emancipatory projects are not separate but deeply intertwined. In fact, Truman was not putting forward a plan for economic development in a vacuum, but rather reacting to emancipatory and radical projects of economic development from the periphery. Leaders in the periphery sought not only to theorize development and underdevelopment, but also to build institutions to challenge that dichotomy, thus also challenging the dominance of the US. One iconic example is the Bandung Conference in Indonesia in 1955, where 29 newly independent countries from Africa, Asia, and the Middle East came together to define the direction of the post-colonial world and to form new rules for the international system (Mkandawire, 2011; C. J. Lee, 2019; Khudori et al., 2022).

However, the development project from the periphery has a longer history that pre-dates World War II (Macekura and Manela, 2018; Thornton, 2023). The calls for development assistance, coordinated through international institutions in which countries of the periphery would have fair representation, started as early as the 1920s – two decades before the establishment of the World Bank and the IMF (Ekbladh, 2010; Helleiner, 2018; Macekura and Manela, 2018; McVety, 2018; Thornton, 2023). There are many examples of this. One is the Chinese nationalist Sun Yat-Sen's 2021 [1923] book proposing an International Development Organization to provide economic development and counter foreign dominance – an idea that was to be picked up by the US economist Eugene Staley in his promotion of US aid (Ekbladh, 2010; Helleiner, 2018). Another example is Ras Tafari (later Haile Selassie) petitioning for Ethiopia's membership in the League of Nations around the same time, to request help with capital and technology, thus proposing that the League support the economic development of countries of the periphery (McVety, 2018). The Indian scholar Benoy Kumar Sarak similarly advocated for

the League to play a role in promoting a "second industrial revolution" in the periphery (Sarkar, 1932; Six, 2018;
Helleiner, 2021). In the regional context of Latin America,
the Pan-American Union, which included Latin American
and Caribbean countries as well as the United States,
put forward a series of proposals to rebalance the global
economy and promote economic development, including
an international clearing union, which was proposed by the
Venezuelan government in 1922.[1]

When faced with scholars and policymakers from the
periphery putting forward projects of economic development
and advocating for specific institutions and infrastructures
that could facilitate such projects at a global scale, officials
in the capitalist center initially responded by rejecting and
deflecting, before, eventually, co-opting those demands to
render them toothless (Thornton, 2023). When the time came
to create new global institutions at Bretton Woods in 1944
– the US official Harry Dexter White, one of the intellectual
founders of the IMF and the World Bank, drew heavily on his
involvement with the Inter-American Bank and his negotiations with Cuba and Mexico about economic development
institutions (Helleiner, 2014; Thornton, 2023). There were
several important interventions made by leaders of Latin
American countries (representing 18 of the 44 countries in
attendance) as well as the Chinese and Indian delegation
during the Bretton Woods negotiations (Franczak, 2017;
Negi, 2017). One of the Mexican delegates, Víctor Urquidi,
had argued in front of John Maynard Keynes that while
European reconstruction was important, "in the long run,
Mr. Chairman – before we are all too dead, if I may say so
– development must prevail if we are to sustain and increase
real income everywhere" (cited in Thornton, 2023). These
interventions from the periphery ultimately led the World
Bank's bylaws being edited to give equal weight to reconstruction *and* development.

Shortly after the establishment of the World Bank and
the IMF, important interventions by India, Brazil, Australia,
Chile, Lebanon, and China were also made to the proposed
new International Trade Organization, especially for the

right of countries of the periphery to have their particular conditions considered, for example through allowing them to protect infant industries (Hudec, 1987; Toye, 2003). Such interventions were ultimately dismissed by US negotiators as being made by "crazy people" fetishizing industrialization (McKenzie, 2020, p. 42). The negotiations ultimately failed and instead of an international trade organization, the General Agreement on Tariffs and Trade (GATT) was agreed on in 1947. Eventually, only after decades of negotiations through the GATT, was the World Trade Organization (WTO) established in 1995.

In 1948, the year before the Truman speech, the Marshall Plan – an economic cooperation act involving more than US$13 billion in assistance for European reconstruction after World War II – had been agreed, while leaders in Latin America had been calling for similar forms of assistance for decades (Thornton, 2023). In fact, the day the Marshall Plan was signed in Washington in March 1948, the US Secretary of State was at an inter-American meeting in Bogotá, Colombia, "fending off calls for a Marshall Plan for Latin America" (Thornton, 2023, p. 39). Many peripheral countries were facing serious crises at that time, which had been exacerbated by the Great Depression (Abreu and Haddad, 2016). In Bogotá, the Mexican foreign minister had urged the US to consider that development is no less urgent in Latin America than in Europe. The response from the US was that it was already overburdened financially so the Latin Americans would need to wait.

With this institutional and political history in mind, Truman's inaugural speech of January 20, 1949, seems a bit less like the beginning of the development era *per se*, and more like a positioning of US hegemony in the development project. Truman declared that financial resources are scarce, but that the US was willing to share technical assistance – thus not only responding to the pressures that the countries of the periphery had been putting on the US and European countries for decades, demanding both financial and technical assistance for the periphery (Thornton, 2023), but also using the moment to establish US hegemony.

After Truman's speech, advocacy for international institutions and global rules that could redistribute surplus capital from the center to the periphery and create a more equal and just world for people everywhere continued among the leaders, scholars, and activists of the periphery. As mentioned, the Bandung Conference in 1955 established the need for permanent sovereignty over natural resources, the economic rights and duties of states, and even a right to development. Bandung was a hopeful anti-colonial moment, when many colonies had gained independence, and others were on the cusp of obtaining it (Amin, 2015).

From the late 1960s onwards, many put hope in the structures of the UN to help to support anti-colonial and anti-imperialist movements and projects. For example, after Ghana became the first African country to gain independence in 1957, its leader, Kwame Nkrumah argued for a refashioning of the UN as an international forum for decolonization. In 1960, Nkrumah gave a speech in the UN that argued that in this new era, "the UN should lead the fight against imperialism by protecting all peoples' right to self-determination and by excluding obstinate imperial powers from membership in the international body" (Getachew, 2019, p. 73). Only three months after Nkrumah's speech, the UN assembly passed the historic declaration on the *Granting of Independence to Colonial Countries and Peoples*, which affirmed "the necessity of bringing to a speedy and unconditional end colonialism in all its forms and manifestations" (UN General Assembly resolution 1514). However, with dominance of the US maintained and affirmed in institutions with real economic and political power, these developments did not fundamentally question US and Europe-led liberal institutions and often strengthened their hegemony.

From 1964 onwards, there was an effort to push for a New International Economic Order (NIEO) within the United Nations Conference on Trade and Development (UNCTAD), a UN institution founded by the Argentinian structuralist Raúl Prebisch. Many regions of the periphery developed their own active intellectual agendas shaping their policy priorities, such as the UN Economic Commission for

Latin America and the Caribbean (CEPAL), established in 1948, and the Council for the Development of Social Science Research in Africa (CODESRIA), established in 1973. However, even within such official institutions concerned with decolonization and development, the more radical anti-imperialist and anti-capitalist strands of scholarship and activism from the periphery tended to be marginalized or neglected. Nonetheless, in the 1950s, 1960s, and 1970s, radical and non-Eurocentric scholarship flourished in universities in the peripheries as well as in the capitalist center, even if it did not become dominant globally.

This alternative to the Truman origin story, which highlights the various political contestations underpinning the development project, demonstrates how interrelated ideas about development are. They did not diffuse neatly from the center to the periphery, nor from the periphery to the center (Kiely, 1999; Go, 2013) but took shape through various intellectual and political struggles. Uncovering the debates about economic development in Mexico, China, Brazil, or India allows us to better understand the debates not only in those countries, but also in the US and international institutions. This institutional history also allows us to see how political the project of economic development was and how tight the connections between academic development economists and policymakers were – and largely remain so today.

The official birth of the development project and the faux anti-colonial turn

Truman's speech is a good illustration of the pervasive use of the value-laden dichotomy of "developed" and "underdeveloped." Although they are presented as value-free, the categories are carefully slotted into a very specific structured hierarchy. They do not simply suggest a difference in the material conditions of the center and the periphery, but they also equate development with capitalist development and underdevelopment with the lack of capitalism, and suggest that underdevelopment and development are consecutive stages of a teleological historical process, one naturally leading to the other.

The developmentalists made some important interventions that took off from the view outlined by Truman. They started by recognizing structural differences between the center and periphery. The most formative intervention in this context was that by the Caribbean economist Arthur Lewis – one of few economists from the periphery to win an Economics Nobel Prize. According to Lewis, a developed economy is characterized by its homogeneously "modern" capitalist economic structure, while an underdeveloped economy is characterized by a fractured – or dual – economic structure, comprising a large "traditional" non-capitalist and a much smaller "modern" capitalist economic sector (W. A. Lewis, 1954). Development, following the Eurocentric teleological view, is defined as a capitalist transition from a dual economic structure toward a homogeneous one along the lines of the advanced capitalist economies – a process commonly understood in economics as structural transformation (Syrquin, 1988). The process of economic growth and capitalist accumulation was viewed as a central driver of this transformation. The ensuing debates in the mainstream have largely been embedded within this frame, asking to what degree the transition has been successful, what the consequences have been, what the roadblocks are, and so on.

There were a variety of approaches within the developmentalist camp. Paul Rosenstein-Rodan's (1944) big push theory called for a coordinated investment in all economic sectors in order to take advantage of externalities and spillovers from different industries, along with import-substitution industrialization. Albert Hirschman's (1961) unbalanced growth theory, on the other hand, recommended promoting high productivity sectors in contrast to a coordinated big push, given the investment constraints in the periphery. Alexander Gerschenkron (1962) emphasized the possibilities of different paths of industrialization, thereby contesting the idea that peripheral economies needed to follow one pre-given path. The debates among the developmentalists were rich, although they all thought of economic development as brought about via techno-bureaucratic fixes (Rist, 1997) and focused on how best to release the constraints on economic growth to promote capital accumulation through structural transformation (A. O. Hirschman, 1981; A. Sen, 1983). The developmentalists were also actively involved in policy institutions, especially UN institutions, and directly advised newly elected leaders of the now independent formerly colonized economies.[2]

Along with the developmentalists, modernization theory became prominent around the same time. One of the famous proponents was W. W. Rostow (1959), who was also national security advisor to President Lyndon B. Johnson from 1966 to 1969. Modernization theory assumed that countries of the periphery would automatically go through the same stages of growth as the advanced capitalist economies – starting with traditional economies and ending in a high age of mass consumption. The economic structures, institutions, and cultures of the periphery are thought to reflect the past of the societies in the center that simply had to be pulled into modern times (Rist, 1997; Danby, 2009).

The developmentalists were critical of modernization theory for not adequately recognizing the structural differences between center and periphery and for assuming the free market would do much of the work to drive the capitalist transition and structural transformation (A. O. Hirschman, 1981; Akbulut et al., 2015). However, even the developmentalists, who saw that peripheral economies were different from those in the center and called for various forms of interventionist policies, still reenforced the binary of capitalist development–underdevelopment, forgetting the histories of colonialism and other exploitative processes that produced both of these outcomes simultaneously. They, too, took a Eurocentric approach in their ahistorical view of development as a techno-bureaucratic project, which involved undertaking the right kind of policies to release the constraints on capitalist accumulation. Any political and social contradiction that was likely to emerge out of this process of capitalist accumulation, such as those associated with transfers of resources and land from the non-capitalist to the capitalist sectors, or dispossession of people from their land or access to livelihoods, were not seriously considered in this narrative (A. Sen, 1983; Akbulut et al., 2015).

The process of development, therefore, became one of transforming the production and labor structures of the economies of the periphery into capitalist processes that were thought to facilitate growth. This was thought possible in the wake of colony after colony gaining independence and seeking sovereign development. Only capitalist institutions, rationalities, and production structures were projected as modern while everything else was deemed as backward. In short, development came to be framed in a way that made it almost impossible to propose an understanding of development that was alternative to capitalist transition and capitalist modernity.[3]

What all these official narratives obfuscate and omit is the common historical process through which both the state of development and that of underdevelopment have been brought into being (Frank, 1967). This included a massive extraction of wealth from the colonies, which was facilitated by widespread dispossession, and a forceful use of slave labor to aid the process of industrial development and wealth accumulation in the center (Naoroji, 1901; Rodney, 1972; Galeano, 1973). This process simultaneously supported the development of industrial capitalism in the center and generated capitalist underdevelopment in the periphery. The mainstream narratives of development whitewashes this violent and extractive history and rather posits development as an apolitical, neutral, and linear process, largely outside the terrain of political contestation.

Relatedly, colonialism created – and imperialism continues to create – obstacles to peripheral industrialization (Chandrasekhar, 2005a). Peripheral economies were shaped to extract and export raw materials and designed to serve the needs of the center. The peripheries usually had a small elite bourgeoisie that consumed imported luxury products, while the majority of the population were poor working class and peasantry that did not demand domestically produced manufactured goods – a structure that did not lend itself easily to domestic industrialization. In chapter

7 we discuss alternative scholarship that identifies structures that reproduce uneven capitalist development globally, blocking the possibility for global convergence (Sanyal, 2007; Amin, 2009 [1988]; P. Patnaik and Patnaik, 2021). Such alternative views about obstacles to development did, however, not make it into the mainstream economic thinking of the capitalist center or into the international development institutions that were setting the rules of the game.

In short, despite recognizing that countries of the periphery were structurally different from the center, the developmentalist tradition failed to break away from the discipline's roots as a colonial intellectual project because of its continued Eurocentric understanding of capitalist development.

The cementing of the sub-discipline's colonial roots

By the 1980s, even the appreciation of structural differences between economies of the periphery and center started to fade away (Fine, 2006; Akbulut et al., 2015). The first of the many shifts in this post-1980s development project was the rise of what came to be known as the *Washington Consensus*. It proposed a standard set of one-size-fits-all policies to bring about an increase in per-capita income and productivity, mainly through markets with minimal state intervention. The mantra underpinning the Structural Adjustment Programs (SAPs) that were rolled out through the IMF and World Bank was centered on liberalization, deregulation, and privatization. These policies were thought to work everywhere, regardless of domestic particularities. However, the SAPs failed to generate growth and alleviate poverty, and in fact in many instances had a hugely negative impact (Demery, 1994; Krueger, 2004; Mkandawire, 2005; Konadu-Agyemang, 2018).

This forced the mainstream of the field to address these failures. It did so, however, firmly in line with late neoclassical thinking. We know this today as *new development economics*, which underpins what came to be known as the post-Washington Consensus (Fine, 2006). Much like the

Washington Consensus, the new development economics was oblivious to any structural differences between the center and periphery. The focus was on market imperfections and information asymmetries, with a program for strengthening institutions, governance, and providing some relief for the poverty that was not alleviated through market mechanisms. The problem of development, then, was reframed as one about correcting imperfections through strengthening institutions so that the capitalist market economy could function smoothly. Instead of focusing simply on rolling back the state as with the SAPs, the post-Washington Consensus brought the state back in to provide the institutions and infrastructure necessary for markets to work well and to provide some safety nets for people excluded from the gains of the development process. Key problems of development that needed addressing within this paradigm were development of skills and human capital, resolving issues of corruption and state inefficiencies, and finding ways to fix the imperfections in the markets (Krueger, 2004; Fine and Milonakis, 2009; Madra, 2017).

When institutions were introduced in this framework, it was in line with New Institutional Economics. This means the capitalist institutions of private property rights – assumed to drive capitalist development in the center – were seen as foundational for economic development (Zein-Elabdin, 2009; Akbulut et al., 2015). Development, therefore, involved aligning the institutions of the periphery with those of the center, especially that of property rights. Even when colonialism is introduced in this analysis (e.g., Acemoglu et al., 2005), it is usually reduced to studying the historical role it played in distorting or facilitating the development of institutions of property rights (Ince, 2022a).

Development economics narrowed even further in the 2000s and 2010s, with an increasing focus on micro-interventions such as cash transfers and micro-credit, meant to alleviate poverty. With this, the discipline moved away from the big discussions about structural transformation that characterized earlier debates (Reinert et al., 2016; Fischer, 2018). A reflection of this is the rise of RCTs.

Since the 2010s, the 2019 Economics Nobel laureates, Esther Duflo, Abhijeet Banerjee, and Michael Kremer, have argued that RCTs are the most rigorous way of approaching localized development problems. For them, development is about identifying a problem in the periphery and undertaking a series of interventions to identify what interventions work to solve that problem. While this new methodological benchmark of development economics is presented as atheoretical, objective, and value-neutral, it is firmly grounded in (late) neoclassical microeconomic theory (Kabeer, 2020; Kvangraven, 2020). The influence of RCTs on policy has been substantial and it extends beyond providing evidence on individual projects and programs to encompass a reframing of the kinds of questions that can be asked in the field (Bédécarrats et al., 2017).

Most funding for RCT-based research has historically come from institutions of the center, particularly the Abdul Latif Jameel Poverty Action Lab (J-PAL) at MIT, often with funding from philanthrocapitalists (de Souza Leão and Eyal, 2019). This means that research questions largely originate in the center, even when the questions are about the lives of people living in the periphery. Rather than taking the realities or knowledge of the communities being studied as starting points, interventions are designed to *test* behavioral responses to pre-defined interventions. In addition, RCTs carried out in the periphery systematically involve lower ethical standards, such as not asking participants for informed consent, thus reproducing the old idea that the colonial subjects are there for the colonists to experiment on (Hoffman, 2020; Wilson et al., 2023). The rising dominance of RCTs and their focus on small solvable problems is squarely in line with the broader trend of marketization, where all solutions to development are meant to be found by correcting market imperfections, tweaking market mechanisms, and nudging people to engage with markets more efficiently (Berndt, 2015).

This evolution of development economics, coming to be narrowly about institutions, market corrections, and poverty alleviation through micro-interventions, marks the absolute demise of development economics as a project related to decolonization. The structural forces that came into being through colonialism and uneven capitalist development, that created the center–periphery relationship to begin with, and that continue to produce poverty, hunger, and dispossession, are papered over or rendered irrelevant. Instead, localized symptoms of underdevelopment such as teacher absenteeism, low vaccination rates, or lack of savings, are treated with targeted interventions meant to make lives more comfortable for people living in poverty. Dispossession and uneven capitalist development that brought about poverty and underdevelopment to begin with are now way outside the frame of reference.

With this final development, the Eurocentric roots of the discipline have been firmly cemented. Capitalism as development is taken as a given and considered all-encompassing, and debates about alternative economic systems and rationalities are considered moot. The only questions left to answer are how to optimize individual, firm, and public sector actions within the system and how to facilitate better markets and institutions. Little space is given to understanding power structures beyond market power, thus keeping economic development analysis firmly within a Eurocentric frame.

From intellectual debates to brute force

The history of the evolution of development economics – from colonial roots, to an opening for recognizing structural differences with independence and sovereignty, to a completely Eurocentric subfield – cannot be studied in isolation from politics. Countries of the capitalist center and the international institutions they dominated worked hard to strengthen their material and intellectual dominance through and beyond the Cold War. The hegemony of Eurocentric thought ensured efforts to envisage radically different alternatives for economic development were marginalized. The expulsion of anti-colonial scholarship and anti-imperialist policymakers across the periphery also happened in violent ways since colonies first gained independence (Getachew,

2019; Khudori et al., 2022; Bianchini et al., 2024). During the Cold War, the United States was determined to end socialism across the globe through any means possible. This quest to squash radical post-independence movements was comprehensive, and included support for a wide range of coups against radical regimes and even direct assassinations and assassination attempts of left-wing political leaders. Famously, Patrice Lumumba, President of the Democratic Republic of Congo, was assassinated by the CIA in 1961, Salvador Allende was killed during the CIA-backed coup by Pinochet in Chile in 1973, and there were many (failed) coup attempts against Cuba's Fidel Castro by the CIA. In fact, the US engaged in at least 64 covert and six overt attempts at regime change during the Cold War (O'Rourke, 2019). The NIEO, which was a proposal to reorient the global economy to provide more autonomy for the newly independent economies of the periphery, was also actively resisted by the capitalist center (Ogle, 2014; Styve and Gilbert, 2023). While UNCTAD was originally meant to be the voice of the periphery striving to create a more just and equal world order in the era of decolonization (Margulis, 2017; Fajardo, 2022), it was actively disenfranchised and weakened by the capitalist center from the early 1980s onwards (Boutros-Ghali, 2006). Anti-colonial and anti-imperialist leaders' trust in the UN system – a system designed to be dominated by the capitalist center – may have been optimistic to begin with. After all, despite the UN resolution to bring colonialism to an end that was passed after Nkrumah's speech in 1960, we still observe colonial occupation to this very day – for example through the Israeli occupation of Palestine – with active political, economic, and military support from the capitalist center.

In the 1980s, the capitalist center's control over the internal affairs of the periphery became easier, as the global debt crisis forced countries to go to the IFIs for support. The SAPs went beyond promoting the market-based policies outlined above to further thwart the more radical post-independence projects many of these countries had embarked upon (Mkandawire, 2005). During SAPs, radical scholarship was also sidelined and marginalized in universities in the periphery (Assie-Lumumba, 2007; Mkandawire, 2014; Stein, 2021; Fajardo, 2022). Many countries in the periphery therefore saw a crisis of universities in the 1980s, partly brought on by donors like the World Bank who pushed for the rationalization and dilution of academic programs, leading to what Mamdani (2007) has described as vocationalization of higher education. Through this crisis, Eurocentric approaches gained ground in economics departments across the periphery, albeit always with pockets of resistance (Mkandawire, 2014; Carvalho and Flórez-Flórez, 2014). While economics departments in the capitalist center have historically had strong ties to institutions such as the World Bank, the IMF, USAID, and the Gates Foundation (Donovan, 2018), these connections became globalized with structural adjustment (Stein, 1995, 2021).

Economic development beyond development economics

The mainstream of development economics has always been limited in its imagination – as the reality of the periphery was always theorized under the shadow of the center. While the post-independence era marked a break in that developmentalists at least recognized peripheral economies as structurally distinct, the discipline never broke away from its Eurocentric foundations. So entrenched have they become that you will rarely see any discussion of how development is theorized in mainstream accounts anymore, as the assumption of development as capitalist transition is thoroughly internalized and pushed into the background to make way for discussions of localized problems in isolation from broader structures. With structural adjustment and austerity programs weakening public sectors in the periphery, and financial aid transfers dwindling, there has been a rising demand for micro-interventions, technical and market-based solutions to problems of hunger, poverty, unemployment, lack of access to housing, healthcare, and education.

This shift of development as localized interventions and fixes makes it easier for the field to pose as apolitical, technical, and ideology-free (Sanyal, 2007; Akbulut et al., 2015). Scholars of post-colonial capitalism, however, have identified these interventions as a way of governing the poor by providing for their subsistence in order to ensure political stability in a context of highly uneven capitalist development (Sanyal, 2007; Chatterjee, 2008). This strategy is not unfamiliar. Earlier, colonial powers often also provided basic needs to their colonial subjects to maintain a labor force that was able to derive some sustenance, first in the interest of capital, and later to ensure political stability and legitimacy for the colonial project (Schmitt, 2020). With this, the colonization of the discipline of development economics stands complete. To the horror of the mainstream development economists envisioning themselves as plumbers, the development project cannot be understood outside of political contestation, violence, subjugation, and struggle for self-determination, liberation, and dignity.

Deconstructing and critiquing development economics with a view to decolonization is not to argue against economic growth, industrialization, or modernity *per se*. Rather, it is about highlighting that there are possibilities for heterogeneous institutions and alternate paths of development and alternatives *to* capitalist development. There is a plethora of scholarship that precisely explores such alternative understandings and that theorizes explicitly about how structural inequalities in the global economy are produced and reproduced, paving the way for different ways of thinking about development and raising serious doubts about the path of development envisaged in the dominant theoretical traditions. The sub-discipline of development economics is thus an apt illustration of how non-Eurocentric strands of economics that challenge colonial standpoints and theories are marginalized and structurally excluded, despite their strong relevance. The systematic exclusion of these strands leaves the Eurocentric view of development largely uncontested within the field of development economics.

–PART II–
Decolonizing Economics

–5–
Heterodox Economics and the Decolonization Agenda

The book so far has criticized economics' Eurocentric theoretical and methodological foundations while highlighting alternative traditions that can contribute to a decolonization of economics. In this chapter, we discuss some of these alternatives and their potential to provide non-Eurocentric insights within a tradition of economics called *heterodox economics*, which is largely ignored in the mainstream.

Heterodox economics is an umbrella term encompassing various traditions of vast, dynamic, and thriving scholarship that together represent different ways to teach and research economics than those we mostly see in what are considered the top economics departments around the world. The term heterodox economics can be traced to Protin (2014 [1863]) who saw orthodox economists as followers of Smith, Ricardo, Malthus, Rossi, and Say, and heterodox economists (the infidels) as "others, bolder or more adventurous" who did not "consent to the theories of the masters, because they find them inadequate, even defective in more than one place" (p. 270). Heterodox economic thinking can also be traced back at least to the nineteenth century in India, with writings by Dadabhai Naoroji, Madan Mohan Malaviya and M. Govind Ranade, although it was not explicitly called heterodox at the time, but rather referred to as "dissenting voices" (S. Sen, 2019, p. 256). The modern origin of the term is often traced to the 1930s with the work of Ayres (1936) or Commons (1932), but gained popularity in the 1960s, mainly as a reaction to economics becoming theoretically and methodologically narrower and more intolerant.

Since heterodox economics refers to a varied set of traditions within economics and to communities following these traditions, there is little agreement about what counts as heterodox (F. S. Lee, 2009; Mearman, 2011; Dobusch and Kapeller, 2012). While these traditions commonly oppose mainstream frameworks, finding theoretical and political common ground among them is challenging (Dequech, 2007–8; Mearman, 2011; D'Ippoliti, 2020). Yet, the problem with seeing heterodox economics only in opposition to the mainstream is that it ignores that heterodox economics is also a positive project with its own thriving research agenda, encompassing many traditions, including Marxist, post-Keynesian, post-colonial, and feminist approaches, as well as the Black Radical Tradition, dependency theory, and theories of post-colonial capitalist development (Tauheed, 2008; Geda, 2011; Mearman, 2011; Fukuda-Parr et al., 2015; Jo et al., 2017; Kvangraven and Alves, 2019; S. Bhattacharya et al., 2022; Chester and Jo, 2022; Agunsoye et al., 2024). This evolving body of knowledge often develops independently of the mainstream of the profession.

While heterodox economics is an intellectual category, it is also a sociological category based on associations, networks, and journals, which typically hold a lower prestige within the mainstream of the discipline. It is worth noting that in this chapter, we take examples from the intellectual category, which means we may refer to scholars who do not necessarily identify themselves as (heterodox) economists or engage with heterodox associations. This is important because a lot of what we would call heterodox scholarship now exists in other disciplines because of the marginalization of the traditions within economics itself. It is also important to bear in mind that there is a huge variety of heterodox scholarship across the world, and there also is a scholarship that has been the most influential in heterodox communities *globally*:

what is often considered the canon in heterodox economics, for better or worse.[1]

Why heterodox economics lends itself to decolonization

Heterodox economics offers several features conducive to a decolonization agenda. First, it prioritizes social relations and structural power in its theoretical frameworks. Second, this emphasis translates into distinct methodological approaches to the so-called economic and non-economic, as well as history. Lastly, politics is embedded in heterodox scholarship from theory to policy implications and knowledge production itself (Resnick and Wolff, 1987; F. S. Lee, 2009; Kvangraven and Alves, 2019; Chester and Jo, 2022), contrasting sharply with mainstream economics where politics often revolves around elections, voting, and formal democratic institutions.

Theoretical focus on social relations and structural power

Heterodox economics foregrounds systemic processes through which economic outcomes are produced, with a central focus on the role of unequal power dynamics (Palermo, 2007). The focus on social relations and structural power makes it more amenable to a decolonization agenda as it challenges the Eurocentric assumption of endogenous, rational, capitalist development based on technological improvements, which conceals uneven power relations underpinning exploitation, oppression, and subordination. Scholarship within heterodox economics, especially the more radical traditions, allows for a recognition of the historical process of large-scale dispossession and other violent processes of restructuring of social relations, through which capitalism was brought into existence (Harvey, 2003; Arrighi et al., 2010; U. Patnaik and Moyo, 2011; Féliz, 2014). The focus on social relations and structural power means heterodox economists begin with entry points that are more likely to expose the underlying dynamics of the economy itself. We can illustrate this using three examples – production, the global monetary system, and discrimination – to demonstrate how differences in entry points lead to different insights and how those insights challenge Eurocentrism in different ways.

In mainstream economics, employer power is often seen as stemming from labor supply exceeding labor demand (i.e., a slack in the labor market). This view assumes that a tight labor market results in equal power between employers and employees. However, this ignores the fundamental dynamics where employers own the product of labor and control decisions about its use and distribution – the decision-making power of what is to be done with the output, including how it is to be divided, rests with the employer and not the laborer. If the labor market is sufficiently tight, labor may have more say in this decision and bargaining power over the output, and some late neoclassical models do acknowledge aspects of bargaining between workers and capitalists. That said, these models still suggest that bargaining leads to a situation where both capitalists and workers can achieve the best possible outcome, given economic conditions. For instance, workers can bargain for higher real wages only to the extent that firms can still maintain their profits and markup; and pushing for higher wages could lead to inflation, ultimately making workers worse off.

Mainstream economics views labor bargaining through the lens of optimally allocating scarce resources, given certain endowments, technologies, and preferences. In contrast, heterodox traditions begin from class to understand production, appropriation, and distribution of surplus (Resnick and Wolff, 1987; Campling et al., 2016). While the mainstream aims for maximum efficiency in the workplace, accounts that consider structural power interrogate how systems of organizations are shaped to let capitalists control labor processes and profits (Marglin, 1974), extending beyond the firm itself. The recognition of an inherent contradiction in the capital–labor relationship from the outset stands in contrast to the idea of the possibility of an equilibrium outcome or an evolutionarily stable outcome in which everyone benefits – or what Madra (2017) would call aggregate rationality, where the individual and aggregate rationality is reconciled.

By starting with class, the issues of distribution and competition for the surplus between workers, capitalists, and other claimants of the surplus are centrally acknowledged, opening room for investigating conditions necessary for production. Heterodox economics emphasize the unequal power between labor and capital even before the surplus is produced, distributed, or bargained for, centering the misalignment of the workers' and capitalists' goals and interests in distribution. Unlike in mainstream economics, the allegedly given endowments of capital and labor that individuals exchange in the free market get problematized, opening space for understanding and contextualizing the violent processes through which the initial endowments initially get produced. Furthermore, the unequal power does not go away in a tight labor market for heterodox econo-mists who tend to see the absence of full unemployment as a feature of capitalism, if anything due to political reasons (Kalecki, 1943).

Historically, capitalists have evaded labor market tightness by leveraging significant political power. By instituting changes in national and international laws and techno-logical changes, they have expanded their reach globally, accessing labor beyond national boundaries and thereby easing domestic labor markets. For example, in the US in the 1960s and 1970s, capital reacted to strong labor movements by becoming more mobile to access labor reserves on a global scale, by facilitating the introduction of laws attacking unions, and by lobbying to reduce corporate taxes domesti-cally (Resnick and Wolff, 2010). Strategies to increase the labor supply also include shifts to more capital-intensive technologies, automation, and a continued dispossession of workers in the peripheries from the traditional resources on which they subsist, making the available pool of labor abundant and redundant (Sanyal, 2007; M. Davis, 2006). The availability of large reserves of (dispossessed) populations in the peripheries for exploitation by capital is evidenced by the prevalence of large swathes of informal labor working under extremely precarious conditions and earning low wages, constituting approximately 70 percent of total employment (ILO, 2022; Ohnsorge and Yu, 2022).

Now, let us consider the global monetary system. Mainstream economic analysis begins with the observation that currencies mediate exchange necessary for settling cross-border transactions. Exchange rates, driven by monetary or financial fundamentals, adjust to restore equilibrium. International monetary arrangements result largely from network externalities, making it beneficial for a country to have a currency that facilitates the settlement of trade and finance with its largest trading partners (Eichengreen, 2019). Currency unions are advantageous when member countries are similar and face similar shocks (Perez, 2018). In recent decades, this mainstream literature has evolved to incorporate an array of market imperfections to explain frictions, fragilities, and vulnerabilities that arise in the system, such as imperfect information, irrational expectations among traders, or misguided government policies. In this scenario, to avoid crises, countries are advised to maintain sound economic fundamentals, develop credible domestic institutions, and roll the state out of the way of the market more generally.

In contrast, the post-Keynesian tradition begins with the observation that currencies are hierarchically structured, which leads to different levels of monetary sovereignty and subordination across the globe (de Paula et al., 2017). The returns of all currencies are assessed in relation to the global money (the US dollar), which has the highest liquidity premium. At the bottom of the hierarchy sit the currencies of countries in the periphery, whose domestic currency functions are often substituted by foreign currencies, including in borrowing practices. An example of this is when a country cannot issue debt in its own currency at affordable rates, which has been called the original sin in the mainstream literature.[2]

Heterodox scholars argue that global markets are shaped by histories of colonialism and empire, leading to a hierarchically structured global system where no amount of market fixing can bring about equally strong currencies (Alami et al.,

2023). For instance, Narsey (2016) argues that the dominance of the pound sterling through the late nineteenth and early twentieth centuries stemmed not from British financial innovations but from Britain's power to maintain colonies on silver standards with coins containing less than the face value of silver, alongside compelling oversubscription to British government securities on its colonies. Similarly, the US dollar's dominance in the currency hierarchy is attributed to US imperialism through selective lender of last resort support to allied central banks (McDowell, 2017; Sahasrabuddhe, 2019; Dutt, 2021), control over multilateral institutions like Bretton Woods that shape conditions for capital accumulation (M. Hudson, 2003), and US hegemonic position in the global economic order more generally (Vasudevan, 2009). See also the case of colonial fixed exchange rate systems, such as the CFA Franc, which still exists to this day. Heterodox scholarship draws attention to the fact that the CFA zone was not an optimal choice based on network externalities, but rather a system of colonial exploitation maintained through economic and political forms of domination (Sylla, 2020b; Pigeaud and Sylla, 2021).

Heterodox approaches to the global monetary system have been better able to uncover structural inequalities produced by the system that take colonialism into account and therefore lend themselves better to a decolonization agenda. This is especially the case for the traditions that tackle the production and reproduction of hierarchy rather than simply measuring its manifestations (e.g., a currency hierarchy).

Finally, let us revisit the example of discrimination and group-based inequalities discussed in chapter 3. Traditions in heterodox economics often address group-based inequalities by examining how they are produced by the structure of the economic system rather than solely by individual discrimination based on identity. This approach emphasizes that the structure of the economy plays a central role in social differentiation. For this reason, heterodox traditions have often effectively engaged with issues such as patriarchy, colonization, racialization, and caste. For example, social reproduction theory has significant insights into the household and its role in the reproduction of the economic system itself (Fraser, 2016a; T. Bhattacharya, 2017; Ossome, 2021). Similarly, heterodox scholarship identifies the structural mechanisms of power that suppress the labor power of certain groups through racialization, as in Wolpe's (1972) work on the apartheid system in South Africa or the Latin American scholarship on internal colonialism, which sees the oppression of indigenous groups as a complex outcome of dependent modernization (C. Kay, 1989). These perspectives enable a structural analysis of wage inequalities (Figart, 2005) that go much deeper than the mainstream explanations focused on employer preferences, which often overlook systemic power dynamics.

This is not to argue that heterodox traditions ignore individuals and individual behavior. But instead of approaching individuals through methodological individualism – which sees individuals as distinct units of analysis that can be analyzed separately from their relationships to others – individuals are analyzed as part of a social structure. The individual and the structure are seen to be co-constitutive, that is, they shape each other (Gibson-Graham, 2006; F. S. Lee and Jo, 2018). Understanding the economy therefore entails understanding both human agency and structural relationships, and how they interact and shape each other in ways that cannot be easily reduced to simple mechanisms of causality (Lawson, 2006; F. S. Lee, 2009; Fleetwood, 2017). As such, individual agency needs to be theorized, studied, and understood in the context of social relations of class, gender, race, and empire, and how these have been shaped politically and historically.

Methodological engagement with history and the non-economic

Heterodox economics understands social phenomena as a cumulative sequence rather than in equilibrium. This leads heterodox economists to often use a range of different types of data to understand and explore underlying processes, mechanisms, and tendencies that may impact social phenomena, rather than attempting to isolate independent variables for hypothesis testing (Lawson, 2013; see also C. Kay, 1989). Many heterodox traditions centrally theorize and empirically explore how institutions of power and economic structures have evolved historically, even in traditions that may not always be thought of as particularly historical, such as post-Keynesian economics (Davidson, 1981; Dow, 1992). Taking a historical approach allows for an investigation into the internal working of economic processes, including the origins of capitalist development itself (Sweezy and Dobb, 1950; Dobb, 1972 [1946]; Brenner, 1976; Fine, 1978; E. M. Wood, 2002).

In contrast, mainstream methods in economics are largely ahistorical (Fine and Milonakis, 2009), and when they do include history do so in a wildly different way than in heterodox traditions. For instance, recall from our discussion about cliometrics in chapter 2, mainstream historical analysis of capitalism emphasizes quantitative changes over shifts in social relations, which significantly limits and distorts the analysis. Another example can be found in how colonial regimes are studied within New Institutional Economics, which often focuses on quantitatively testing the impact of different private property rights systems under different colonial regimes to establish strong property rights as the causal mechanism for explaining long-term growth (see Acemoglu and Robinson, 2012).

Heterodox economists are more concerned with how colonial institutions led to different kinds of regimes of accumulation (centered on trade, concessionary companies, or labor reserves) that lent themselves to different kinds of economic structures and institutions, which in turn endure to this day (Amin, 1972; Mkandawire, 2020). In this historical method, the nature of social relations and their evolution over time are explored, emphasizing structural power dynamics rather than hypothesis testing. The implication is that social relations can be uncovered and analyzed, going beyond understanding domestic institutions through a quantifiable index to represent institutions of private property rights, and taking us away from Eurocentric under-standings of history.

The other implication of heterodox methodologies we wish to highlight is the broad engagement with social dimensions that construct reality, unlike the mainstream focus on separating economic and non-economic spheres. In heterodox economics, solutions to economic problems are viewed as inseparable from their specific historical, political, and social contexts. For example, utility-based marginalist theory in mainstream economics often reduces economic issues to a constrained optimization problem. Take unemployment, which was largely absent from the mainstream macro-economic dynamic stochastic general equilibrium (DSGE) model (Galí and Gertler, 2007) before the 2007–8 sub-prime mortgage crisis and subsequent recession. Post-crisis, models began explicitly incorporating unemployment as arising primarily from a variety of labor market frictions. Only more recent developments have even allowed for the possibility of involuntary unemployment, which in some models is considered to be the result of changes in the markup over wages (Galí et al., 2012).

In contrast, heterodox traditions tend not to separate the economic from the political, insisting on the political dimensions of labor market tendencies and the persistence of unemployment. Moving beyond the economic–non-economic binary, some heterodox economists analyze capitalism as prone to overproduction and demand constraints, where involuntary unemployment is expected and observed as a systemic outcome of the system rather than an imperfection to be fixed through wage or markup adjustment (P. Patnaik, 2009). They also recognize that economic policies aiming to reduce unemployment can be politically unattractive for policymakers, given the potential destabilizing power of a strengthened working class (Kalecki, 1943). In contrast, mainstream economics tends to depoliticize these outcomes, often superimposing market-like interactions to analyze behavior in non-market spheres.

The difference in both method and theory on this point has significant consequences. In heterodox frameworks, solutions to economic problems are often tied to historical and political contexts, linking them to systemic issues. For example, mainstream RCT-driven development literature sees poverty and deprivation as simple shortfalls in earnings to be fixed by transferring cash, productive resources, or skills to individuals or small groups. In contrast, heterodox economics sees it as an outcome of the continual dispossession of people from resources and land without providing stable alternate livelihoods, of a system that produces unemployment and exploits labor, and a system that requires a reserve army of labor to maintain its stability (P. Patnaik and Patnaik, 2021). For this reason, as we found in the previous chapter, while mainstream development economics focuses on identifying the impact of narrow interventions to reduce poverty, heterodox economics focuses on uncovering the mechanisms embedded in the economic system through which such poverty arises (Sanyal, 2007; Reinert and Kvangraven, 2023).

Politics in heterodox economics

This brings us to the third and final key feature of heterodox economics that lends itself to a decolonization agenda, namely, how politics is embedded in heterodox scholarship and practice. Heterodox economists often explicitly identify the political implications of their theories and recognize that these stem from their theoretical vantage point. Different political implications, whether explicit or implicit, result from what processes each framework highlights, which originate in deeply embedded normative considerations. Unlike mainstream theory, which often suppresses debates about normative values (as discussed in chapter 3), heterodox economists tend not only to centrally embed issues of power in their analysis, but also to highlight the importance of such political factors for understanding society and possible ways to change it. This embeddedness is not accidental and is intricately linked to how theory is approached in heterodox economics.

As noted earlier, in the mainstream, which starts with individuals, preferences, and endowments, structural power is not actively present. When inequalities in power and distribution are recognized, they often appear as inequalities that can be resolved through adjusting institutions and markets or through providing better conditions for individuals to themselves act (e.g., through training, bargaining, or more equal inclusion in institutions). Consequently, the political implication of much mainstream economic scholarship tends to be centered on market-based solutions within the system. Let us take research on global value chains (GVCs) as an example. In the mainstream, the global division of labor through GVCs allows for economies of the periphery to achieve industrialization via upgrading within the chain, with the state's role being limited to facilitating this transition by alleviating market imperfections (e.g., Lin and Chang, 2009). In contrast, heterodox approaches show how GVCs reinforce colonial patterns of specialization, with the center countries continuing to hold intellectual property rights and erecting barriers to technological advancements and upgrading globally. Firms in the capitalist center continue to undertake the higher value-added tasks in the value chain and exploit workers of the periphery, who remain further down the chain (Suwandi et al., 2019; Durand and Milberg, 2020). Moreover, capitalist competition reinforces such uneven development across the world (Shaikh, 2016).

In their approach to politics, a fundamental difference between heterodox and mainstream economists is that the latter assume that such unequal outcomes *can* be resolved through the system, whereas the former considers unequal outcomes as endogenous to the system itself. These unequal outcomes are a feature and not a bug. Political implications in heterodox traditions thus go far beyond market-based solutions to a fundamental rebalancing of political forces – ranging from state-managed capitalism in post-Keynesian economics to challenging capitalism itself in the more radical traditions (Campbell, 2019; O'Kane, 2020; P. Patnaik and Patnaik, 2021). Relatedly, in addition to how politics is embedded in heterodox theory and methods, heterodox economists are keenly aware of the politics of knowledge production itself, given the exclusion many heterodox economists experienced in the process of narrowing and cementing of Eurocentrism in the discipline (F. S. Lee, 2009).

Eurocentrism in heterodox theory

While heterodox economists may be more willing and open to challenge Eurocentrism in their own approaches (Kvangraven and Kesar, 2023), the most influential heterodox scholarship in the capitalist center also presents Eurocentric ideas about how capitalism evolved and functions globally. This scholarship also tends to neglect processes of social differentiation and structural oppression beyond class, such as colonialism, racialization, and patriarchy. For example, some Marxist traditions of heterodox economics see countries of the periphery as existing in a prehistory of capitalism, expecting them to transform along the lines of the center economies as capitalism spreads, thereby sharing teleological foundations as modernization theory (e.g., Warren, 1980).[3] In this type of analysis, even if capitalist development is not the end point, it is considered a necessary stage. Such Eurocentric heterodox analysis views oppression beyond only class as peripheral in the analysis and tends not to account for the specificities of post-colonial capitalism, thereby failing to understand global capitalism itself.

Anti-imperialist Marxist scholarship, such as theories of neocolonialism (Nkrumah, 1970 [1965), imperialism (P. Patnaik and Patnaik, 2021) and dependency theory (Amin, 1974; Marini, 1978) acknowledge a central role of colonialism – and the continuing role of imperialism – in producing underdevelopment in the periphery, but such scholarship has been relatively neglected within heterodox economics globally, especially in the capitalist center. Similarly, scholarship that focuses on the particularities of capitalist development in the periphery has also been relatively neglected, such as Latin American structuralism (Prebisch, 1950; Furtado, 1970; Tavares, 1985), scholarship on modes of production (Banaji, 1972; G. Kay, 1975; U. Patnaik, 1990), and recent interventions on post-colonial capitalist development (Sanyal, 2007).

While these heterodox traditions may be deeply familiar to Latin American or Indian economists, they remain at the periphery of the global heterodoxy.

Another dimension of Eurocentrism that stands out in heterodox economics is the relative absence of concerns with structural forms of oppression integral to the workings of capitalism such as racialization and patriarchy. While the rational white man is typically the starting point for theoretical analyses in mainstream economics, the theorization of the Western working class tends to be blind to race and gender in heterodox representations. Many differentiations within the working class are often ignored, even when including them would improve the economic analyses (Reich et al., 1973). Given how capitalism has produced or reshaped processes of racialization, patriarchy, and imperialism, a focus on the working class that is blind to other forms of oppression neither allows us to fully understand all the dynamics of capitalism nor to address their impacts.

Even though late neoclassical economics and Marxist economics differ substantially, both tend to view households as largely cooperative and altruistic units – at least certain Marxist traditions do (Folbre, 1986). While Marxist economics has a well-developed theory of conflict, inequality, and exploitation, intrahousehold conflict is often absent. In addition, Marxist theories often implicitly and sometimes explicitly assume that household space is extra-economic and does not contribute to market production. There are, of course, some important Marxist feminist traditions that do integrate domestic labor into economic analysis (Gibson-Graham, 2006; T. Bhattacharya, 2017; Fraser, 2016a), but they are less prominent in most heterodox spaces. For example, Fraser (2016a) finds that the production of commodities in the market crucially rests upon care work in the household and that extraction of resources from households can potentially destabilize reproduction in the market as well. She argues that this destabilization is often managed by creation of global care chains, where households of the capitalist center pass the burden of care to the immigrant, racialized women from the periphery.

Some heterodox work in Marxist and Keynesian traditions on the role of workers' bargaining power in determining the functional distribution of income suffers from similar shortcomings. While this scholarship allows for analysis of the relationship between income and wealth inequality and bargaining power of the working class (through unemployment levels or strength of labor unions, for example), it often remains insufficient for explaining inequality within the working class, especially along the lines of caste, race, and gender. How can we explain the systematically higher unemployment rate and structurally lower incomes and wealth among women and marginalized communities when our primary unit of analysis is an undifferentiated working class?

Another drawback is how some Keynesian and Marxist economic traditions consider capitalist economies of the center to be isolated systems, thus distorting the analysis. For example, in determining inflation in the capitalist center, heterodox economists do not tend to consider the role of the periphery in stabilizing the system. Prabhat Patnaik (2009) has long argued that the stability of prices in the global capitalist economy requires petty producers of the periphery to suppress commodity prices through suppressing local demand. One of the mechanisms described by P. Patnaik (2009) is as follows: in the face of various inflationary pressures, in order to maintain the value of capitalist investments, the demand in the global economy is suppressed by curtailing the purchasing power of the petty producers in the periphery via destruction of their livelihoods. Such dispossession is not seen as a failure of the system, but as necessary for its stability. Under colonialism this was done through dispossessing petty producers and imposing colonial taxes, directly contributing to the drain of surplus from the periphery, while in the contemporary economic order this is done indirectly through neoliberal policies that also suppress incomes in the periphery (P. Patnaik and Patnaik, 2021). The capitalist center's reliance on cheap commodities outside of its frontiers is generally left out of most heterodox models.

A related problem is that the particularities of the center are sometimes universalized in heterodox economics. Heterodox macroeconomics, for example, like mainstream macroeconomics, essentially places the center economies at the core of their analysis, leaving the periphery to development economics. Generally, well-developed labor markets tend to be assumed in much of heterodox economics, leaving the realities of labor markets in the periphery – such as the persistence of non-capitalist, self-employed, and family-based informal sector activities – out of the analysis. Especially post-Keynesian models based on the capitalist center have often been applied to economies of the periphery with little understanding of the post-colonial realities. There is also a Eurocentric assumption underlying much of post-Keynesian theory in particular, which is that the world is composed of discrete societies rather than being deeply interconnected (Danby, 2004). This leads to a distorted view of how economics in general works, let alone how economies in the periphery work.

One can find many more specific examples of concepts that are often universalized based on experiences in the capitalist center. For example, an important insight in heterodox economics is that money is endogenous – that is, that much of the liquidity in an economy is not effectively controlled by the central bank, but by financial markets (Minsky, 1986). Specifically, if there is additional demand for money that the central bank does not supply, the banking system will simply create it by creating new financial instruments or by drawing on existing ones to push on the limits set by the central banks (Lavoie, 2000). However, in the absence of highly developed financial markets, as in many economies of the periphery, it is not obvious that money will always be endogenously created. Scholars who do discuss the conditions under which money is endogenously created in the periphery are not widely read, especially if they are not based in or from the capitalist center. For instance, Joseph Pouemi (2000 [1980]) – a Cameroonian scholar who wrote in French and is yet to be translated into English – observed that money in the CFA currency zone in West Africa is highly credit constrained overall, due to the colonial monetary arrangement (Koddenbrock and Sylla, 2019; Perez, 2023). The implication is that domestic banking systems do not provide sufficient credit to meet demand from domestic enterprises, bank interest rates tend to be high because of the anti-inflationary policies pursued by the central banks, which contributes to repression of domestic economic activity. As such, Pouemi's theorization about endogenous money under the constraints of internal and external repression remains relevant for understanding certain peripheral economies, especially for those that do not control their own monetary policy.

Another strand of post-Keynesian economics, Modern Money Theory (MMT), makes the argument that governments that issue a sovereign currency do not have intrinsic financial constraints but rather a real resource constraint – the availability of labor, equipment, raw materials, etc. In their case, there is no risk of insolvency but a risk of inflation. As such, the argument goes that monetarily sovereign governments should care about real outcomes rather than about arbitrary financial rules (Kelton, 2020; Felipe and Fullwiler, 2022).

Even if there are several national governments that issue their own currency without pegging it (to another currency or to gold) and that borrow essentially in their own currency (that is they enjoy monetary sovereignty in an MMT sense), they often still face real institutional constraints on expanding spending, even if inflation is low. For example, in a peripheral setting, a high level of fiscal deficit and public debt, even if it is sustainable, can lead to capital flight and a loss of confidence in a country's currency, which can make the situation unsustainable (Dutt, 2021). As such, the original insights of MMT are not directly applicable beyond a few countries in the capitalist center. Nonetheless, although the MMT literature has been mostly US- and UK-focused to date, there is an emergent literature where authors expand on the questions of sovereignty, monetary subordination, and the relevance of MMT more generally in the periphery (de Rezende, 2009; Sylla, 2020a; 2023; Deos et al., 2021; Gadha et al., 2021; Deos and Gerioni, 2022; Gimene et al., 2022;

for critical engagement, see Vernengo and Caldentey, 2020; Copley, 2024).

When approached from the periphery, MMT takes on a slightly different character. Some MMT-inspired scholarship argues that the external debt problem of peripheral economies reflects their lower degree of economic and monetary sovereignty (Sylla, 2020a; Gadha et al., 2021). The Senegalese economist Ndongo Samba Sylla (2024), for example, argues that MMT can aid in clarifying the difference between a situation of technical and material dependence, international payment problems, and political economy considerations. This is of crucial importance in a peripheral setting, he argues, where foreign exchange shortage is often pointed to as a reason for countries in the periphery to issue external debt, without considering development problems that arise from the structure of ownership and distribution of the country's real domestic resources. However, while MMT as a frame offers compelling critiques of mainstream understandings of economic policy constraints and an alternative way of conceptualizing various development problems, it remains fairly ahistorical and often removed from deeper power relations that play out globally. This may be why Sylla (2023, 2024) has argued that MMT is a useful lens through which to highlight the differences between various constraints but combines the lens with dependency theory to aid in theorizing the dynamics of development and underdevelopment. This MMT scholarship that attempts to theorize from a vantage point that includes the periphery is still relatively marginal, but it could potentially challenge some of the Eurocentrism embedded in the dominant approach to MMT.

An engagement with methodological and theoretical issues that emerge when thinking about heterodox economics from the periphery is necessary not merely in its own right and for understanding development in the periphery, but also because it is centrally important for understanding the implications for global capitalism. Leaving out these neglected issues is not simply a blind spot to be corrected within Eurocentric frameworks. On the contrary, the Eurocentric theories produce distorted and partial understandings of economic systems and should rather be re-conceptualized within a decolonization agenda – as we shall soon lay out in more detail in chapter 6.

Reflections of Eurocentrism in the heterodox community

While heterodox economics may be more conducive to a decolonization agenda, there has been a marginalization of non-Eurocentric understandings in heterodox knowledge production. In other words, at a sociological level, even when heterodox economists do engage with theories that are amenable to decolonization, such as theories that do center structural power and various axes of oppression, they tend to omit scholars and scholarship that comes from the periphery. As such, Eurocentric structures are not only reflected in certain heterodox theories – as discussed above – but also in the marginalization of scholars and scholarship based in or from the periphery. These two issues are closely related.

As mentioned, with the term heterodox economics we refer both to intellectual scholarship as well as the scholars who produce it. It is important to consider the latter given that one cannot ignore that how scholars understand and interpret the world is likely to be impacted by their own contexts and perspectives (Fourcade, 2009). For example. it is no accident that it was women economists who first recognized and engaged with problems associated with excluding household work from GDP (Waring, 1990; Folbre, 2012) or that one of the classic theses on caste was written by Dr. B. R. Ambedkar (2014), a Dalit scholar and activist.

Moreover, even the nature of heterodoxy is quite varied in different country contexts. For example, Baumol (1995) argues that Europe is much more heterodox when it comes to research subjects and methods when compared with the United States. Meanwhile, countries like Brazil and India have had a long history of critical anti-colonial heterodox theoretical frameworks being taught in many public universities that has only recently been increasingly abandoned with the privatization and liberalization of education (Sharma, 2020; Guizzo et al., 2021). Unfortunately, however, much like the community of economists in general, the global intellectual community of heterodox economists suffers from a lack of diversity. What can be called top heterodox institutions (journals, departments, conferences) are characterized by the overrepresentation of white men based in the capitalist center. The heterodox economics textbooks, journals, and speakers invited for seminars and conferences are overwhelmingly written by, articulated by, edited by, white men based in the United States and Western Europe. This is despite the existence of important centers of heterodox economics in the periphery, heterodox women and heterodox scholars of color that continue to write prolifically on important economic issues.

For example, there is an overrepresentation of journals published in the capitalist center in directories of heterodox journals, and the journals based in the center tend to be ranked higher than those in the periphery by heterodox rankings (F. S. Lee and Cronin, 2010). This impacts the way hiring and promotion practices are carried out, where publishing in journals of the center is more highly valued, further reinforcing the marginalization of scholars who publish in journals based in the periphery. Furthermore, there is evidence of strong and persistent research and collaborative ties among white heterodox men based in the capitalist center (Brites et al., 2022), which serves to exclude women, minorities, and scholars from the periphery from editorial boards of journals based in the center.

The homogeneity among the body of heterodox economists is also evident in heterodox teaching. For example, in macroeconomics, students of heterodox economics are regularly recommended to engage with thinkers like Keynes, Kalecki, Kaldor, and Robinson, while the engagement with Patnaik, Chakravarty, dos Santos, and Bambirra is rarely considered indispensable to understanding macroeconomic questions. Similarly, even when teaching political economy, students are primarily recommended to engage with Marx's original work and Western interpretations of it, while anti-colonial Marxist work such as that by Lenin, Rodney, Nkrumah, and Fanon are rarely attributed the same importance. It is not that these thinkers are not studied at all in heterodox economics, but these are considered readings on special topics of imperialism, or development, rather than as theorists of capitalism itself. Notably, despite these biases, many heterodox economists are not at all concerned with Eurocentrism in economics teaching according to a recent survey.[4]

Therefore, the colonization of heterodox economics is a sociological and political problem as well as a theoretical issue. Given the commitment among heterodox economists to attempt to expose the structural processes of oppression, its marginalization of women, people from underrepresented communities, and those who theorize from a vantage point that includes the periphery, is particularly shocking. It may be the case that in their attempt to protect their constantly narrowing space as the mainstream excludes them, they become excessively protective of their networks. However, this sometimes results in yet another white men's club that is especially persistent and resistant to change in the relatively smaller heterodox economics community.

In need of non-Eurocentric heterodox economics

It is telling that heterodox economics, despite its relative compatibility with a decolonization agenda, presents several shortcomings in terms of an embedded Eurocentrism that bears a similarity to mainstream economics. Given the heterogeneity within heterodoxy, some strands are relatively more Eurocentric than others. However, even parts of the most radical schools within heterodox economics that are staunch critics of capitalism as an exploitative system are often unable or unwilling to extend the critical interrogation of exploitation to other axes of structural power. As such, they, too, end up placing at their locus a partial European experience of capitalist development. They, too, have remained quite insular to processes of colonialism, gendering and racialization, and the specificities of post-colonial capitalist development that other radical traditions have highlighted.

The strengthening of heterodox economics within economics then becomes a necessary – but not sufficient – condition to drive forward an agenda for decolonization. However, given the features of heterodox economics we have highlighted here, it should be amenable to decolonization. Heterodox economics can help us better understand the structural relations of power that underpin all economic processes and how they interact with both micro elements and macro dynamics, which is the first step toward challenging the inequalities and injustices we see in the world. This is essential for shedding light on the underlying forces and contradictions that shape our crisis-ridden economies.

–6–
Toward a Decolonization Agenda

The decolonization of economics would require different theoretical frames and tools than what are currently acceptable or available within the mainstream of the discipline. Economics – in its contemporary hegemonic form – is intransigently Eurocentric. Any additions or adjustments to hegemonic economic thinking that are positioned as an attempt towards decolonization will likely be superficial if the Eurocentric frameworks remain intact. Ultimately, the dominant approach to economics ties an economist's arms behind their back, as it makes it almost impossible to uncover the underlying logics of economic processes and how they relate to observed economic outcomes. Expanding a Eurocentric economic framework to incorporate issues associated with decolonization at the margin of economic theory, such as colonialism, race, or gender, will not contribute toward the decolonization of economics. Therefore, studying colonialism in a framework of New Institutional Economics, studying women's empowerment using randomized controlled trials, studying race within a neoclassical framework, or studying the slave trade's impact on the development of capitalism through cliometrics as an approach to economic history, is not enough.[1]

As outlined previously, that economics is a Eurocentric discipline means it idealizes a particular view of capitalist economies of the center and sees it as the norm, while considering all else that breaks with this norm as an aberration. The aberrations are, allegedly, in need of development to become more like the norm, as they are seen as lacking for being not adequately capitalist, or, alternatively, lesser beings who should learn to be rational, modern, and in line with the optimizing and modern behavior of the capitalist individuals and firms. We can think of the norm and the aberrations as a mirror image of the capitalist center and the periphery, where the center and periphery are not geographical locations *per se* but rather visions of Eurocentric expectations for (capitalist) development. The norm – the center – is conceived of as the essence of capitalism, where modernity and rationality have reached commanding heights, and the peripheral others are seen only in relation to the center, representing a lack or deviation for not being adequately capitalist. Implicitly, these elements serve to legitimize the dominance of the capitalist center, as this idealized view does not consider the underlying forms of exploitation, expropriation, and oppression through which the two states are constructed. The economics discipline universalizes this distorted – and partial – view of the capitalist center in its use of Eurocentric frameworks.

The economics field, based on a mechanistic and positivist approach to science, involves ordering and categorizing difference in hierarchical terms, normalizing peripheral economies as social formations lower down in the hierarchy in relation to the center. A decolonization agenda for economics unravels this apparatus of power in which the capitalist center and periphery are placed and shows how these hierarchies are constructed and maintained. With such an agenda, it becomes apparent that categories that we use merely descriptively in economics, such as class, gender, race, or developed/developing, are by no means simply descriptive.

Capitalist and colonial exploitation *created* both these states – the center as well as peripheries, which were then legitimized through colonial and racist discourse and the categories and frameworks employed to analyze them. The categories, in turn, *reinforce* such hierarchies. This is why the project to decolonize economics is not simply an epistemological issue. The decolonization agenda seeks both to expose the categories through studying them, but also to challenge the process that brought them into existence and to put forward alternative explanations for the hierarchies in the world today.

Key features of a decolonization agenda

How can we theorize and research economics in a way that is in line with a decolonization agenda? Before laying out our general reflections on what this would entail, three caveats are important. First, there is no recipe for decolonizing economics and the book thus far has not been the 100-page equivalent of a food blogger telling you their life story before getting to the recipe for producing a decolonized economics. However, we do propose some general reflections that can help to think critically about decolonization with reference to a concept, theory, method, and context. Second, decolonizing economics is not just an academic project, but a political one as well. And as the agenda gains recognition, there is a real possibility that the agenda is depoliticized – as has happened with the concept of *intersectionality* (Erel et al., 2011). The concept of intersectionality – which we shall see is also central for a decolonization agenda – has been so successful in becoming dominant across much of the social sciences that it has in many cases been stripped of its radical transformative power and analytical potency (Charusheela, 2013). A lot of the scholarship that inspires a decolonization agenda emerged in political struggle against capitalism, racism, patriarchy, and imperialism, and it is important to not attempt to separate the theories and concepts of this scholarship from their political foundation. Third, the post-colonial turns in other disciplines often came with the marginalization of questions of radical political economy that moved the disciplines to focus instead on representation and discourse.[2] We need to avoid this in economics, as a move toward greater representation and a critical economic discourse, even if an improvement, will be far from sufficient for its decolonization.

The universal and the particular

Universalism in the mainstream of the economics discipline is Eurocentric. Eurocentric universalism in economics is a partial and distorted view of the world and is based on the idea that capitalist development will diffuse across the world in a way similar to how it evolved in the idealized understanding of Europe. Universal principles in economics therefore contend that if such a diffusion does not happen, this is aberrant behavior that must be explained in reference to the (Eurocentric) benchmark of a harmonious and linear capitalist development. Therefore, universalism in economics is not universal at all, but the imposition of a Eurocentric myth on all theorizing, with perhaps a few adjustments for local contexts. This must be rejected.

But this does not mean all attempts to provide universal theorization, categorization, knowledge, or political projects should be eschewed in favor of only particular analysis. This could risk going down the exclusively particularistic or relativist route, which can essentialize, romanticize, or exoticize all that comes from the periphery (Majumdar, 2021; Larsen, 2022; Smith and Lester, 2023). This is theoretically and politically dangerous as it has the potential to place too much emphasis on the pre-colonial, pre-modern, pre-capitalist, or native, as the ends of development and decolonization. Unsurprisingly, such approaches to decolonization have recently been co-opted by several right-wing politicians of the periphery for nativist ends (A. Lewis and Lall, 2024). Instead, a decolonization agenda necessarily rejects nativism and any kind of ethnocentrism in favor of a global, transnational analysis, also laying the basis for transnational solidarity. In fact, Samir Amin (2009 [1988], p. 214) saw nativism as "inverted Eurocentrism" and called for critical examination of such a mode of thinking. Cultural relativism also makes it difficult to expose oppressive structures and relations when they occur in the periphery. A decolonization agenda is therefore anti-relativist in its insistence on uncovering and analyzing all forms of domination, not only domination by the capitalist center (Charusheela, 2004). Instead, the agenda opens for exploring and challenging multiple sites of oppression (Parashar, 2017), and how they are embedded within the overall system to produce a social totality.

We caution against complete epistemic relativism – the idea that all ways of knowing are necessarily partial and that therefore there can be no single way superior to another. Different ways of knowing are geared toward revealing certain aspects of the social reality while occluding others. In this context, the hegemonic way of doing research in contemporary economics is actually inferior to many other modes of theorizing because of its rigid Eurocentrism that does not lend itself readily to studying systemic processes of exploitation, extraction, and oppression, which other frameworks readily reveal. Indeed, many Latin American intellectuals' efforts to decolonize the social sciences were explicitly aiming at constructing better theories to the dominant Eurocentrism, rather than promoting pluralism for the sake of pluralism (C. Kay, 1989). With a decolonization agenda, we seek to establish helpful ways of evaluating and conducting research that can help us sort among different claims to knowledge to more clearly articulate why we choose certain frameworks.

What we need instead of Eurocentric universalism is a kind of universalism that seeks to study capitalism – as the dominant global organizing system of production, distribution, and the organization of life – in its historical and geographical totality. This takes different forms in different places, and has different implications for different social groups, but this universalism needs to be based on the recognition that capitalism is a global system, and not just a "Western" one (Majumdar, 2021, p. 18). What is produced in the peripheries is also very much capitalism and not a lack of it. We should strive towards general comprehension of economic issues in a universal manner, including shared criteria for evaluating specific research endeavors, so that it is possible for scholars from different theoretical and methodological traditions and geographies to communicate with each other (Alatas, 1987). Aspiring to universalism does not mean that social science is frozen, or that its universality cannot be constantly expanded, refined, and contested.

It is possible to recognize differences across cultures, while also striving to find common humanity in spite of differences (Buck-Morss, 2009). Majumdar (2021) calls this a "radical universalism" and points out that this was also embraced by many anti-colonial thinkers such as Frantz Fanon, Amílcar Cabral, and C. L. R. James. Take, for example, the concrete history of the Haitian Revolution of 1791–1804, in which black slaves overthrew their colonial masters to establish the Haitian state. The slaves did not do this in the defense of a pluriverse or based on their own cultural values; instead, they were defending freedoms that had not been extended to them despite the French Revolution's language of universal freedom (Buck-Morss, 2009). The Haitian constitution, then, became the first in the world to enshrine the principle of *universal* freedom in a genuine manner, meaning the legacy of universal freedom originates not in Europe but on the "barricades of subaltern struggle" (Wilson, 2022, p. 155). Such common humanity that arises amidst revolutionary upheaval has been conceptualized in terms of an *insurgent universality* (Tomba, 2015). A decolonization agenda can open the possibility for discussion around what a different, non-Eurocentric kind of universalism entails, one that, for example, centers issues such as humanism (Charusheela, 2004), truly universal freedom (Buck-Morss, 2009), or an internationalist struggle in the name of a global proletariat (Moore, 2022).

Therefore, localism and universalism need not be delineated as an "exotic and essentialized localism" and "a Eurocentric universalism" (Majumdar, 2021). A universalist view of a social science project can be adopted for a decolonization agenda. However, it needs to be an open one where the uniqueness of each society or of historical developments is not denied, rather one where this uniqueness can be identified in terms of general concepts that can specify ranges of forms of difference. This differs from a particularist social science where distinctive concepts are needed to suit a particular situation, making communication across space and time difficult. A particularist social science can only establish absolute difference, whereas a universal one can identify differences systematically.

The vantage point of theorization

While we have documented how the mainstream of the field theorizes from a Eurocentric vantage point of the capitalist center, a decolonization agenda is one that lays the foundation for theorizing in a way that includes the vantage point of the periphery. This is not to suggest that those at the periphery necessarily know better because of their positionality. Rather, the focus is on frameworks that allow us to adopt non-Eurocentric standpoints, thereby allowing for accounts of society that can better capture structural processes relevant for understanding economic outcomes (Harding, 1997). It is not a vantage point *from* the periphery, but as a vantage point that *includes* the periphery, to allow for a fuller understanding of both global connections and forms of structural marginalization. An example is theorization from the perspective of global history (Amin, 2010) to better understand the way that capitalism evolved historically with different impacts for different locations across the globe, or accounting for colonial histories and empire in our theorization to better put forward a reparatory social science (Bhambra, 2022).

Feminist political economists, drawing on feminist standpoint theory, argue that *strong objectivity* is where the researcher recognizes their vantage point for theorization, while *weak objectivity* is where the researcher's vantage point is obscured and when research rests on technique rather than a reflection of theoretical entry point (Harding, 1992, 1995; Wolff and Resnick, 2012). The idea here is that by making the researcher's vantage point clear – rather than claiming neutrality – we can improve objectivity of research (Harding, 1992). Crucially, it is not enough to reveal our vantage point for theorization if that vantage point remains Eurocentric. If one wants to uncover the oppressive processes that have been camouflaged by Eurocentrism, one must include a vantage point that can uncover oppressive structures (Harding, 1992; Hartsock, 2006). This means that theorizing from the vantage point that includes the periphery leads to more relevant insights for a decolonization agenda. Unfortunately, the kind of objectivity that prevails in the economics discipline is in line with what Harding calls weak objectivity (Kvangraven and Kesar, 2023).

We are therefore trying to provincialize Eurocentric theorization as the locus of our understanding of the economy (Chakrabarty, 2008), and utilize frameworks that study capitalist exploitation, patriarchy, racial capitalism, imperialism, and caste as constitutive elements comprising the contemporary economic system. This is not only relevant for understanding the periphery or outcomes for marginalized groups but will also provide better analysis of the lives of white men, white women, or black men, as their lives cannot be easily understood without considering exploitation, racialization, or patriarchal structures either (Charusheela, 2013). A decolonization agenda thus challenges the way that we understand the economic order *generally*, not only in relation to colonialism, the periphery, or marginalized groups.

Methodological reflexivity and rigor

Working toward a decolonization agenda also requires a reconsideration of the methodology of economics. Generally, there is a strongly entrenched epistemology of positivism in academic research. This assumes that there is social distance in the relationship between the researcher and the research subject (McCloskey, 1994) and that anyone can discover the truth "out there" through scientific enquiry. Economists' view of themselves as objective observers uncovering the truth through social experiments and econometric analysis stands in sharp contrast to critical reflexivity on the part of the researcher that is emphasized in other disciplines (Hunter,

2002). Critical reflexivity in research involves attentiveness to the researcher's own location within structures of power and attentiveness to the politics of knowledge production, given that the researcher's location shapes both the process of undertaking research and interpreting the material (Charusheela, 2013). It is important for researchers to be clear about the hidden assumptions they are making that impact their investigation and their theoretical and political worldview. Even Nobel laureate Amartya Sen (1992) argued that recognizing one's own positional perspective is crucial for improving research objectivity. This can make the researcher more aware of how they are constructing knowledge and the influence of their own beliefs, backgrounds, and feelings on the research process to assess how their subjectivities affect their way of seeing the world (Wasserfall, 1997; Shilliam, 2012; Bhambra, 2014; Reyes and Johnson, 2020). This may often also involve addressing power differences between researchers and their participants, especially when there are added layers of differences such as in terms of race, class, and gender (L. T. Smith, 1999).

Reflexive research accounts for researcher's own frames of reference, given that these frames may often reflect the hold of oppressive structures on our understanding of the world. For example, from one frame of reference, bringing women into the workplace may be a sign of liberation, whereas from another, work may be a marker of exploitation (Charusheela, 2013). Contrasting theories of feminist economics that center patriarchal structures tend to lead to wildly different findings about the effects of development interventions on women's empowerment than late neoclassical theories that take the individual as a starting point for interpreting the findings (see Kabeer, 2020, for example).

A researcher interested in pursuing economics within a decolonization agenda can employ various methods depending on their questions and categories (Charusheela, 2013).[3] Quantitative research is useful for tracking the effects of differences on groups, keeping categories intact. Qualitative research helps understand the processes through which these differences are created and experienced. Discursive methods reveal the assumptions underlying the categories and how they become stabilized and normalized. Additionally, oral traditions and archival work are valuable for recovering economic and human history (Falola, 2001). As Charusheela (2013, p. 38) puts it, scholarship drawing on combinations of such methods "can illuminate the structural origins of social difference." Unlike the positivism and weak objectivity of the mainstream of the field, a decolonization agenda should ideally be informed by a better form of rigor and stronger objectivity (Kvangraven and Kesar, 2023).

The role of positionality and identity

A decolonization agenda aims to address the structural marginalization of voices typically unheard in the hegemonic capitalist center. However, merely addressing this marginalization is insufficient. A common pitfall in recent attempts to "decolonize" the social sciences is reducing the problem to one of identity alone.

Historical and ideological factors obstruct the possibility of marginalized groups in the periphery being heard in economics research. Academic institutions are plagued by steep hierarchies based on race, gender, caste, and imperialism. Those closest to the ideal type of *homo economicus* – white, heterosexual men from the capitalist center taking Eurocentric approaches to research – are more likely to be recognized as academically excellent. This is linked to what others have termed *cognitive imperialism* (Mentan, 2015), *cultural imperialism* (Said, 1993), the *metaphysical empire* (Thiong'o, 1986) or the *white gaze* (Pailey, 2020), and it makes furthering a decolonization agenda even more difficult because of its silencing of voices from the periphery with different theoretical starting points.

The silencing associated with an uneven intellectual division of labor enables multiple levels of academic extraction (Hountondji, 1990). Within development economics, extraction takes a particularly egregiously colonial form with scholars from the capitalist center traveling to study people of the periphery, producing studies guilty of Eurocentrism, orientalism, and racism (Cornwall, 2007; Hoffman, 2020). The hierarchies in economic theory are completely reflected in the functioning of academic economics as well as in the world at large. They create additional barriers to challenging Eurocentrism and moving toward the decolonization of economics (Gani and Marshall, 2022).

That said, there are many pitfalls related to reducing the problem of decolonization to identity and positionality. The problem is not simply about who is in a department, a panel, or a workshop (the very understandable outcry against *manels*), or who can speak about what, although those issues are also important. Structural hierarchies in academia and the world do marginalize certain voices, but a decolonization agenda is not merely about elevating indigenous, native, or peripheral knowledge above others. Elevating scholars or scholarship solely based on the author's identity risks politically problematic conclusions that do not evaluate research on its own merits (Hull, 2021). Focusing too narrowly on one identity group – such as scholars from the periphery – risks being singularly influenced by hegemonic thought from that group, neglecting the diversity within the periphery as well as other marginalized groups in economics.

Furthermore, a decolonization agenda is about reflexivity, responsibility, and rigor in research, and not about policing identity (Moghadam, 1989). If we reduce research simply to who is allowed to say what, we move into murky territory of having to decide who is sufficiently a part of the *Other* to qualify for being allowed to speak or to study the other. Not only is this unnecessary, but it also solidifies the self/other distinction (Abu-Lughod, 1990) and distracts from the issue of the quality and objectivity (as defined above) of the research itself and the dignity with which it was carried out. Rather than thinking about positionality solely in terms of geography or identity, it is important to focus on the vantage point of theorization for uncovering structures. For instance, simply theorizing from a woman's perspective is insufficient to understand gendered inequalities. A decolonization agenda requires theorizing from a feminist vantage point that identifies and analyzes the patriarchal structures shaping the economic system. This includes understanding the role of social reproduction – mostly carried out by women – in sustaining capitalist accumulation, and thus comprehending gendered experiences and economic outcomes in that context. Similarly, theorizing from the periphery of the global economy improves our understanding of peripheral conditions by considering structures of colonialism, imperialism, and racialization, as well as enhancing our general comprehension of how global capitalism functions.

While it is tempting to reduce the problem to either identity discrimination or epistemological colonization, a decolonization agenda compels us to situate the hierarchies of identity and Eurocentrism within a broader understanding of the world. The discrimination and epistemological imperialism in the economics discipline cannot be addressed without also tackling the hierarchical nature of the global economy itself.

Deconstructing and reconstructing categories

While categories create analytical elegance and neat distinctions, using them also risks reifying the differences (Charusheela, 2013). However, ignoring those categories risks failing to account for and address existing inequalities. To advance an understanding of unequal economic outcomes in a world where Eurocentric categories and analysis dominate, several tasks stand before researchers committed to a decolonization agenda. The first is deconstructing the dominant Eurocentric categories to assess how they come into being. The second is to study the impact of the categories to trace their effects on specific groups. The third is advancing alternative forms of understanding socioeconomic outcomes that may involve employing different categories from the ones that are dominant in the economics discipline.

When constructing alternative categories, it is crucial to keep in mind that economic categories and processes are not fixed across time and space. We must be wary of institutionalizing one alternative way of studying economic processes, given that "institutionalizing the frame can freeze categories of analysis as researchers simply apply the frame" (K. Davis, 2008, summarized in Charusheela, 2013, p. 41).[4]

A decolonization agenda requires that we think carefully through which kinds of structures and categories may be most helpful for uncovering economic processes, and exposing and interrogating the ideological baggage of structures and categories that we use in research and analysis. This may call for a *counterdisciplinary* approach (Zein-Elabdin and Charusheela, 2004, p. 10) or *anti-disciplinary* approach (McKittrick, 2015, 2021; Gilmore, 2022; Kvangraven and Styve, 2024; Nasong'o and Ikpe, 2024) because it requires thinking that goes beyond disciplinary boundaries. This is not about simply learning from other disciplines, as many disciplines have colonial foundations, leading scholars to argue that "discipline is empire," more generally (McKittrick, 2021, p. 36).[5]

The need to transcend disciplinary boundaries has long been recognized by scholars dedicated to advancing decolonization. One example is the Dar es Salaam School, which hosted many anti-colonial scholars, including the Tanzanian legal scholar Issa Shivji; Walter Rodney, who wrote *How Europe underdeveloped Africa* (1972) while based in Dar es Salaam; Ruth First, one of the most prominent white South African communists in the anti-apartheid struggle, who spent a semester at the university; Angela Davis, who came from the United States to deliver an address on the question of global black solidarity and anti-imperialism at the university; the South African Pan-Africanist Archie Mafeje, who spent less than two years at the university, but a very formative period of his career and at the height of anti-colonial debates at the university (1969–71); and the women's liberation theorist Marjorie Mbilinyi, who eventually gave up her American citizenship to become Tanzanian (Al-Bulushi, 2023; Ndlovu-Gatsheni, 2023).[6] The Dar es Salaam School re-organized knowledge into *fields of study* rather than narrow disciplines, as a way to better grapple with the most pressing issues of post-colonial development.[7]

As discussed in chapter 3, one of the key characteristics of the separation of economic questions in the social sciences into disciplines was the separation of social spheres, such as the state, the market, and non-market spheres. This sustains economists' focus on the market while considering social phenomena as external to economic processes (Brown and Spencer, 2014). Such separation compromises our ability to understand the social formations underlying socioeconomic processes, particularly as we delve into the patriarchal, colonial, and racialization of capitalism itself.[8] A decolonization agenda calls for a unified approach to the social sciences that avoids the separation of social formations into separate spheres (Wallerstein, 1996).

The hierarchies of economics

Economics has been based on constructing dualisms, or dichotomies, since its inception as a discipline (Dow, 1990). These dualisms serve to perpetuate Eurocentrism. To expose processes of dichotomization and hierarchy within economic theory that we find essential for the work of decolonization, we draw on a range of existing critical traditions that focus on various axes of oppression, such as class, race, patriarchy, and empire.[9] Each of these traditions have their own particularities, specificities, and diversity within them.

As we discussed, the center–periphery binary is pervasive globally, manifesting also in gender differentiation, racial differentiation, distinctions between traditional and modern, and the economic and non-economic. Wherever such hierarchies are constructed, they are juxtaposed against an idealized capitalist center positioned at the apex of the hierarchy. This process of dichotomization legitimizes one singular, universal form of knowledge that elevates the idealized notion of the capitalist center, while delegitimizing others. It is, therefore, a Eurocentric dichotomization that we will examine closely in this section.

Although the dichotomies are presented as neutral, they are based on a long-drawn and ongoing process of differentiation, whereby all phenomena, systems, and institutions that do not align with a Eurocentric vision of capitalism, including femininity, non-heteronormativity, non-whiteness, socio-economically disadvantaged castes groups, and traditional and non-capitalist structures, are ascribed the status of *others* that are lacking in various ways. While these categories exist in the discipline of economics, the process of polarization and suppression of the *other* is also to be found in the real world, and this subordination and the institutions supporting it play a crucial role in sustaining an imperial, racialized, Brahmanical, and patriarchal capitalist system. As such, a decolonization agenda also seeks to uncover how such hierarchies reinforce systemic inequalities and thus have material effects on people's lives. In line with the key features of a decolonization agenda that we have identified, we take on the task of deconstructing Eurocentric categories, exploring how they are produced and reproduced, and evaluate what alternative categories in line with a decolonization agenda might look like.

Key to this thesis is the idea that capitalism as an economic system can reproduce itself through a class system based on worker exploitation, supported by a web of inequalities shaped by racialization, patriarchy, imperialism, and casteism (Federici, 2004; Bhattacharyya, 2018; Fraser, 2019; Dilawri, 2023). Interrogating the ways that capitalist social relations shape economic processes is therefore crucial for a decoloniz-ation agenda given that we live in a society where capitalism is the dominant form of production. This certainly does not mean reducing all forms of domination to capital, but considering how capitalism enables or interacts with other forms of domination and recognizing that there are also non-capitalist exploitative social relations to be uncovered (Charusheela, 2000, 2010).

The concept of *homo economicus* – the rational economic man – exemplifies this. *Homo economicus* is central for economics, even for behavioral economists who spend their careers studying why people do not behave in the way that economic theory would predict. In this example, the rational economic man represents the center – a hyper-rational, modern, and capitalist, heterosexual, male agent that exists completely independent from social structures (Nelson, 1995; Kaul, 2007). Behavior not aligned with *homo economicus* is considered to be imperfect and in need of correction through incentives. Beyond the racialized, colonial, and gendered dimensions of the rational economic man, it is worth also discussing how a key problem with the concept is that it neutralizes and depoliticizes behavior itself, given that it conceals social structures that shape the individual's actions. This depoliticization is central for all dualisms in economics. For example, the worker is posited as selling their labor on the open market, whereas the capitalist is posited as a mere buyer, concealing the power relationship between capitalists and workers, which is fundamental for understanding how capitalism works. As such, the economics field – despite its origins in political economy – has found a way to depoliticize class itself by assuming all individuals – whether workers or capitalists – have equal power in the marketplace, or, at least, when the system works fairly this power can be equated, without a need to fundamentally challenge the ownership structures. A decolonization agenda brings the political power of capital and class, as well as other structural processes such as colonialism, white supremacy, and patriarchy, to front and center of the discussion in economics.

1. Colonial hierarchies

Colonial dichotomizations are pervasive in economics, including in categories of traditional–modern, culture–economy, developed–underdeveloped, and colonizer–colonized. These categories implicitly or explicitly underlie a lot of economic theorizing, and they are being continuously reproduced along a Eurocentric center–periphery axis.

The construction of colonial categories

By and large, the economics discipline has a straightforward, uncritical view of the path of economic development. The assumption is that the lagging peripheral economies will teleologically follow the paths of a capitalist transition toward the economies of the capitalist center. A powerful binary emerges: the developed and underdeveloped, which exists in parallel with the colonizer–colonized and center–periphery binaries. Here, the former is celebrated for its homogeneous modern and rational capitalist structure and the latter is considered lagging because it is not capitalist, modern, or rational enough. A singular path of economic development, understood as synonymous with capitalist transition, is thus assumed to be available to the periphery – one that accepts a Eurocentric understanding of how capitalism evolved in the center – based on improved rationality, hard work, and endogenous technological improvements. All the alternative visions of development that exist across the world are marginalized and considered virtually non-existent in the top echelons of the discipline. As such, the discipline puts forward a colonial discourse by writing off the history of colonialism that materially impoverished and institutionally weakened the formerly colonized economies and views them as simply being at an earlier stage of historical development (Callari, 2004; Zein-Elabdin, 2011).

Closely linked to developed–underdeveloped dichotomy is the traditional–modern binary. In this characterization, modernity is based on a social vision that includes a liberal democratic state, a capitalist economy, and a series of other specific institutions of public life that are associated with the capitalist economies of the center. Capitalist modernity is usually perceived as a normative ideal, where societies are ranked based on their closeness to or distance from it (Dussel, 1995; Charusheela and Zein-Elabdin, 2003; Quijano, 2007). Consequently, the economics field itself can be considered a hegemonic modernizing discourse, which adopts a particular vision of modernity based on a Eurocentric understanding of capitalism and rationality (Zein-Elabdin and Charusheela, 2004). The peripheral economies, their economic structures, institutions, and other elements of cultural and social spheres are viewed as traditional or primitive, without an analysis of alternative forms of modernization that align with those contexts.

This dichotomy dates to the Enlightenment period, which laid the basis for thinking about Europeans as producing logic and science, whereas the *others* produce myth and superstition (Said, 1979). The dichotomy has been cemented with the establishment of economic behavior that aligns with capitalist institutions as rational, and all those that digress from it as non-rational (Quijano, 2007). While the rational agent is considered abstract and universal, it is predicated on the exclusion of all characteristics, experiences, and subjectivities that are considered non-rational, non-masculine, subjective, and/or non-European (Lugones, 2010).

Within the traditional–modern dichotomy, there is also the separation between the economy and culture, where the market economy is generally considered the rational, modern sphere and culture is considered the traditional and irrational sphere. Although culture is most often absent or undertheorized in economics, when it is theorized, it tends to be conceptualized as a constraint on welfare-maximizing behavior (Zein-Elabdin, 2009). As such, welfare-maximizing behavior is viewed as a universal form of rationality that is separate from culture. Alternative understandings of rationalities and how culture impacts economics directly challenge such Eurocentric views of behavior. An example of such alternate understandings is the concept of hybridity[10] – a concept that attempts to make sense of crossings of indigenous and colonial legacies with contemporary cultures – which directly challenges the idea that there is one predictable historical path where the traditional will eventually wither away to make way for the dominance of capitalist rationality and modernity (Canclini, 1995). Understanding the possibility of hybrid social formations also shifts our understanding away from categorical dualisms and allows for alternative social formations and rationalities that break with the Eurocentric vision (Zein-Elabdin, 2009).

Colonial hierarchies produced and reproduced

Colonial forms of knowledge, which are apparent in economics, are rooted in material and violent projects of colonialism and imperialism. Therefore, colonial discourse can itself be considered an apparatus of power, as it construes the colonized as degenerate types based on their racial otherness, which in turn justifies conquest and systems of administration and instruction (Bhabha, 1994, p. 70). Its perpetuation in economics discourse is striking.

First, the concept of *development* is itself a discourse of power, rather than a culturally neutral and scientifically knowable path for an economy (Escobar, 1995). As noted earlier, non-Eurocentric scholarship has argued that under-development is not simply a lack of capitalist expansion, but rather that it is produced precisely because of it. Indeed, it is the common process of capitalist expansion that produces uneven development globally (Frank, 1967). Even within the economies of the peripheries, capitalist expansion continually produces conditions of development and underdevelopment (Sanyal, 2007; P. Patnaik, 2009). Acknowledging the problems embedded in this discourse, which reduces development to a lack of capitalist expansion enables us to also challenge the spread of the narrative globally, which has had devastating impacts as governments are coerced into following policy prescriptions based on a Eurocentric idea of development (H.-J. Chang, 2002; Cooke, 2003; Mkandawire, 2005).

Second, the dichotomy of traditional–modern, where capitalist modernity associated with the center is seen as the goal of development, has complicated and devastating consequences. In a Eurocentric view, it is assumed that modernization will only occur through contact with the modern capitalist center and that the countries of the periphery would learn from the center in all ways, including in terms of better facilitating capitalist development as well as modern attitudes to human rights, women, and minorities (Cowen and Shenton, 1995; Bergeron, 2004). While this categorization of the traditional backward former colony and enlightened modern former colonizer is prevalent across the fields of economics and development today, it has been heavily resisted since its inception. Anti-colonial nationalists recognized that colonial powers had plundered and not developed the colonized, and there is no doubt that the center economies have always also exploited and subordinated people within their own territories. Values such as human rights and women's rights are often associated with Western modernization even though this rights narrative was not always a force for liberation for people of the colonies, and colonial rule often led to severe marginalization of women economically and politically.[11] Thus, the liberatory narratives about modernity obscure realities across the periphery, where there were many struggles for self-determination and against oppression before, during, and after the colonial period. This is not to romanticize the pre-colonial or pre-capitalist forms of social formations, but to highlight two key insights that are lost in the current economics narrative. First, social organizations, institutions, and cultures that deviate from the Eurocentric norm in economics may be more or less amenable to supporting free and emancipated lives of people – they will not *necessarily* be better or worse. A decolonization agenda must be open to understanding institutions and social processes on their own terms, moving beyond the modern–traditional binary. Second, narratives of modernization completely neglect the exploitation and expropriation that is associated with colonial and capitalist expansion, with devastating consequences for understanding existing social processes. While capitalism produced exploitative structures everywhere, capital accumulation in the colonies played out much more brutally, which also "called for different frameworks of justification" (Ince, 2018, p. 4). A decolonization agenda must take this reality into account when evaluating the ways in which modernity has been employed as a proxy for capitalist development and expansion.

Finally, let us consider another category: that of the nation-state, which was often produced as a result of, or as a response to, colonialism. The category of the nation-state has been vigorously resisted by many anti-colonial movements and scholars, despite the obvious existence of national boundaries across the periphery. Anti-colonialism was in many moments a deep rejection of the boundaries of the nation-state, calling for Pan-Africanism (Nkrumah, 1970 [1965]), a new global world order (Nyerere, 1980), international socialism (James, 1963 [1938]), worldmaking (Getachew, 2019), and/or a better understanding of colonial global connections in order to challenge them (deGrassi, 2023). Many anti-colonial and anti-imperialist scholars thinking from the periphery challenged the idea of the Westphalian nation-state category precisely because of the colonial connections that produced hierarchy in the global economy, making autonomous national development in the periphery impossible (Amin, 1972; T. Dos Santos, 1970; Rodney, 1972; Bambirra, 1978). These critiques are also related to the problems of methodological nationalism – the notions that states are the most relevant units of analysis. Methodological nationalism is prevalent in a lot of economic theorizing and is problematic in terms of papering over hierarchies both within and between countries (Pradella, 2014). Many anti-colonial scholars rejected methodological nationalism to rather theorize the global structures that underpin the international system of exploitation.

That said, anti-imperialist nationalism has also been used to challenge the subordinate position that former colonies find themselves in in the global economy at large. This is relevant for many aspects of society, including universities. After the end of formal colonialism in Africa, there was a nationalist turn across universities on the continent, which challenged Eurocentrism and approached history and theory from an African vantage point (Olukoshi, 2006, p. 534). This has been considered a kind of nationalist humanism (Zeleza, 2006, p. 113), where the project was not about carving out an exclusive space for African intellectuals, but rather to challenge patriarchy, capitalism, and imperialism more broadly (Kimambo, 2008; Mamdani, 2016). Despite the radical intentions, however, it is questionable to what extent this actually led to freeing intellectuals in Africa from the imminent logics of colonialism and imperialism (Ndlovu-Gatsheni, 2023). As the Cold War intensified, imperialist forces made it increasingly difficult for these institutions to develop strong and well-resourced radical academic programs in line with a decolonization agenda (Mkandawire, 2005; Zeleza, 2009; Kamola, 2019).

2. Patriarchal hierarchies

Gendered categorization is also pervasive in economics, and it also relies on Eurocentric dichotomization. Feminist economists have been pioneering in their critique of economics as a masculine discipline and have fundamentally challenged the discipline's claim to neutrality and objectivity (Nelson, 1995; Hewitson, 1999). Feminist scholars have also pointed out gender biases in data collection, construction, and analysis (Waring, 1990; Criado Perez, 2019).

The construction of patriarchal categories

In economics, masculinity is valorized and is projected as the ideal or the norm that is aligned with the center that represents the essence of capitalism, while femininity is devalorized and viewed as peripheral. This represents yet another dichotomization that is embedded in the relationship of power, where the market production due to its valorization under capitalism is celebrated, while social reproduction outside the market, which is mostly done by women, is neglected.

Adding to the critique of *homo economicus* introduced earlier, it is essential to add that the concept is patriarchal as well (Nelson, 1995). In economics, characteristics of masculinity tend to be attributed to capitalist rationality and modernity, including self-interest, maximizing behavior, and calculative individuals unbound by social ties. This rational agent has no explicit gender and generally exists in economic models unencumbered by gendered social roles guiding or constraining behavior. Based on what are considered traditionally gendered attributes, it is evident that the rational masculine agent with capitalist rationality has formed the basis of economic modeling in mainstream economic theory. On the other hand, characteristics traditionally attributed to femininity, such as altruism, others-regarding preferences, subjectivity, and relationality, are devalorized and considered aberrations from this rational and autonomous individual that should ideally be corrected. How these different subjectivities and rationalities are constructed is not a question of interest to most economists.

The way both identity and socialization are conceived of within late neoclassical economics serves to reinforce a patriarchal and methodologically individualistic approach to economics. In neoclassical accounts, a person's identity is used interchangeably with ego, as it represents the psychological motivations for behavior and links to fixed social categories that people "slot into" (Kaul, 2007, p. 161). Underlying this is the image of an abstract, essentialist individual version of identity, where the identities are different but not systematically hierarchical or structurally produced. This conceptualization does not allow for power or oppression, as people are merely acting according to rational empirical motivations. Conceiving rational economic men in such an atomized manner, disconnected from imperialist, racialized, and gendered structures, is in line with what Hobbes found to be an apt starting point for understanding human behavior, namely considering men to be as if "sprung out of the earth, and suddenly, like mushrooms, come to full maturity, without all kind of engagement to each other" (cited in Nelson, 1995, p. 135).[12] Such asocial analyses make it impossible to study or consider the social structures in which individuals find themselves, which are crucial for understanding issues such as structural discrimination, but also how we are socialized to behave in particular ways through our family, cultural, and community bonds.

Furthermore, in economics, and in society, the market-place – representing the masculine sphere of economic production – is viewed as the primary economic sphere, whereas the household – representing the feminine sphere of social reproduction – is viewed as peripheral. Although feminist political economists have documented carefully how social reproduction of labor (power) forms the basis of market production, in economics it is still viewed as subordinate in mainstream economics (Federici, 2004; Naidu, 2016; T. Bhattacharya, 2017; Ghosh, 2021; Ossome, 2021; Cantillon et al., 2023). The subordination of reproductive activities in economics often means devaluing women's labor as a fragmented, marginal, and inconsequential noneconomic *Other* (Gibson-Graham, 1996). As a result of this subordi-nation, social reproductive work, including housework, care work, and subsistence production, is not counted in national GDP, the person providing non-market care is not viewed as a worker, and even when care work is provided by the market, it is undervalued (Waring, 1990; Benería, 1992; Folbre, 2012). Notably, this bias is also reflected in the division of labor in the economics discipline itself, with research on topics such as care work (Folbre and Nelson, 2000), discrimi-nation (Figart, 2005), development of gender-aware theories (Barker and Kuiper, 2003), being understudied and under-valued. To the extent that women's subordinate role in the labor market is acknowledged, as was the case in the recent Nobel to the feminist economist Claudia Goldin, it is in the narrow terms of women's entry into the productive sphere of the markets, that is, the valorized sphere in economic theory.

The category of the nation-state that we discussed also tends to be conceived of as a masculine concept in economics, as the imagined community of the nation continues to be based on "making much of women's work invisible through masculine notions of economic activity and economic citizenship" (Bergeron, 2004, p. 3). Stretching the analysis to the global level, we can, further, see that patriarchal, racialized, and colonial discourses come together to represent countries of the periphery as the feminized, racialized Others that stand in contrast to the modern, autonomous, capitalist, masculine countries of the center (C. Scott, 1995). This analogy also works at the micro level, where the woman of the periphery is often portrayed as the most backward in her society, "ignorant, poor, uneducated, tradition-bound, domestic, family-oriented" (Mohanty, 1991, p. 56). The assumption is that she could only be empowered by integration into the capitalist labor market (Bergeron, 2004).

Patriarchy reproduced

Similar to colonial categories, the patriarchal categories in the economics discipline are not merely discursive; they are rooted in material hierarchies continuously produced and reproduced in real life. The issue is that these patriarchal categories fail to capture the processes through which these inequalities are created and sustained.

For example, consider the elevation of the market sphere in economics. Due to the primacy of the market, economists often advocate for women's empowerment by way of entry into the market sphere. This approach, prevalent in global development projects, is marked by a Eurocentric view of paid labor as representing "autonomy, choice, and self-esteem for people otherwise trapped by home, culture, or tradition" (Carrasco-Miró, 2022, p. 775). However, this perspective fails to challenge the false separation of market and non-market activities and tends to reproduce patri-archal power relations within the market sphere rather than challenging them (Elson and Pearson, 1981). As women increasingly join the market workforce, they often face the dual burden of work in both the home and market spheres (or sometimes a triple shift, including the emotional labor they disproportionately shoulder) and women are often faced with much harsher working conditions than men in the labor market (Bambirra, 1972; Oakley, 1972; Duncombe and Marsden; 1993; C. Wood, 2003; Ghosh, 2009; Barrientos, 2019; Tontoh, 2022). Whether this approach to labor results in women's empowerment depends on whether you view empowerment primarily as obtaining work in the market sphere or something else (Cornwall, 2018; Kabeer, 2020). In many cases, this empowerment agenda mainly provides cheap, exploitable labor to capital, often even from within the household (Mies, 1986). This example clearly illustrates how the elevation of the market sphere is both reflected in the Eurocentric economic categories of the discipline and repro-duced with real-world consequences for women globally.

To understand how such gender hierarchies are produced and reproduced, we also need to understand the complex ways that patriarchal relations played a key role in development of capitalism (Federici, 2004; Fraser, 2016a; T. Bhattacharya, 2017). Social reproduction theory is one way to connect patriarchy and capitalism, as it focuses on behind-the-scenes processes that are key for the worker to reproduce (and sell) their labor power (T. Bhattacharya, 2017). Through this specific framing, social reproduction comes to be seen as an integral part of capitalism that sustains its drive for accumulation, instead of simply being a parallel system existing alongside the economic system (S. Ferguson, 2016). Such an approach rejects the separation of the productive as economic and the reproductive as non-economic, and rather sees all these processes, including those of gendering and racialization, as internal to the reproduction of the capitalist economic system itself.

Although dominance of gendered categories in economics makes it more difficult to challenge patriarchal structures and even to imagine alternatives (Gibson-Graham, 1993; K. Chang and Ling, 2000; Bergeron, 2004), feminists worldwide have long contested patriarchal and Eurocentric views of capitalism, capital, and globalization, offering alternative perspectives (Jayawardena, 1986; Gibson-Graham, 1993; Rowbotham and Mitter, 1994; Basu, 1995; Afshar and Barrientos, 1999; Runyan, 1999). It is important to note that these feminists do not necessarily form a unified global voice against capital. Constructing a unified global voice risks being dominated by feminists from the capitalist center who may not account for the diversity of women's experiences with global capital (Grewal and Kaplan, 1994) and might silence women from the periphery (Minh-Ha, 1987).[13]

These complex axes of power are central for understanding the different forms of oppression that someone faces and are therefore also central for the decolonization agenda we are developing here. A decolonization agenda encourages an intersectional analysis that tackles the many dimensions of oppression, such as patriarchy, heteronormativity, and casteism, that play a central role in *producing, reproducing,* and *sustaining* capitalism (Federici, 2004; Fraser, 2016a; T. Bhattacharya, 2017; Carrasco-Miró, 2022). Taking an intersectional approach allows us to speak to economic questions in a range of new ways, including by bringing in work on race, class, caste, sexuality, and disability (Butler,

1990; Deshpande, 2002; Meyer, 2002; Ruwanpura, 2008; Gupta, 2010; Taylor et al., 2011).

3. Racialized hierarchies

Building on the colonial and patriarchal hierarchies, we now interrogate racialized hierarchies, and the concept of intersectionality can help us here. Intersectionality captures the fact that multiple forms of oppression cannot simply be considered as the sum of two or more axes of oppression but that their *intersection* must be understood as co-constituting and shaping each other (Crenshaw, 1989).[14] The insight is in some ways simple: we cannot effectively address – or even understand – one axis of oppression on its own without also addressing – or understanding – its interactions with other axes. Therefore, liberation requires the destruction of a *structure* that bell hooks (2000) famously came to call "white supremacist capitalist patriarchy" (p. 159) and it is what Kimberlé Crenshaw (1995) refers to as structural intersectionality. This structure is also key to challenge within a decolonization agenda. As such, a decolonization agenda responds to Syliva Tamale's (2020, p. 9) challenge to "connect the ideological dots of racism, colonialism, capitalism, sexism and heterosexism."

The construction of racialized categories

During early periods of colonialism, the dichotomization between colonized and colonizer were often framed in terms of the universal and civilized on the one hand and the particular and uncivilized on the other, but this dichotomy also assumed racial dimensions in the early twentieth century (Anghie, 2005; Getachew, 2019). In W. E. B. Du Bois' (1995 [1900]: 639) formulation of the problem of the twentieth century being "the problem of the color line," he linked the racial domination he saw unfolding to the new era of imperial expansion of the late nineteenth century. This process of racialization placed different groups in a hierarchical framework of power, with more or less complete beings, sub-beings, and non-beings, with the latter two kinds of beings assumed to have no history, reason, rationality, or knowledge, and the former analogous to the rational economic man of the capitalist center (Ndlovu-Gatsheni, 2018). As such, the "color line" is tightly linked to an "epistemic line," which determines how humans are conceptualized in the social sciences (Ndlovu-Gatsheni, 2023, p. 3).

The color line extends to theorization about economic behavior, as the underlying assumption is that the rational agent is white, and that the individual exists free from any structural societal constraints on their behavior (Watson, 2018). In most cases, race is only implicit, but when it is explicitly addressed, it is often treated as a fixed identity, neglecting that racialization is socially produced and evolved in specific historical social structures and institutions. This aversion to the complexities of social institutions is so strong that standard economic textbooks often use Robinson Crusoe as a metaphor for individual behavior, given the desert island context (Watson, 2018). This isolated context conveniently supports a theory that is committed to understanding economic relations separately from all social relations of power, including imperialism and white supremacy. The focus on individualized rationalities, fixed categories, and individual behavior obscures how racialization was constructed through strong (capitalist) institutions (Bonilla-Silva, 2003; Tilley and Shilliam, 2018).

The category of race as it is employed within economics leads to methodological problems. In econometric studies, race is often viewed as an unalterable characteristic of an individual, rather than a social construction. Even when the social construction of race is acknowledged, it is often framed in terms of the independent evolution of norms (as in Akerlof and Kranton, 2010), rather than as a product of racialization under the Transatlantic Slave Trade and capitalism through active use of power and violence. This leads to inconsistencies because race is not consistently defined as a variable across time and space and because it limits the researchers' ability to understand the dynamics of racialization (Zuberi, 2001;

Zuberi and Bonilla-Silva, 2008). Within these frameworks, most of the explorations of racial disparities in economic outcomes lie outside the model, meaning race is considered an exogenous variable (Darity, 1975b; Spriggs, 2020). The implication of treating race as an exogenous variable is that "the model begins with a fallacy that assumes racial differences as natural order" (Spriggs, 2020, pp. 1–2).

This is particularly problematic because these analyses tend to draw conclusions about the *effect* of race, without being clear about what exactly they mean by this (Zuberi and Bonilla-Silva, 2008). For example, when an economist says that the effect of being Black on mortality is equivalent to over five years of increased age, do they mean it's the blackness that causes mortality or that Black people are more likely to engage in particular behavior? In both explanations race rather than racial relations are seen as the causal factors. Another problem with this method is that these kinds of causal arguments in economics depend on counterfactual reasoning, and such reasoning entails the construction of fictions about what would have happened or would happen in the world absent an event that is taken to be causal (DeMartino, 2020). It is quite clear that the fact that economists start with a racially biased view of the world shapes their analysis of race. As Zuberi and Bonilla-Silva (2008, p. 7) put it simply: "if we begin with a racially biased view of the world, then we will end up with a racially biased view of what the data have to say."

Racialization produced and reproduced

There are at least two important ways that the world economy is racialized, which a decolonization agenda must grapple with. The first is the development of capitalism, where racism was produced during the Transatlantic Slave Trade and in conjunction with colonialism (Rodney, 1972; Du Bois, 1999 [1920]; Robinson, 2000 [1983]).[15] This means it is impossible to understand capitalism without understanding racialization and vice versa. The second is the ways in which capitalism reinforces and reshapes these hierarchies.

First, the construction of a racial hierarchy, where whiteness is at the top and blackness is at the bottom, in such a rigid and universal manner is a relatively modern phenomenon that arose during the Transatlantic Slave Trade and the development of capitalism (Padmore, 1936; Williams, 1944; Nkrumah, 1963). As Du Bois (1999 [1920], p. 17) put it, "the discovery of personal whiteness among the world's people is a very modern thing – a nineteenth century and twentieth century matter." Even when slavery ended officially, the extension of citizenship to former slaves in the Americas ended in "new structures of racialized political and economic domination" (Du Bois, 1920], p. 20). Given the centrality of capitalist expansion in the creation of the black–white dichotomy, it is important to delve into the relationship between capitalist expansion and racial ordering.[16] As social categories are not fixed but socially constructed, analytical vocabulary such as racial formation, rather than simply the category race, can be helpful in advancing a decolonization agenda.[17]

Second, capitalism reinforced and reinforces existing hierarchies along lines of racial or other constructed categories of differentiation in social grouping. As radical political economists have long observed, constructing structural difference between the global proletariat, where some social groups see their labor power devalued, secures a degree of stability of the capitalist system, and it helps to prevent the working class from coming to a consciousness of itself as a social class (Leibowitz, 2003). As Roediger (2017, p. 26) put it, wherever in the world capitalism sets its roots, it "sought, exploited, needed and created difference."

This means that the process of dichotomization and creation of hierarchies extends beyond colonizer–colonized hierarchies to various processes of internal colonization and construction of social difference within the periphery (and within center) as well (González Casanova, 1965; Wolpe, 1975; C. Kay, 1989). Seeing capitalism as exploiting difference stands in contrast to the idea that capitalism wipes out hierarchies that existed under feudalism or other pre-capitalist societies. However, capitalism did not eliminate the existing hierarchies of feudalist social orders, but rather extended – and rewired – many of these social hierarchies into capitalist social relations (Robinson, 2000 [1983]). For example, feudal social structures such as caste, "in many ways predetermined who would collaborate, who would profit, and who would labor in India and beyond" (M. Khan, 2021, p. 96). Existing relations of indebtedness in India enabled plantation owners to access cheap labor provided by peasants and other landless villagers that was organized along caste lines (M. Khan, 2021; J. Raj, 2022). Local hierarchies such as caste have by and large been incorporated into the logics of global capitalism more generally (Dilawri, 2023).[18]

There is a resurgent literature on the relationship between race and caste, emphasizing that these categories are not merely comparable but also genealogically entangled, inter-secting with capital (Loomba, 2009; Dilawri, 2023). This challenges the treatment of caste hierarchies as Indian-subcontinent-bounded, feudal remnants and interrogates how caste helps explain socially constructed hierarchies within global capitalism. Radical scholarship on caste attempts to upend the common assumption that "the inter-section of colonialism, capitalism and race is primarily an Atlantic phenomenon" (Ince, 2022b, p. 144). Instead, Ince puts forward a *capital theory of race* by incorporating work on European imperialism in Asia which saw civilizational categories applied to the capitalist organization of land and labor, not simply based on colonial binaries, but on graded categories that were incorporated into capitalist logics. As with other socially constructed categories of identity, a decolonization agenda requires us to situate racial categories within a historical structure of capitalist exploitation, rather than one single axis of power (Lazarus, 2011; Melamed, 2015).

The fixing and individualization of race in economics has several real-world implications. As we discussed in chapter 3, because of the discipline's reliance on methodological individualism, discrimination is often ascribed to individual behavior – and often reduced to either taste and preferences (e.g. Becker, 1957) or statistical discrimination (e.g. Arrow,

1998), meaning it becomes rational to discriminate in the face of incomplete information, if the employer is unable to have access to complete information about the productivity of the individual. However, this can work to normalize discrimination until the market system is aligned to counteract it. Indeed, in many cases, economic studies of race create realities that serve the ideological interests of the dominant group, or what Hunter (2002) calls neoliberal positivism. This is evident, for example, in how racialized crime statistics are often used to reinforce racist perceptions of minorities (Austin, 2008). The way in which it does so is by putting forward an epistemology of colorblindness, which makes institutionalized racism invisible (Neubeck and Cazenave, 2001; Gordon and Gordon, 2006). Mainstream economists tend to propose policies designed to nudge individuals toward more rational behavior or to correct market failures by providing better educational opportunities for groups racialized as Black, rather than addressing the structure of white supremacy itself. For example, in the wake of the Black Lives Matter protests in 2020, economists attempted to address structural racism with individualized interventions aimed at nudging police officers toward better behavior (Wilson and Buchholz, 2020). Stratification economics, now a recognized tradition within mainstream economics, represents a step forward from individualized approaches by centering groups to explore inter-group inequalities as the long-term effects of historical dispossession (Darity et al., 2015; Chelwa et al., 2022). But it still falls short of interrogating how racial inequalities support and co-evolve with capitalist accumulation and the broader economic structures that sustain such inequalities (Darity et al., 2020).

An emerging framework of analysis

One implication of a decolonization agenda, as we have outlined here, is that we cannot analyze structures of oppression – such as capitalism, patriarchy, or white supremacy – completely in isolation from one another. This calls for an intersectional and counter-disciplinary framework of analysis that centers power structures in its analysis. In terms of concrete alternatives, there is much to learn from anti-colonial, anti-imperialist, post-colonial, feminist, and other theoretical traditions in terms of which categories can best capture the processes we are interested in. Generally, constructing categories that align with the structures outlined in this chapter can help to shed light on the *processes* through which certain social and economic outcomes are generated – namely through the production of capitalist, patriarchal, racialized, and colonial hierarchies. As such, understanding these power relations helps us go beyond simply describing outcomes – such as inequalities between groups – to explaining them. The key is to move beyond both methodological individualism and well as methodological nationalism, to understand connections across the globe and the dependencies that are reproduced globally and in conjunction with multiple systems of oppression.

All these critiques we have put forward of the economics discipline so far are structural, methodological, historical, or theoretical. At no point does anyone claim that economists are *themselves* racist, although this may also be the case. This may seem like a trivial point, but perhaps because of the individualizing, universalizing paradigm inherent in economic theorizing, with its Eurocentric framing, economists themselves tend to misunderstand critiques of the discipline as personal attacks on economists. This has led this disclaimer to come up in a lot of critical literature; for example, Zuberi and Bonilla-Silva (2008) reassure their readers that they are not calling quantitative social scientists racist and Zein-Elabdin (2009) emphasizes that she does not mean that development economists are themselves racist or driven by a desire to colonize. As DeMartino (2011) puts it, the "tragedy of economics lies in the fact that economists often cause harm as they aspire to do good."

–7–

Exploring the Decolonization Agenda

Scholars from across the globe, and especially scholars based in the periphery, have long been carrying out scholarship that can contribute to a decolonization agenda – even before the idea of decolonizing the academy first emerged in the 1960s. This means they have been theorizing from a vantage point that includes the periphery and situating their theorization within the power structures that shape our global order. They have been contributing to uncovering the apparatus of power that constructs and maintains hierarchies in our world today. We have mentioned some of these throughout the book already. For example, we wrote about how the care crisis in North America and Europe may be best understood by connecting it to global processes such as imperialism and global care chains in chapter 5 (Fraser, 2016a). We also wrote about how mainstream theorizing of inflation fails to address the ways in which dispossession in the periphery contributes to keeping inflation stable in the center (P. Patnaik and Patnaik, 2021). We argue that economic phenomena everywhere can be best understood when situating them within relevant power structures such as capitalism, imperialism, racialization, casteism, and patriarchy.[1] In this chapter, we discuss a few examples of this kind of work and explain how it provides completely different insights from what mainstream economics does.

We start with the fundamental question in economics: growth. What are alternative ways of theorizing growth? What about related issues, like trade and structural transformation? Then, we discuss the very foundation of production, namely labor. Can we expect labor across the world to be absorbed by the formal sector? Why may we not be seeing the transition to formality across the world as one might expect with capitalist development? Finally, we discuss rationality and institutions. What are other ways of thinking about human behavior beyond the concept of utility maximization as a universal principle or even beyond behavioral economics? How do institutions impact human rationality and what happens when we try to understand institutions on their own terms, rather than as deviations from a Eurocentric benchmark? Analyzing these themes in economics using a decolonizing agenda makes a huge difference in our understanding of the world.

Growth and structural transformation

An underlying assumption that is made in most mainstream models and theories of growth is that countries of the periphery will transition – or undergo a structural transformation – toward a full-fledged homogeneously capitalist economy in the same manner that economies of the capitalist center did. This is reflected in an underlying teleological assumption about a shared path to capitalist modernization, growth, and industrialization. The starting point for many theories of economic development is that countries of the periphery are characterized by a dual economy, which comprises a large, traditional, pre-capitalist and informal sector and a much smaller modern, capitalist, and formal sector. Economic development should become possible through capital investments that release the constraints on growth, in part through the development of markets. Development is expected to transform this dual economy into a homogeneous, modern capitalist structure that absorbs all labor in the economy. In this process, the economies of the periphery are expected to become richer and develop institutions like those of the capitalist center – a process often referred to as convergence. This teleological view of capitalist transition has been challenged by many theoretical frameworks that predominantly originated in the periphery, and that take seriously the ways in which colonialism, capitalism, and other power structures shaped these economies and their integration into the global capitalist order.

The current state of underdevelopment of the periphery cannot be reduced to a prehistory of the capitalist center. Rather than viewing the global economy as one where any country can develop through a series of stages, dependency theorists – theorizing in a way that includes the vantage point of the peripheries – saw, quite vividly, how colonialism on one hand played a critical role in transferring resources to the center, contributing to capitalist development there, while, on the other hand, erecting internal and external economic structures that produced capitalist underdevelopment in the periphery (Amin, 1974; Marini, 1978). As the dependency theorist Andre Gunder Frank (1966, 1967) put it, based on his historical study of the growth processes in Chile and Brazil, the processes of development and underdevelopment both emerged as an outcome of a common historical process.

This explicit recognition of dependence stands in stark contrast to the idea of delayed development in the mainstream literature, which suggests that the challenges of development are a result of simply arriving late to the game rather than being structurally disadvantaged in the process of capitalism's development. It also stands in stark contrast to mainstream assumptions that greater integration into the global market will facilitate trade, investment, and growth, and that eventually capitalist development will materialize if the right kind of policy mix and techno-bureaucratic fixes are adopted.[2] Insights in line with a decolonization agenda challenge these mainstream understandings in two significant ways. First, they center power and imperialist relations in their understanding of capitalism and capitalist growth, trade, and structural transformation. Second, they analyze post-colonial capitalist dynamics not simply as aberrations to how capitalism was thought to unfold, but rather as outcomes of the nature of post-colonial and global capitalism.

Growth, trade, and uneven development

The persistence of unequal trade relations between the center and periphery presents a major challenge to (late) neoclassical trade theory, which is founded on the Ricardian assumption of equilibrating trade in the long run. According to Ricardian trade theory, when countries produce and export the goods in which they have a comparative advantage and trade and import goods in which they do not have a comparative advantage, then these countries will gain from trade, or at least not be worse off. The exchange rate – if allowed to move freely – should lead to the needed adjustments so that trade balances.[3]

Structuralists in Latin America were pioneers in exposing and challenging the unrealistic assumptions of Ricardian trade theory. The Argentinian economist Raúl Prebisch – who first used the term periphery to discuss post-colonial economies' structural disadvantage in global capitalism already in 1944 – was originally convinced by Ricardian economics until he observed first-hand the deteriorating terms of trade for Argentina's exports during the Great Depression (Love, 1980). It then became impossible for him to justify free trade policies, which led him to develop alternative theories of growth and trade.

Prebisch (1950) and Singer (1950) observed that while workers in the center can absorb real economic gains in economic booms, trade unions are weaker in the periphery and therefore absorb most of the system's income contraction.[4] They also found that the income elasticity of demand was higher for industrial goods – mostly produced by the center – compared with agricultural goods, raw materials, or low value-added manufacturing exported by the periphery. These were key reasons, they argued, for both falling terms of trade for periphery exports and for the higher volatility of prices of exports from the periphery. Because the international institutions of the time failed to consider and act upon the unequal terms on which Latin American countries had been integrated into the global economy, Latin American countries pushed for the establishment of CEPAL in Santiago, Chile, in 1948, to "fill that void" (Fajardo, 2022, p. 55). CEPAL swiftly became the institutional center for a homegrown Latin American intellectual project that analyzed problems of development from and for the periphery. As Cristóbal Kay (2009, p. 159) has argued "[t]he Latin American Structuralist School is one of the first major attempts by scholars and development practitioners from the developing world to systematically analyze the development processes and problems of their region from their own perspective instead of relying on those from the developed world."

Latin American structuralists formulated alternative theories and policy recommendations that took the structural specificities of the periphery into account and promoted structural transformation of the periphery through interventionist policies such as import-substitution industrialization. They challenged the standard narrative that Latin American and Caribbean underdevelopment was due to market imperfections or economic policy distortion, and rather argued that the region's economic problems were founded on structural issues rooted in the region's history (C. Kay, 1989; Fajardo, 2022).

However, in the 1960s and 1970s, dependency theorists started to contest the premises of the structuralist *cepalino* development project, which assumed that the gap between the periphery and capitalist center could be closed through a combination of national industrialization policies alongside improved international economic cooperation. Dependency theorists built on center–periphery thinking inherited from the structuralists but took a more critical view of the unevenness of global capitalism. In simple terms, dependency theory emerged as a research program theorizing about the unevenness of global capitalism that considered the specific constraints faced by the periphery (Kvangraven, 2021; Katz, 2023). It approached questions of uneven development through a historical understanding of capitalism from a vantage point that included the periphery.[5] According to dependency theorists, development and underdevelopment in different parts of the world must be considered two sides of the same coin. Catch-up growth and convergence would not be possible, even if countries of the periphery employed interventionist policies as promoted by the structuralists – because uneven development was built into the system itself.

Insights from both structuralists and dependency theorists have important implications for debates about growth and development today. For example, a key assumption in mainstream economics is that wages in the periphery are low because productivity is low, since workers' wages are assumed to be determined by their productivity. However, unequal exchange scholars of the dependency tradition saw that productivity may be lower in the periphery, on average, but that the difference in wage rate between center and periphery tends to be larger than the productivity difference (Emmanuel, 1972a).[6] The existence of average wage differences greater than productivity differences has become more or less accepted as an empirical global phenomenon now, despite the inability of mainstream traditions to explain it. Milanovic (2012) noted that unskilled workers' wages in the center versus periphery often differ by a factor of 10 to 1, meaning wages are ten times higher in the center.

Structuralist scholars and dependency theorists also found that given that an increase in productivity in the industrial sector in the periphery did not necessarily translate into increased wages for workers, the expansion of the domestic market and the potential for growth was severely limited (Ruccio and Simon, 1986). Instead, the surplus from the industrial export sector of the periphery tended to be channeled to the center and shaped by unequal trade relations, thereby limiting the re-investments made in the periphery. Therefore, a balanced growth and structural transformation remained elusive despite increases in productivity.

Many dependency theorists brought class into their analysis of wages and labor as well. For example, Marini (1978) saw the exploitation of the working class in the periphery taking specific and particularly acute forms, which he theorized

through the concept of *super-exploitation*: "a higher exploitation of the workforce, either through increasing its intensity,
or through lengthening of the working day, or, finally, by
combining both procedures" (2011 [1973], p. 146, authors'
translation). Given that countries in the periphery did not
depend on internal consumption to generate the demand for
products that were exported, the wage was often not even kept
at a level adequate for the social reproduction of the worker.
Indeed, as we discussed in chapter 5, P. Patnaik and Patnaik
(2021) argue that deflating incomes of workers and peasants
in the periphery has been a necessity for the stability of the
global system since the emergence of capitalism. Extremely low
incomes and a wage–productivity gap are not anomalies here,
but integral parts of the uneven capitalist system. Bambirra
(1972, p. 84) extended the category of super-exploitation to
also consider the particular burdens of working-class women
in the periphery, as they are both "exploited in their class
and they are exploited as women." As such, there was early
intersectional analysis to be found in the radical dependency
theories of the 1970s (Antunes de Oliveira, 2021).

The unevenness identified within the tradition of
dependency theory also manifests itself in areas beyond trade,
labor, and production, such as technology and finance. For
example, Theotonio dos Santos (1970) explains the nature
of structural transformation of the peripheral economies in
terms of their technological dependence on the center. He
argued that need for advanced capital goods constrained the
development or transformation possibilities of the periphery
even if they protected their industrial sector via import
substitution industrialization, given the need to import the
advanced technologies needed to support industrialization
from the center (C. Kay, 2020). Over half a century after dos
Santos's (1970) intervention, peripheral economies have been
largely unable to significantly climb up the value chain ladder
despite the global dispersion of manufacturing through the
development of extensive networks of global value chains
(Caraballo and Jiang, 2016). The production structures
of the periphery have remained largely concentrated in
low technology production and services, providing support

for the original insights of Latin American dependency theorists (e.g., Sunkel, 1969; T. dos Santos, 1970; Furtado, 1970). Even when countries of the periphery do manage to achieve high-tech industrialization in certain sectors of the economy, the gap between them and those same sectors in the capitalist center keeps widening, reflecting a continuation of technological dependence (Shie and Meer, 2010). Given the stringent rules regarding trade-related intellectual property rights (TRIPS), the possibilities for technological advancements in the periphery are further strangulated, perpetuating the global hierarchy (Durand and Milberg, 2020).

Dependency scholarship has also highlighted new and old forms of financial dependency, building on the pioneering work of Tavares (1985), who argued that the limits to development in the periphery lay in unequal access to stable and affordable finance, rather than in inequalities in labor structures, competitiveness, and access to technology.[7] For example, Musthaq (2021) expands Samir Amin's original work on unequal development in production systems of the periphery and center, by exploring how the global financial system produces rents for the center in a situation where relatively higher interest rates are offered in the periphery (she calls this financial arbitrage). Meanwhile, Reis and Antunes de Oliveira (2023) argue that financialization has reproduced and heightened the super-exploitation of labor in Brazil and Mexico because of the significant changes in the role of the state and class relations that the era of financialized dependence entails. Such specific characteristics of peripheral development show why theoretical concepts related to financial and monetary systems in the center are not easily transportable to situations in the periphery where financial systems have different characteristics and constraints (Chandrasekhar, 2005b; Powell, 2013; Koddenbrock et al., 2022).

Failed structural transformation or post-colonial capitalist development?

Other notable scholarship from the periphery has focused on the internal dynamics of capitalism within post-colonial economies to answer why the process of capitalist transition – or structural transformation – has not borne out. As mentioned, structural transformation refers to a transition from a fractured economic structure to a homogeneously modern and industrialized one. The process, according to mainstream approaches to economics, is facilitated by a shift of production factors – especially labor, capital, and land – away from traditional non-capitalist activities and sectors with low productivity to modern industrial capitalist sectors with higher productivity (Rodrik et al., 2013). This results in a withering away of the traditional non-capitalist sectors as labor is absorbed in the more productive capitalist sectors. Any persistence of non-capitalist sectors is seen as a marker of underdevelopment.

Within the mainstream of the economics discipline, it is generally accepted that some extent of market failure-correcting industrial policy would be necessary for structural transformation to occur (Lin, 2011; Aiginger and Rodrik, 2020). Given that more than half a century has passed since most of the last remaining colonies gained independence while underdevelopment has persisted, there has been a puzzle posed in economics, asking why structural trans-formation – or capitalist transition – in the periphery has remained an "illusive quest" (Geda et al., 2018), "stalled" (Resnick, 2016), or why there has been a "lack" of it (Alessandria et al., 2023, p. 459). The question posed by this literature is why the traditional, low-productivity, non-capitalist economic sectors have not withered away with capitalist growth.

Perspectives in line with a decolonization agenda have taken a radically different approach to characterize the economic structures in the peripheries and to explain this lack of capitalist transition. They raised other important questions about how to characterize the economic struc-tures of peripheral economies: are these economies likely to undergo a capitalist transition along the lines of the capitalist center or are there dynamics internal to the peripheral economies that would inhibit such a transition? If the latter is the case, what is the nature of these dynamics? Rather than assuming that limited structural transformation is simply a lack of growth, or the right kind of policies or institutions, scholars observing the world from a vantage point that includes the periphery theorized the structures and dynamics of post-colonial capitalism on their own terms. The scholarship and debates that followed are now known as the *mode of production debate.*

The mode of production debate, centered on critical interventions from scholars based in South Asia, Africa, and Latin America, appeared in various publication located in the periphery,[8] and focused on the specificities of the production structures of peripheral economies. In Marxist political economy, a mode of production is the way production is organized, including the relationship between the owners of the means of production and the laborers, and how the value produced is appropriated and distributed. The capitalist mode of production is one whereby the conditions of capitalist class processes dominantly prevail. In a capitalist class process, a capitalist organizes production, advances the means of production, purchases raw materials, and hires labor at a wage, while the labor exerts their labor power to produce the final product by enhancing the value of raw materials. The value produced by labor is appropriated by the capitalist who then decides how to distribute it, and it is the profit motive that drives the capitalist. The implicit assumption in mainstream approaches to development is that countries will undergo a transition from various pre-capitalist modes of production to the capitalist mode. However, building on arguments from dependency theory, the mode of production debate explored how production in the periphery was structured in a manner distinct from that of the capitalist center, explaining why they may not undergo a capitalist transition in the same way as the center.

The original insights from the scholarship on modes of production on the economic structures of the periphery can be summarized as follows: first, they center the imperialist structure of the global economy and its impact on shaping internal structures of peripheral economies (Alavi, 1975); and second, they open for the possibility of the co-existence of various modes of production within one economic system, albeit with the capitalist mode of production remaining dominant (Ruccio and Simon, 1986).[9] Scholars within this debate attempted to explain the persistence of non-capitalist modes of production in the periphery in different ways (Banaji, 1972; G. Kay, 1975). One camp argued that despite the expansionary tendencies of the capitalist mode of production, capitalist transition could be delayed or thwarted if the pre-capitalist modes offered a strong resistance to the capitalist mode. One such form of resistance could be the dominance of merchant capital – or traders – in the peripheries, who lose power in a capitalist transition.[10] Another camp argued that the non-capitalist sphere of the economy had a functional role within capitalism and remained intact to satisfy certain needs of capital. These needs could include the provision of cheap wage labor, the provision of cheap raw materials, or both. It was in the interest of capital for these non-capitalist modes to continue to exist, but at a level subservient to capital's needs (Wolpe, 1972). Given that capitalist relations and modes of production were impacted by the imperialist nature of the global economy and shaped by colonial relationships, scholars of the modes of production school argued that separate sets of concepts were needed to characterize the economic structures and modes of production in the periphery (U. Patnaik, 1990).

Yet another explanation for the persistence of non-capitalist sectors and lack of capitalist transition or structural transformation comes from a more recent intervention on post-colonial capitalist development initiated by Sanyal (2007). In this view, the persistence of non-capitalist sectors in the periphery is seen as the outcome of contemporary capitalist growth and accumulation processes in post-colonial economies, rather than due to a lack of it. In his view, unlike the mode of production school, the non-capitalist sector is, for the most part, not considered economically needed by capital. In the process of capitalist growth, the accumulation-driven capitalist sector encroaches upon the resources in the subsistence-driven non-capitalist sectors of the economy and in the process dispossesses those that subsist on it. However, the dispossessed are not transformed into wage labor in the capitalist sector, as expected within Eurocentric frameworks. Much of this dispossessed population is instead rendered surplus – and is not needed – for the process of capitalist production. This population is then forced to find ways to sustain themselves by carrying out income-generating activities, often as small non-capitalist family-based self-employed enterprises that do not employ any wage labor and are mainly driven to satisfy the consumption needs of the household without any explicit profit motive. Such enterprises comprise the vast informal sector in the periphery and are continuously reproduced as the process of capitalist expansion continues to encroach upon non-capitalist sectors and dispossess the people subsisting on it. Sanyal argues that unlike the European experience of capitalist transition, the process of primitive accumulation, or the process of dispossession of labor from traditional livelihood sources and their transformation into wage labor in the capitalist sector, remains ever-incomplete in post-colonial economies.

Given the widespread dispossession and difficulty sustaining livelihoods in the informal, non-capitalist space, the state often steps in to support the dispossessed population to ensure political stability and to maintain the legitimacy of capital (Sanyal, 2007). This is usually done through providing transfers in the form of small loans or cash transfers to allow the dispossessed masses to acquire the means of production or some limited means of survival in the form of self-employment in the informal sector. The non-capitalist part of the economy serves a political role as it absorbs the surplus population that is dispossessed in the process of capitalist accumulation, but it is not functionally necessary to sustain accumulation in the capitalist sector (Chatterjee, 2008; S. Bhattacharya, 2017; Kesar et al., 2022).[11] The persistence of the non-capitalist space and lack of structural transformation is, then, an outcome of successful capitalist accumulation and growth, rather than due to a lack of it.

From structuralism and dependency theory to debates about modes of production and post-colonial capitalist development, these non-Eurocentric insights make important contributions to a decolonization agenda. They challenge the linear teleological understanding of economic development that is implicit in Eurocentric frameworks, and instead focus on the common processes through which development and underdevelopment are produced. More importantly, perhaps, they can explain the highly uneven nature of economic development that can be observed globally and within the periphery.

Labor and informality

The way labor has been conceptualized in mainstream (and parts of heterodox) economics debates has not escaped Eurocentrism. In the process of development-as-capitalist-transition or structural transformation, the excess labor in the non-capitalist sector of the economy was expected to be absorbed by the capitalist sector as wage labor. This was the expected route to enhance welfare since wage employment in the capitalist sector was assumed to be secure and the wages were expected to be linked to increasing productivity. A dominant capitalist sector characterized by stable wage employment was considered the ideal model that capitalist countries of the periphery were moving toward – and what was already the dominant model of the European and American economies in the post-war period and until the 1970s (Munck, 2002; Denning, 2010; Breman and Van der Linden, 2014). The notion of wage employment as the route to welfare was normalized and labor relations in the periphery – often marked by an absence of wage work – were seen as aberrations to be corrected with a capitalist transition. Scholars theorizing from non-Eurocentric starting points, however, have poked holes in this Eurocentric framework for understanding labor.

Across the periphery, despite a transition away from agriculture and the growth of the capitalist sector, people have often not been able to find productive employment as secure wage workers. Instead, people often find themselves in urban and non-agricultural sectors without wage work, often relying on small income-generating activities – such as setting up a small mechanic shop, or a banana-selling cart, tea stall, or other small service units. These activities are driven by the need to satisfy the economic needs of the households using family labor, run on an income-sharing basis, without engaging in wage labor and without a profit motive. Such non-capitalist activities, characterized as the informal sector, are a common sight in the landscape of peripheral economies. There is a shift in spatial location of labor as people transitioned out of traditional agriculture, but not a shift in the organization of their production, which remained akin to activities they had transitioned away from (McGee, 1973). As a result, non-capitalist activities mushroomed even within the industrial, urban areas, which were also sites for modern capitalist economic activities. These informal activities are considered a roadblock to capitalist development from mainstream economic perspectives. In fact, the International Labour Organization (ILO) organized several missions to different African economies to study this apparently anomalous phenomenon (Rakowski, 1994; Bangasser, 2000). They reported back having discovered that what they called the *in*formal economy was characterized by non-standard, precarious, low productive work. The dynamics of the process through which these informal sectors of the economy came into being, and how they interacted with the growth process more generally, was not interrogated. Instead, a hierarchy of formal–informal was constructed, and the persistence of informality was deemed a temporary holding ground for the transition population waiting for capitalist expansion and the promise of formal and secure wages.

What the ILO considered standard work (formal wage labor) was never standard in the periphery, where informal employment has long been the most common form (Munck 2013; S. Bhattacharya and Kesar, 2020). Even in the US, what is considered the standard form of work – work with secure wage contracts – was only the standard form of work in a very specific period in history and in part driven by strong labor movements – rather than being the natural state of capitalism (Breman and Van der Linden, 2014). In the post-war period, capitalist wage relations were not all-pervasive as there were several informal, non-capitalist spaces co-existing alongside secure capitalist wage work (Tabak and Crichlow, 2000; Gibson-Graham, 2006). These realities are erased from the Eurocentric narrative of capitalist development in the center.

Scholars theorizing from non-Eurocentric starting points and from the vantage point of the periphery have long studied informality as a part of the dynamics of the capitalist growth process. Some of the arguments from the debates we discussed earlier are relevant here: the informal sector could be considered as existing to serve the needs of the formal sector to provide cheap raw materials, cheap wage goods, and cheap labor to keep the cost of production in the formal sector low (Rakowski, 1994; Wolpe, 1975; U. Patnaik, 1990), or, it could be considered as a sector continually reproduced due to the nature of the growth process in the periphery, which dispossesses workers deriving livelihood from the traditional sectors of the economy but without being absorbed into secure employment in the formal sector (Sanyal, 2007; S. Bhattacharya and Kesar, 2020; Kesar, 2024). However, informality can exist in both the non-capitalist and capitalist sectors, so the processes of informalization/formalization do not map neatly onto processes of capitalist transition or non-transition, although there are some parallels. In mainstream understandings, there is an assumption that there will be a transition both toward formality from informality alongside a withering away of non-capitalist sectors of the economy.

As the mainstream perspectives fail to take into account the consequences of continued dispossession, limited labor demand in the formal capitalist sectors, and the alternative logics under which labor in these informal sectors may operate, they focus their attention on supply side factors such as providing better credit facilities for entrepreneurs, training of potential entrepreneurs and workers, and developing stronger subcontracting linkages to increase the productivity of domestic firms and aligning them better with capitalist market dynamics (Ranis and Stewart, 1999). The extreme end of this spectrum is represented by Banerjee and

Duflo (2014), who characterized the informal enterprises as reluctant entrepreneurs that need to be nudged to expand and grow, assuming away the structural dynamics that produce and reproduce the informal sector to begin with.

With this rich history of thought on informal labor in mind, scholars of the capitalist center characterizing the rise of informality as a "new" dangerous working class (Standing, 2011) reeks of Eurocentrism and lack of a global and historical understanding of labor. Generally, even when economists in the capitalist center study informality, precarity, and working conditions, they tend to erase the long lineage of academic debates on informality in the periphery that has engaged with this question. The rise and spread of informal wage work have characterized work in the capitalist center as well as the periphery in recent decades, also shaped by new informal wage work such as platform and gig economies (S. Bhattacharya et al., 2022; Kassem, 2023). Globally, jobs have become increasingly insecure, real wages have declined, the productivity–wage gap has risen, and bargaining power has become more and more diluted (Stansbury and Summers, 2020; Farber et al., 2021).

Faced with these changes in the world of work, mainstream economists have responded in a few different ways. On one hand, many economists continue to trust the underlying assumption that the market will adjust demand and supply of labor to reach an equilibrium wage rate. This is the underlying theoretical frame that justifies economists calling for deregulations of labor (e.g., Besley and Burgess, 2004),[12] which continues to be reflected in the conditionalities of IMF programs in the periphery (Reinsberg et al., 2019; Ortiz and Cummings, 2022). Others in the mainstream do recognize that market mechanisms do not automatically lead to good working conditions, and rather explore the issue of employer power, reformulating the late neoclassical models to study the impact of progressive labor policies, which has led to a justification for unionization and artificially setting a minimum wage above the market clearing rate (Card and Krueger, 2000; Dube et al., 2007; Bassier, 2023). From a decolonization perspective, a few issues need reckoning with. The first is to consider the limits of local or national policies if capital is global and there is a large global reserve of labor. The second is to not neglect the unequal power dynamics of the capital–labor relation and to consider the political reasons for why labor tightening cannot be sustained on a permanent basis (Kalecki, 1943). The third is to recognize that informal employment is not a temporary glitch due to lax labor regulations or temporarily weak labor markets but rather produced through processes of dispossession that continually make labor, especially in the peripheries, redundant and superfluous (Sanyal, 2007; U. Patnaik, 2009; Li, 2010).

Institutions and rationality

The concept of rationality, as understood in mainstream economics, is a specific form of rationality, that is, a capitalist rationality expressed in terms of a maximizing agent operating within a capitalist sphere – that can be reconciled with an aggregate rationality in the form of a stable equilibrium (as discussed in chapter 3). This maximizing, rational behavior is theorized as a universal rationality, whereby individual behavior is determined through essentializing, abstract, and universal human characteristics and motivations relevant across all geographies and social spaces. Deviations from this universally assumed behavior are often considered traditional, backwards, or simply irrational, which presumably leads to non-optimal outcomes (Zein-Elabdin, 2009). The rational economic agent has been modified in mainstream economic theory in a variety of ways, including by introducing bounds on rationality or through introducing institutions as variables shaping behavior. We discussed in chapter 3 how the dominant approach, even with these modifications, is an idealized and Eurocentric approach to individual rationality and institutions that support it. Behavior and institutions that deviate from this ideal rationality are considered aberrations, often regarded as traditional and primitive, creating transaction costs, and thus in need of modernization or fixing to allow for maximizing behavior and ultimately efficiency gains.

Scholarship that theorizes from a vantage point that includes the periphery, however, explores alternative institutions and rationalities on their own terms (Zein-Elabdin, 2009). Here we first consider alternate ways of understanding behavior and then institutions, before briefly considering why we need to locate the problem not only in how individual rationality is conceptualized but to open up for an exploration of systemic rationality.

There is a range of alternative ways of representing and analyzing individual rationalities that move beyond the rational/non-rational and capital/non-capitalist dichotomies. For example, the African philosophy of Ubuntu (in Zulu) or Utu (in Kiswahili) is one of these, where the wellbeing and behavior of one person is intimately tied to the wellbeing of others (Menkiti, 1984; Mbiti, 1990). From this perspective, you are what you are through your relationships with other people. Because of the centrality of this alternative way of viewing individual rationalities (as not individual at all, but deeply connected to the community), Africana scholars have called for discussions on how to incorporate such a collective and connective perception of behavior into scholarship (Ramose, 1999; Mũgo, 2021).[13] If we take this understanding of rationality as a starting point for theorizing, we may prioritize communal resources over private property, communal ways of organizing production over private ownership, and a more equitable distribution than what is commonly considered desirable in mainstream economics.

Another example can be found in Marxist theorization of human behavior as understood as a product of various social processes linked to class, including natural, cultural, political, and economic (Wolff et al., 2012). Human behavior thus becomes the outcome of these interconnected processes and motivations cannot be reduced to only one type of process, unlike in the rational economic agent, who is primarily motivated by the economic. Individuals are governed by conflicting desires, so individual preferences are rarely the stable and consistent foundations for decision-making that is implied in late neoclassical theory. This Marxist framework opens up the possibility of individuals being governed by different behavior depending on their positions in the economic system (Gibson-Graham, 1993) and of their having multiple identities (J. B. Davis, 2003). For example, a woman could be having her labor appropriated within the household, while simultaneously being someone's employer in the capitalist sector (Gibson-Graham, 1993). These different class positions may be governed by different forms of rationality, making it impossible to ascribe one singular form of rationality to any one individual – be it self-interested, maximizing, or altruistic.

There are also crucial non-Eurocentric ways of theorizing institutions that take seriously the possibility that various ways of organizing society in our world are not necessarily best understood through the lens of the capitalist center. An example is the concept of hybridity, which studies how institutions may be shaped by multiple forces, where market motives or optimizing rationality may be only one of several (Bhabha, 1994; Zein-Elabdin, 2009). This stands in contrast to Eurocentric conceptualizations of behavior and institutions being either modern or traditional, which tends to lead to an othering of alternative institutions and behavior. As Zein-Elabdin (2009, p. 1164) argues, this lens of hybridity allows subaltern culture to "genuinely participate in the global construction of the terms of being because then a lower level of material consumption, strong kinship ties and social commitment could be viewed as serviceable ethics rather than remnants of obsolete tradition." To give you a sense of how such alternative views of institutions radically change the way we see those that are studied by economists, consider social insurance and education.

When theorizing from a vantage point that includes the periphery, one can see that social insurance is not necessarily always primarily governed by market rationalities. In fact, it is often organized in the form of solidarity among kin or ad-hoc rules, rather than strictly based on market principles. As such, the institution of social insurance is heavily shaped by social obligations and cultural considerations (Zein-Elabdin, 2009). Understanding social insurance on its own terms helps us better predict the outcomes of individual failures such as unemployment or bankruptcy, as it expands our understanding of where individuals may receive support beyond formal institutions such as banks and the government.

Second, education can be understood in a radically different manner than through the frame of human capital as in the mainstream, where education is meant to allow individuals to accumulate human capital to qualify for higher-paying jobs, depending on the level of the education and/or training (Schultz, 1961). This is an instrumentalist view, as education is primarily seen as an instrument to prepare students for jobs in the labor market, rather than an institution of politicization and socialization. Even feminist scholarship within the capabilities approach tradition tends to view education in this way, as literacy itself is seen as the basis for women's equality and political engagement, and emancipation (e.g., Nussbaum, 2003). Such scholarship is rather Eurocentric as it views individuals as workers-to-be and the ultimate form of empowerment to be free to sell your labor and cast your vote in formal spaces, which is how individuals were thought to be emancipated during the development of capitalism – brushing away the exploitation, inequality, and subordination that came with it. Within this Eurocentric view, education is considered formal training for the reproduction of the capitalist system itself. Alternative, non-Eurocentric approaches, on the other hand, have argued that education, as provided under capitalism, can be a means for indoctrinating students and shaping them to be good, subjugated subjects of capital and other oppressive structures (Freire, 1970). Other approaches also consider alternative educational institutions and take certain forms of informal education seriously as well (Charusheela, 2009). For example, Nzegwu (1995) shows that Igbo women in Nigeria, despite being illiterate, were politically conscious and organized themselves for the causes of gender equality, while the literate upper-class women lacked political consciousness, in comparison. She foregrounds the traditional institutions that play a strong role in creating both productive workers as well as socially and politically conscious individuals. This demonstrates that there are aspects of education, training, and empowerment that mainstream metrics of literacy and formal education level fail to capture (Charusheela, 2009). This is not about celebrating the pre-modern or advocating for going back to traditional ways of living, but rather about seeing the institutions in the world for what they are and uncovering what goes amiss when theorizing from a Eurocentric vantage point.

The concept of rationality in economics can be extended from individual behavior to the system itself. Systemic rationality encompasses the rationality of the competitive capitalist market economy, with all its contradictions. The rationality of the competitive market economy is one that subsumes even non-rational kinds of preferences and behaviors, as long as they don't challenge the continuing functioning of the capitalist system itself.[14] This is not to say the market will produce the most efficient outcomes or that it is all-encompassing or without contradictions, but rather that there may be certain rationalities that govern the political economy at a systemic level (Carroll and Manne, 1992).

Not everything is guided by capitalist rationality in the world, and people do not live their lives only according to the market. For example, many aspects of our lives, such as family, marriage, and friendship, are not guided by capitalist rationalities. But this type of behavior will always be circumscribed by the capitalist market. For example, philanthropic giving by firms is only feasible insofar as it does not undermine the ability of firms to make a minimum level of profit. Irrational behavior of individuals within the stock market is also perfectly consistent with the systemic rationality of the market as a system and has been widely observed. Household production or non-capitalist production also tends to be organized around kinship relations and is driven by the logic of household subsistence rather than capitalist rationality (Sanyal, 2007; Fraser, 2016a; T. Bhattacharya, 2017; P. Patnaik and Patnaik, 2021). However, all these alternate rationalities are compatible with the reproduction of the capitalist system itself.

The rationality of the system, additionally, tends to permeate into spaces that were previously not shaped by capitalist motives. This is, for example, evidenced by the increased commodification of care labor as more women have entered the labor force while the state has increasingly withdrawn from care services. Similarly, education is increasingly being commodified as it is moved from public to private institutions or public institutions underpinned by market incentive structures. There are opposing forces, or a double movement, at play here (Polanyi, 1944): while we can observe a tendency of capitalist rationalities taking over more and more spaces of human life, this tendency is also met with resistance, forcing the system to give in to certain social demands to stabilize society.

A decolonization agenda deconstructs and challenges the Eurocentric conceptualization of (capitalist) rationality that dominates in economics and which pins rationality to optimizing behavior of individuals that is meant to produce optimal systemic outcomes if coupled with efficient institutions. There is a series of alternate behaviors and institutions that exist across the world that are completely compatible with capital's rationality – its drive for profit. These cannot be understood only as deviations from a Eurocentric ideal and they cannot be expected to fully wither away as capital expands. On the contrary, alternate rationalities and institutions are not only compatible with capitalist growth, but they often also directly support it. Understanding capitalist rationality at a more systemic level allows for an uncovering of certain tendencies of the system, while also recognizing the contradictions that it encompasses.

Toward a better general economics

We live in a world where economic relations are embedded in a global and imperialist economic order. Decolonizing economics entails *both* theorizing from the relevant vantage point of the economic phenomenon at hand *and* situating this phenomenon within this global order to better grasp the underlying structural processes of power at work and their implications. This matters for understanding both international economic processes, like trade and value transfers, and for understanding situations and relations that don't align with Eurocentric capitalist expectations, such as informal labor, human behavior, rationality, and institutions.

The point is that the Eurocentric economic theory presents a particular, limited, and distorted worldview. Decolonizing economics necessarily moves us toward more general theories of economics, by adopting theoretical approaches that are more amenable to clarifying the dynamics of the economic system that are not revealed by a Eurocentric approach. Therefore, a decolonization agenda is not merely relevant for understanding conditions in the periphery better, but it is about understanding the global economic system and the variety of social relations underpinning it. We have selected only a few themes in this chapter to demonstrate this as a taster, but we encourage you to read further and beyond this book.

–8–

What Is to Be Done?

Eurocentrism is embedded in economics and permeates all spheres of life – the classroom, the university, policy landscapes, and society. Eurocentrism in economics compromises scientific quality, creates a distorted understanding of the world, and leads to economic policies that are at best ineffective, or at worst harmful for large sections of society. As Lenin (1902) famously put it, "what is to be done?" is the burning question of our movement and it is the question with which we end this book. Decolonizing economics entails challenging Eurocentric, universal, and seemingly objective claims by dismantling structures, theories, and practices that scaffold and facilitate the maintenance of the status quo in economics. However, the call to decolonize economics cannot be detached from the wider social struggles against the imperialist, capitalist, and unequal system that the economics discipline serves to legitimize. That is, decolonizing economics is also ultimately a movement to reverse structural oppression that has material impacts on people across the globe. Therefore, decolonization is a political, uncomfortable and, at times, even a violent process, given that it ultimately aims to disrupt existing power structures.

Decolonizing economics is crucial for the classroom and the university, as how economics is taught and researched in the academy shapes how people think about policy, and how people see the role of economists in society. However, decolonization must also extend beyond the classroom if it is to be a transformative movement that unites with decolonization efforts in society.

Decolonization is clearly a much larger project than improving diversity within economics. The lack of diversity among economists is merely a reflection of both the Eurocentric knowledge production in the field and the unequal power relations underpinning the global social fabric. To meaningfully diversify the field, then, its decolonization is a necessary condition.

Decolonizing economics education

In discussions about decolonizing academia, the classroom is the center of attention. There is a burgeoning literature on decolonizing pedagogy, although it has barely made it to economics (Kvangraven and Kesar, 2023). As educators, economists need to reckon with Eurocentrism in the field and counter it – in pedagogy and in the curriculum. However, as we have mentioned before, there is no unique path or recipe for decolonizing economics and the same is true for decolonizing education.

Decolonizing pedagogy in economics

While much of mainstream economics teaching leaves its pedagogical approach – and the assumptions behind it – undiscussed, it is generally consistent with instrumentalist pedagogy, where students are trained in concrete, identifiable skills, such as problem-solving, specific techniques, and application of theory. This approach to pedagogy coincides with understanding knowledge as a set of objective truths and tools that the student must be helped to acquire. Many economists also opt for a more liberal approach to pedagogy, where the goal is for students to develop intellectual open-mindedness and intellectual capacities of critical, evaluative, and comparative thinking, rather than simply learning pre-defined models, tools, and methods.

Heterodox economists, on the other hand, are more likely to opt for a critical approach to pedagogy, which aims to liberate those oppressed and excluded by the system (e.g., Freire, 1970, hooks, 1994; Mearman et al., 2018a; Kvangraven and Kesar, 2023). This approach is student-centered, involves critiquing everyday concepts, and provides frameworks that enable critical reflections on power structures in society. Fewer heterodox economists adopt a decolonial approach to pedagogy, which is about promoting an "ecology of knowledges," which counters Eurocentric epistemic monocultures by identifying "other knowledges and criteria of rigor and validity" (de Sousa Santos, 2014, p. 176). A decolonial approach involves pluralism but goes beyond it by establishing alternative criteria for rigor rather than placing all approaches on an equal plane. A decolonial approach involves de-canonizing and de-centering the Eurocentric mainstream as the master texts. Decolonial pedagogy assumes a connection between the social and political structures of colonialism and Western regimes of knowledge and representation (Tejeda et al., 2003). To expose this connection, frameworks of decolonization (as discussed in chapter 6) are needed to understand the Eurocentrism of dominant knowledge regimes.

Approaching pedagogy from the perspective of a decolonization agenda – as outlined in this book – can draw from both critical and decolonial pedagogy. While it is fruitful to draw on the emphasis on class and capitalism from critical pedagogy, a decolonization agenda ensures that we grapple with class, colonial, racial, and gendered structures, as well as other relevant forms of oppressions in the context in which the teaching is taking place (Wheiler, 1991; Grande, 2004). Within a decolonization agenda, learning is considered a transformative process, rather than simply a rationalist acquisition of knowledge. Therefore, decolonizing economics pedagogy involves directly dealing with and questioning power relations that sustain economic and epistemic structures.

As an instructor, it is important to align pedagogy with a decolonization agenda. This does not mean throwing out at once all structures that guided your approach to teaching or dropping all the white male authors from the capitalist center from your syllabus. It means connecting the critical re-examination of thinkers and political ideologies embedded in your teaching with the de-canonizing and de-centering of Eurocentric mainstream as master texts and thus challenging the Eurocentrism of dominant knowledge regimes and knowledge that is usually presented as value-free and the outcome of an even battlefield of ideas.

Decolonizing the economics curriculum

When it comes to curricula design, a critical approach is required at three levels: criticality within theory, criticality between theories, and critiquing economic thinking more broadly. The first level may be the easiest to achieve within a mainstream curriculum. It involves teaching students to think critically about mainstream theories and how they are applied to the world. The second level requires exposing students to a plurality of theories and encouraging them to develop critical thinking through comparing frameworks and considering their different implications. Finally, at the third level, students are exposed to critiques of knowledge creation more broadly and are encouraged to engage in critiques of economic thinking and the philosophy of knowledge. Decolonizing the economics curriculum will necessarily involve all three.

The path for decolonizing economics will look different and will depend on the current state of economics education in a particular context. However decolonizing economics will necessarily require centering structural power, recognizing that economics is normative, challenging Eurocentric universalism, placing content in theoretical, political, and historical context, and encouraging political engagement.

Centering structural power
We have argued that we cannot meaningfully understand economic dynamics without understanding structural power.

Therefore, structural power needs to be incorporated into teaching economic theory. Incorporating theories and methods from heterodox traditions is a good starting point but is ultimately insufficient. Instructors need to ensure that non-Eurocentric scholarship, which is marginalized even within heterodox economics, forms a central part of the curriculum.

For example, scholarship on caste in India remains underrepresented. Even when it is included, it mainly uses contributions that analyze it through a narrow Eurocentric lens. Scholars on caste, such as Dr. B. R. Ambedkar, Kancha Illaiah, Anand Teltumble, among others, who provide critical perspectives to challenge the structure that produces caste disparities remain largely excluded. Challenging structural exclusion, therefore, requires work to locate silenced or trivialized voices in economics, while also signaling to students from marginalized groups that non-white experts and knowledge produced by scholars from marginalized groups is valued. Therefore, texts from researchers that belong to minority groups, but more significantly, texts based on historically excluded theoretical frameworks, need to be included. Lowering the drawbridge to cross the moat around the traditional repertoire of articles in economics and standard textbooks and exploring radical scholarship in other disciplines is necessary.

If we recognize that there is a specific problematic understanding of knowledge in academia that abstracts from power dynamics – including underlying discriminatory structures resulting from colonial legacies – then diversifying the field through better representation will not be enough to decolonize the curriculum. There is a great degree of standardization in economics education, with the abstract principles of economics being taught globally, and excellence in economics research defined very narrowly in Eurocentric standards. Therefore, academic research in economics in the periphery can be and often is Eurocentric. The matter then is not simply one of adding to the curriculum scholars based in the periphery or from marginalized backgrounds.

Recognizing that economics is normative
There is no such thing as a value-free neutral economics. Therefore, it is imperative that the vantage point from which theorization is taking place is interrogated in the classroom. As Morrison (2001) argues, the genesis of all higher education is value-ridden and value-seeking. It is only that some values in economics are seen as values (normative) while others are embedded in theory (positive). Therefore, it is imperative that instructors identify for students the embedded theoretical framework and the political and historical context in which the ideas emerge. We must explicitly connect content and context and not allow the mainstream canon to retain a "privileged place of neutrality" (Dennis, 2018, p. 196).

Instructors can fruitfully weave in discussions of the values we take for granted within a mainstream economics framework. This could include questions like what does development entail, what are the political underpinnings of how development is characterized and is it desirable? Are there different ways of knowing and experiencing the same material reality and are these different ways of knowing commensurate with each other? It is worth educators also examining and bringing their own values to the classroom. As Toni Morrison argued, the values we hold seep through into our work, and "we teach values by having them" (Morrison, 2001, p. 277).

Instructors need to find an appropriate space to speak about decolonization explicitly in the course – and how it relates to research and pedagogy. Addressing decolonization does not mean necessarily embracing the view that a scientific method or tradition is necessarily colonial in nature, but rather to critically engage with the canon and how it came about, and to uncover the myriad realities with no common ontological basis (Arsel et al., 2021).

Challenging the starting point in much of the economics curricula – the rational individual, for example – involves recognizing the axes of social differentiation that shape structural inequalities, such as race, class, caste, ethnicity, nationality, and gender. All these axes of social differentiation and the hierarchies they produce shape socioeconomic processes in fundamental ways. Therefore, it is important to address the underlying processes that create the power relations embedded in gender, race, caste, and class and their relation to capitalism, in addition to those in colonialism and empire, given that economics does a singularly poor job in theorizing these aspects of structural power.

Challenge Eurocentric universalism in economics
In economics, core microeconomic and macroeconomic theory is presented as universal, and is taught as if it is universally applicable with a few adjustments depending on peculiarities of specific contexts. Studies of the periphery from such a Eurocentric standpoint are only seen as useful insofar as they can uncover aberrations to the norm of the capitalist center. In the classroom, we must interrogate whether key points raised by a text are universal and if they reflect the experiences of a limited group of people in specific circumstances embedded in particular social structures and partial idealized understandings. This is crucial in economics teaching where insights are often taught as universal principles rather than reflections emerging from a particular historical moment.

As we discussed in chapter 6, this is not a rejection of universalism, but specifically discarding distorted Eurocentric universal categories, according to which capitalism develops and unfolds seamlessly in a teleological, peaceful fashion, removed from violence, dispossession, or colonialism. Therefore, the idea that if countries in the periphery could just build enough of the right institutions, or if ethnic minorities could just get enough education, or if women could earn high enough incomes to outsource their childcare, then progress can be achieved, needs to be discarded along with the Eurocentric universal principles that lend themselves to such deterministic and linear narratives. Instead, decolonizing economics requires a radical universalism, which Majumdar (2021, p. 11) describes, in the context of literature, as "a universalism rooted in local realities but also capable of unearthing needs, conflicts, and desires" that are common among various contexts and times.

Place content in theoretical, political, and historical context
The theories and methods taught need to be placed in their
historical and political context to dismantle Eurocentric
understandings of the economy that abstract away imperialism, class struggle, racialization, and patriarchy. Rigorously
teaching economic history and the history of economic
thought can potentially expose the Eurocentric nature of
core theoretical concepts in economics and challenge their
apparent neutrality. To illustrate this, we give below three
concepts as examples, namely, comparative advantage, game
theory, and unequal exchange.

Comparative advantage: Teaching Ricardian principles
of comparative advantage along with the context of the
political economy in which Ricardo was writing would
not only help students understand the concept better, but
also challenge its neutrality. The theory of comparative
advantage teaches us that if countries produce and export
goods in which they have a comparative advantage and
import goods in which they do not have a comparative
advantage from other countries, everyone benefits from
trade. Therefore, removing barriers to trade would improve
overall welfare in the economy. Ricardo opposed protec-
tionism, especially for agriculture. He was particularly
opposed to the British Corn Laws, which involved imposing
tariffs on agricultural products – and he happened to be a
large landowner himself. It is also important to consider that
by the time Ricardo published *The Principles of Political
Economy and Taxation* in 1817, British industry was highly
competitive on the global market and, as is made clearer by
List (1841): it is once a country has attained the summit of
greatness that it tends to start advocating free trade policies
internationally. In List's time he was referring to Germany's
need to develop its own competitive firms while the United
Kingdom was advocating free trade after having already
built up a competitive export industry. This argument has
later been made by many scholars critical of the capitalist
center pushing free trade on the periphery through the
World Trade Organization and regional trade deals (e.g.,
H.-J. Chang, 2002).

Game theory: Although game theory has been used in interesting ways to analyze bargaining, it often does not interrogate how the unequal power relationship underpinning the game is produced and reproduced, at least in geopolitical analyses. While game theory is often presented as a neutral and objective way to model strategic behavior, teaching students the context in which such thinking became dominant can provide useful insights into the history of the ideological underpinnings of the theoretical framework's development. As Mirowski (2002) details, there was a close link between the development of game theory and national security concerns, where the RAND Corporation[1] and the Cowles Commission[2] – which both received US military funding during the Cold War to further the geopolitical interests of the United States – played a pivotal role. At the time the US wanted to show that it was always prepared for whatever happened, a notion that game theory offered. The details of the Cuban Missile Crisis, for example, were framed in terms of rational models of individual decision making rather than the ideological and geopolitical battles between the US and the Soviet Union. Consequently, economists were supported to do research that demonstrated that everything about nuclear war could be understood using the core principles of rational choice theory. Game theory helps us conclude that irrational, unpredictable, and ideological actions often lead to sub-optimal outcomes. In response to irrational behavior, it is important to have a credible strategy to counteract an opponent's potential irrational behavior, such as stockpiling nuclear armaments as a credible deterrent. Geopolitical analyses done using game theoretic frameworks are unsurprisingly still based on methodological nationalism and rarely consider aspects of structural power. Conflict is often seen to arise from incomplete information or distrust (Acemoglu and Wolitzky, 2014), and rarely because of structural violence or resistance to structural violence. Economists often use the game theoretic framework in their geopolitical analyses, but these are, as a result, reductive and not very insightful.

Unequal exchange: When teaching radical concepts associated with dependency theory, such as unequal exchange, the context of their theoretical development is important. In the period after formal independence from colonial powers, developing countries were expecting to reverse their colonial ties and pursue sovereign and autonomous national projects. While theories emerging largely from the capitalist center suggested that this could only happen through capitalist transitions and modernization (see chapter 4), it became increasingly obvious that instead of catching up, many developing countries were still experiencing enduring dependencies on capital and technology. This ultimately put them in a weak position in the global economy and inhibited their possibilities of capitalist transition along the lines of the center. Arrighi Emmanuel observed settler colonialism in South Africa, Rhodesia, and Israel, as well as attempts to set up an apartheid state in Katanga, Democratic Republic of Congo (DRC) (Emmanuel, 1972b), and later went on to theorize what he saw as a system of economic apartheid at a global scale through a theory of unequal exchange (Emmanuel, 1972b).[3] This theory attempts to explain the unequal situation in a world of mostly independent states and to explain value transfers from the periphery to the core, which were seen to maintain an international division of labor and a geographically uneven distribution of wealth (see also Amin, 1974).

Encourage political engagement
Economists and economics teaching typically puts a high premium on the allegedly politically neutral nature of economics. As we have demonstrated, this is a fallacy, and late neoclassical economics that still dominates economics reflects a particular theoretical and political orientation. Therefore, it is important to impress upon students that not only is it desirable to engage with explicitly political texts and arguments but also recognize the political nature of mainstream economics.

To create economically literate, critical, socially conscious, and engaged citizens of the world, it is crucial for both lecturers and students to analyze where they fit into the larger political economy, and how they benefit from or are harmed by the structures they study and critique. This includes understanding how advancing certain kinds of knowledge and frameworks can help facilitate structural inequalities. One fruitful strategy is to bring other voices representing other forms of knowledge into the classroom, such as community organizers and examine how and why their approach may differ from the approach in the textbooks.[4] Professors and students can also discuss how to address social issues and problems, not just in the classroom, but also through political and social movements. For instance, a formal education on economics of the labor market could be greatly enriched by involvement in their own workplace union, apart from increasing their collective bargaining power vis-à-vis their employers.

There are many movements around the world that are at the forefront of calls to restructure and decolonize the university along these lines and that could be brought into the classroom. For example, as we mentioned in chapter 1, the #RhodesMustFall and #FeesMustFall campaigns in South African universities, campaigns against caste prejudice in Indian universities, and the "Why is my Curriculum White" and #LiberateMyDegree campaigns in UK universities (Ndlovu-Gatsheni, 2018; Cini, 2019; Economic and Political Weekly, 2021) helped move the needle on debates about decolonizing the university. These movements are tied to concrete demands for ways that teaching, pedagogy, and curricula can be reformed. Decolonization can entail encouraging students to understand and be a part of these and other such movements or start their own.

Decolonizing the curriculum itself is crucial, but there are issues to consider beyond the curriculum as well, such as addressing discrimination in the classroom, reforming pedagogical practices such as assessments and learning strategies, and creating freedom to learn for everyone in the classroom. In fact, many of the constraints that will necessarily arise to decolonizing economics are beyond the classroom, and therefore also require our attention and energy.

Decolonizing the university

Since teaching and research in economics largely occurs within the structures of a university, we examine the constraints university structures place on the decolonization project. The structures of universities reflect their relations with the society in which they are immersed, and the contradictions associated with their establishment. The historical circumstances of the establishment of many universities often make them sites of status quoist conversations, with limited potential to be engines of transformation.

Historically, the university was a key site through which colonialism was institutionalized and naturalized (Bhambra et al., 2018). Some of the oldest and most prestigious universities in the center have a history grounded in slavery and colonialism (Wilder, 2013). Many of these universities were centers of scientific racism, which is the pseudoscientific belief that racial hierarchies have objective and scientific bases. These were the centers providing ethical, intellectual, and ideological justification for slavery, racial hierarchy, colonialism, gendered and racial segregation, dispossession, oppression, and domination of colonized subjects. It is no surprise that many of them have buildings, schools, and institutions named after notorious figures who played a key role in furthering the imperial agenda of several nations, such as Cecil Rhodes, or are named after racist figures, such as Woodrow Wilson.

Universities in the colonies were either created or (re-) structured to serve the empire during the colonial period, designed to "cultivate the morals and the minds of the young men who would lead the economically successful colonial societies" (Pietsch, 2013, p. 5). While Britain invested in its colonial universities, especially in its settler colonies, there was no doubt that they operated in a world of limitations, such as limited research funding, laboratory space, materials, and access to networks. University networks centered around Britain reproduced "hierarchical constructions of race that legitimized certain (white, Global North-centric, gendered) kinds of knowledge at the same time as they erased others" (Pietsch, 2013, p. 6). For example, universities of the settler colonies such as Australia and Canada were included as serious actors in the British imperial academic network, but universities in Africa, the Americas, and South Asia operated at the edges. While settler colonies were able to negotiate benefits from being a part of the network, scholars such as Dadabhai Naoroji and Jomo Kenyatta found themselves "virtually off the map" (Pietsch, 2013, p. 200).

The British academic world also resembled "a sophisticated tool of social and imperial rule" (Pietsch, 2013, p. 7). It exploited and appropriated work done by female, local, and marginalized workers. At the same time, it also cultivated the scholarly dependence of settler universities by drawing into the metropole the best colonial graduates and sending out young British students and academics to gain experience and conduct fieldwork in the colonies. This description by Pietsch (2013) is of British academic networks in the nineteenth and early twentieth centuries, but one can certainly identify parallels to how universities operate globally today.

Today, many disciplines acknowledge both that "assumptions regarding racial and civilizational hierarchy informed a lot of thinking about how the world worked, what was worth studying in it and how it should be studied" (Sabaratnam, 2017), and that the historically exclusionary practices of universities toward women, racial, ethnic, and caste minorities are reflected in the proportionally fewer students, faculty, and administrative staff from these groups in universities today. Universities continue to elevate Eurocentric universality and other concepts associated with European rationality (Maldonado-Torres et al., 2018). Classrooms often remain spaces of marginalization and alienation, especially for underrepresented groups (Bhopal, 2018). Unless these colonial roots and their permeation into the curriculum and research practices are actively challenged, it seems impossible to think of universities as a place where anti-colonial and anti-imperialist scholarship, and other scholarship associated with a decolonization agenda, can flourish.

This situation has been compounded by the commodification of higher education seen in the neoliberal era,
that is, higher education has become a commodity to be
provided through market transactions, transforming students
into consumers and universities into sellers. Increasingly,
justified by market-based principles such as competition
and efficiency, this commodification is driven by the profit
motive, which is typically seen as the best arbiter of the needs
of an ever-changing society. Among the many implications of
this process is that education is increasingly seen as a private
good that must be acquired to move up the social ladder.
In this context, the most critical features of universities
are lost and the instrumentalization of education is exacer-
bated (Hartley, 2006; T. E. Lewis, 2020). That is, going
to university is considered important for building human
capital – an intangible asset obtained through education,
training, skills, intelligence, and health – which creates a
financial value out of a worker's experience and skills. As a
result, areas and disciplines that can be easily assessed against
their economic returns to students are prioritized. Therefore,
science, technology, engineering and mathematics (STEM)
disciplines have been prioritized by sidelining humanities,
arts, and critical scholarship more broadly. The proliferation
of short-term higher education and distance learning degrees
also reflects the drive to ensure that higher education is
enhancing economic competitiveness and productive development of the workforce.[5]

Universities are now full of managers and there has been
a vast increase in university bureaucracy, reflecting the flour-
ishing of a managerial ideology in this sector (Gornitzka
et al., 1998). Commodification of higher education has also
meant universities are increasingly being run like businesses,
with a sharp focus on their income and costs. With SAPs
imposed on governments of countries across the periphery,
and budget cuts being implemented by governments in the
capitalist center, public funding for universities has been
deprioritized since the 1970s. Even before the pandemic,
one in eight country governments were spending more on
debt service than on education, health, and social protection

(UNICEF, 2021). This situation has worsened since then. As a result, university administrations face the pressure to impose high fees and thus extract as much money as possible from students who very often are only able to afford higher education through high levels of debt. Just as producers often need to rely on financial markets to purchase capital for production, in the neoliberal logic, it makes sense that students purchasing their human capital may need to rely on bank loans. However, debt is a disciplining mechanism (Gilmore, 2011) and ensures that many students focus on preparing to obtain jobs rewarded by the market to pay back their loans after they graduate, instead of thinking critically and creatively at university without constantly considering how to instrumentalize their education. The emphasis has shifted from "pedagogies that unsettle common sense, make power accountable, and connect classroom knowledge to civic issues" to "mastering test-taking, memorizing facts, and learning how not to question knowledge or authority" (Giroux, 2014, p. 6). This imposes higher costs on those from marginalized groups, and often makes premier institutions less accessible to them. Education then becomes a means of ossifying group differences rather than facilitating mobility.

The other side of this coin is poor remuneration of staff and increasingly relying on early career scholars and graduate students on precarious contracts to teach, research, and do administrative work (Gallas, 2018). As a result, academics either do not have the time or the resources to innovate in their teaching practices, and when they do, are incentivized to conduct research according to increasingly narrow standards (Muller, 2021). This leads to demoralized faculty members increasingly beholden to corporate, neoliberal, and even imperial interests (Giroux, 2014). In this neoliberal atmosphere, critical engagement with social issues related to decolonization in the universities is discouraged or even silenced. Academics engaging in discussions of the Israeli occupation of Palestine and Israeli settler colonialism, for example, have been increasingly under threat in recent years, leading to a culture of fear on many university campuses

(Salaita, 2015; Landy et al., 2020; Sukarieh, 2023; Renton, 2024).

The emancipatory potential of universities

On a brighter note, there have also been moments that generated critical consciousness which led to the rethinking of universities, allowing them to break away from reproducing the dominant social structure (Ribeiro, 1969). It is unsurprising then that some see classrooms as "the most radical space of possibility in the academy" (hooks, 1994, p. 13). Universities can also become places where it is possible "to reflect on the values, goals, and interests of a social order too frenetically bound up in its own short-term practical pursuits to be capable of much self-criticism" (Eagleton, 2015).

As Darcy Ribeiro observed in his seminal *A Universidade Necessária* [*The Necessary University*], when universities start questioning the given social order, there is a continuous challenge related to whether universities contribute to keeping things as they are or to changing them according to new aspirations. He argued that:

> From that moment onwards, the university [comes] to be represented by a lived consciousness that sought to discover which traditional interest groups it serves and which are the directions to which its trends of change lead it. Opinions are divided, generating two types of dissatisfaction that are increasingly conflicting: those who want to reform the university to make it more accommodating and conservative, and those who want to see it transfigured into a trench of revolutionary struggle, even if it is the only barricade that stands against the global social order. (Ribeiro, 1969, p. 35, our translation)

Inclusive universities are spaces where people who otherwise might never meet can interact, learn, think, and work together. Historically, universities are the places where many key thinkers and leaders of liberation movements have met and developed their analyses, contributing to anti-colonial thought and practice (Gilmore, 2011). They are also spaces where many anti-colonial and anti-apartheid protests have taken place and there are strong movements for BDS within universities that attempt to push them to end complicity with the contemporary settler colonial regime of Israel.[6] Universities can be centers of critique, centers of civic education, and a crucial public good (Giroux, 2014), and reclaiming this emancipatory potential is a key part of a decolonization agenda.

We situate our call for decolonizing economics – and therefore also the university – within the broader anti-colonial, anti-racist, and anti-imperialist struggles in society. The university's potential for radical change, and thereby also of society, is an incentive for us to push for decolonizing economics within universities and beyond. The main obstacles in this path are the colonial roots and legacies of universities, the strong dominance of instrumentalist education in universities, and the commodification of education, which all weigh on the side of keeping the universities more accommodating and conservative. Working to decolonize economics and the university means pushing to tip the balance back toward making universities vibrant liberatory public spaces.

Here's what you can do to decolonize the university

Following Steve Salaita's (2024) recent intervention – "So you're a professor? Here's what you can do to oppose genocide" – we have put together some suggestions on how you can contribute to decolonizing the university, even as we recognize that no such recipe exists and any attempt to put together a checklist will be incomplete and insufficient.

Challenging colonial legacies of the university requires structural changes that go far beyond any single academic institution. Therefore, forming alliances across universities to strategize and work toward decolonizing university spaces is crucial. The responsibility and power for this lies with all members of the university community: students, professors, researchers, and administrators alike. In fact, it is likely to take a collective effort to move university policies and practices closer to being consistent with a decolonization agenda. We have put together three examples to consider below, but these are in no way comprehensive. In addition to the below, there are, for example, important discussions for academics to have regarding how to organize conferences, journals, and academic societies in anti-racist, anti-sexist, and anti-colonial ways.

1. **Challenge the neoliberal and colonial university.** We cannot let the decolonization agenda be co-opted by neoliberal logics of the university. This is incredibly difficult since even critical academics tend to internalize the market logic of neoliberalism, rather than meaningfully challenging the very structures of which they are a part (Bacevic, 2019). The seemingly meritocratic ideology of individual achievement that underlies the neoliberal university and that frames success and failure as purely individual, provides a justification for inequalities in representation. It suggests that white men are overrepresented in economics because they are simply smarter, work harder, or are better suited for economic research. The low status of teaching in the current academic system also disincentivizes efforts to decolonize teaching and pedagogy, given the amount of time needed to do it well and the little recognition instructors get for it. The neoliberal and colonial university excludes already marginalized groups in many ways, for example through not covering the excruciating visa costs for students and scholars, through not being able to retain students from working-class backgrounds, and through unsustainable workload models that have ensured that mental health has become a major concern among both students and staff (Bhopal, 2018). Finally, to challenge the neoliberal and colonial university, it is also necessary to look at how universities actively contribute to imperial and colonial practices, such as through contracts with ministries of defense, national security agencies, and the military. Student movements have taken universities to task for the damage they do to society at large, with perhaps the most well-known and successful

campaigns being the ones targeting universities' investments in fossil fuels (Everson, 2022).

2. Support and strengthen institutions of the periphery and heterodox economics departments. Decolonizing the university entails challenging the material inequalities between institutions in the capitalist center and the periphery, as well as challenging the marginalization of non-Eurocentric scholarship in the periphery. This involves working to reverse the underfunding of universities in the periphery and working toward more equal partnerships with institutions and academics in the periphery. This requires academics in the capitalist center to actively advocate against structural adjustment programs in the periphery, so that robust government investment in universities is not sabotaged. Universities will need to forge different kinds of partnerships and undertake efforts depending on the context and needs of the institutions. Examples of efforts to consider are locating main disciplinary conferences in the periphery, providing institutional support for journals in the periphery – especially non-Eurocentric ones – changing the institutional environments and incentives in both the center and the periphery to make it more attractive to publish in journals in the periphery from a career progression perspective, work to make journals and databases open access, and find ways to avoid extractive exchanges and partnerships (e.g., where institutions of the periphery are seen primarily as vehicles to facilitate data collection). However, as we know power inequalities permeate all institutions, including institutions in the periphery, any attempt at decolonization must go beyond challenging only the center–periphery hierarchy to also acknowledge and challenge the hierarchies that exist within both the center and the periphery, like hierarchies related to gender, race, class, and caste.

3. Promote more inclusive recruitment and promotion practices. This involves, for example, breaking away from a narrow Eurocentric definition of academic excellence as defined by the top five journals in economics, and recognizing and rewarding research based on its contribution to knowledge production. Economics needs to be open to approaches that align with a decolonization agenda, like feminist, radical Black, anti-colonial and heterodox scholarship and scholars, to move beyond the rigid hierarchy in mainstream economics. Promoting more inclusive practices must also involve recognizing contributions in heterodox and non-Anglophone journals and even non-academic publications. Even seemingly neutral policies for promotion and recruitment often have negative impacts on women, minorities and scholars working in non-Eurocentric traditions. The reform of these practices starts from interrogating how and why the hiring and promotion practices may be implicitly racist, sexist, elitist, or Eurocentric, and then move to assessing how this can be changed structurally (Croom, 2017). Specific steps could involve, for example, hiring people on permanent positions rather than precarious contracts, addressing the hostile seminar culture in economics to ensure more openness to alternative ways of doing economics, addressing the harassment in the field, and addressing broader structures of discrimination such as women facing higher publishing standards than men, being less likely to get credit for their work when they coauthor with men, Black professors in the UK facing more bullying, stereotyping, and institutional neglect than other academics (Rollock, 2019), and caste-based inequality in promotions in Indian academia.[7]

An example of a university's decolonization agenda

An example of a university that attempted to take a comprehensive approach to decolonization is the African Leadership University in Mauritius. Auerbach (2018) outlines the seven commitments to decolonization that the university has been working toward:

1. To commit to only assigning open-source material to students. This is to be achieved through negotiations with publishers and writers in an attempt to undo centuries of knowledge extraction from the continent with little benefits to Africans.[8]

2. To commit to teaching material in languages other than English. Concretely, the university aspires to assign students at least one non-English text per week.
3. Equitable student exchanges. Rather than support unequal distribution of opportunities (ten Americans to Ghana for each Ghanaian to the US), the university operates on a strict 1:1 ratio.
4. Beyond text sources. In line with African intellectual history, and to instill deeper knowledge and awareness to context and content among students, the university has committed to making sure students are assigned at least one non-text source of history, culture, and belief a week.
5. Collaboration. Students are given a central role in contributing to the university's outputs.
6. Producers, not just consumers. Students are given the space and tools to contribute to and shape the public dialogue about Africa through platforms such as op-eds, podcasts, and YouTube videos.
7. Ethics. The university is committed to both doing no harm and being an impetus for good and is committed to ensuring that students learn to think and act to high ethical standards.

Economics beyond the university: Decolonization and economic policy

Bringing a decolonization agenda to global, international, regional, and domestic policy requires examining how such policies may be based on Eurocentric ideas and interrogating how they support structural oppression. A decolonization agenda draws our attention to the power relations underpinning specific institutions, which in some instances may entail their abolition rather than reform. There are some fields that are more obviously Eurocentric than others. For example, the international development industry has obvious colonial dimensions (Escobar, 1989; Cowen and Shenton, 1995; T. Khan et al., 2023; Kesar and Kvangraven, 2024). However, there are other policy areas as well where the need for decolonization may not be immediately obvious.

If we want to analyze global policies within a decolonization framework, outlining how economic policies can be anti-colonial, anti-imperialist, anti-racist, or serve a decolonization agenda is essential. Some will argue that there is a case to reject all institutions that came out of colonialism, given the difficulty involved in reversing their colonial roots (this includes universities as well as international financial institutions). Arguably, colonial institutions cannot be decolonized, and decolonization means their dismantling, not reform. Others argue that, given how likely it is that universities and other institutions in the capitalist center will continue to hold massive amounts of power in the near future, it is necessary to demand decolonization processes within these institutions. Many policy organizations and universities can play a transformative and instrumental role in supporting a decolonization agenda. No doubt, decolonization will mean different things in different contexts and there will inevitably be debates about what the best way forward is.

Principles related to a decolonization agenda can be applied in many areas. Questions to ask in the pursuit of a process of decolonization include: Does this policy – or institution – address or reverse legacies of structural oppression, including those of class, colonialism, and imperialism? Is it *anti*-colonial and/or *anti*-imperialist? Does it engage and consider the views of the people it is trying to reach? We investigate this briefly in a few policy areas where decolonization is not discussed as much: Climate change, international finance, evidence-based policymaking, and health policy.

Climate change. Climate change impacts us all and is perhaps the biggest and most complex emergency we'll face in our lifetime. However, while the struggle against the unfolding ecological crisis is global, the impact is not equally distributed, and the burden not equally shared. Asking how climate change policies are anti-colonial or anti-racist leads to fruitful and important discussions. It leads us to recognize that colonialism and its legacy has had adverse environmental consequences and that environmental projects remain colonial in many ways (Asiyanbi, 2019). To decolonize climate policies is to explore and address how colonialism left legacies of extraction and vulnerabilities that impact post-colonial countries' abilities to cope with climate change today, as well as to understand the degree to which it is in fact the former colonizers that are mostly responsible for climate change. Several activists are therefore calling for reparations from the polluters and colonizers based on *climate debt* and *ecological debt*, concepts that address the unjust power relations between the capitalist center and periphery (Dengler and Seebacher, 2019). Metrics on which climate policies are based continue to be on current levels of absolute levels of production, without considering per capita measures of both current and historical levels of both the production and consumption emissions. The latter metrics are starkly biased against the economies of the center, with economies of the periphery often being used as a dumping ground (Azad and Chakraborty, 2021; Dorninger et al., 2021; Perry, 2023).

An approach to climate change in line with a decolonization agenda, then, involves addressing the unequal power relations that have led to the current crisis and what can be done to reverse them. This includes considering issues such as reparations, compensation, and recognizing that multinational companies drilling for oil and leading deforestation activities contribute to increased worldwide greenhouse gas emissions. It also involves working toward more humane and just policies for climate refugees fleeing from the countries that are impacted the worst, to transfer wealth and technology to the areas that are in most need of mitigation and adaptation, and to generally reverse the unequal structures created by colonialism, imperialism, and capitalism, that impact how countries are affected by climate change (Sealey-Huggins, 2017; Ajl, 2021; Huber, 2022; Táíwò, 2022). To best understand how to approach climate adaptation and mitigation, we can learn from scholars theorizing from a vantage point that includes the periphery who were quick to notice that capital accumulation comes at the expense of planetary destruction, given the brutal

ways that environments across the post-colonial world have
been destroyed historically (Furtado, 1974) and continue
to be destroyed through ongoing processes of imperialism
(Ajl, 2021; Hamouchene, 2023; Perry, 2023) and settler
colonialism (Braverman, 2023). A decolonization agenda
for climate change would take a radically different approach
than how the contemporary economics discipline currently
conceptualizes environmental and climate issues (Chen,
2022; Işıkara, 2023; Christophers, 2024).

International financial institutions. On the global stage,
international financial institutions such as the IMF and the
World Bank are often held up as institutions that are at the
forefront of alleviating poverty and assisting countries in the
periphery. However, they were set up to preserve economic
stability in the centers of capital and are dominated by
capitalist center countries in their very structure. Since they
were founded in 1944, these institutions have arguably
contributed to a structural economic dependency through
requiring *structural adjustment* of developing countries
– which hinders these countries' abilities to put forward
sustainable developmental agendas. What can decolonization
look like in such a context, beyond the option of abolition?

Lukka (2020) suggests a series of policies that the World
Bank and the IMF could pursue to take a more reparatory
development approach. These include: (1) assessing the
historical impact of slavery, colonialism, and neocolonialism
in order to re-envision financial assessment practices;
(2) assessing the need for repudiation of debt where communities continue to endure injustice and marginalization
because of their post-colonial trajectory – this would involve
the IMF and the World Bank examining the impacts of their
activities on post-colonial countries, evaluating when and
where they may have caused harm, and how such harm can
be avoided in the future; (3) governance reforms that redistribute power, including giving up power to UN institutions,
where countries have equal votes.

Debt repudiation is a broader concept that goes beyond
just the IMF and the World Bank, especially since it challenges
their legitimacy. It entails questioning the legality of debts

owed by countries in the periphery to countries in the capitalist center. Instead of trying to fix the system, the repudiation and reparations approach sees the system itself as the problem. An example of such an effort can be found in Tunisia's Truth and Reconciliation process. Tunisia's Truth and Dignity Commission announced in 2019 that the IMF and World Bank bore a share of responsibility for social unrest that led to the revolution in 2011 (and ultimately to the Arab Spring), because of pressure the institutions put on the Tunisian government through structural adjustment to freeze wages and reduce subsidies on basic consumer goods, which in turn led to social crises and conflicts. The commission called for an apology, financial compensation to the victims, and a cancellation of Tunisia's multilateral debt to the IMF and the World Bank (Lukka, 2020).

Evidence-based policy. The dominant methodological approach of evidence-based policy helps to preserve the status quo and to avoid addressing the impact of colonial legacies and structural racism in the design of policies. Proponents of evidence-based policy often present their quest for evidence as neutral and in everyone's best interest, despite the specific (Eurocentric) knowledge system it promotes at the expense of others (Kvangraven, 2020). Evidence-based policy is very often based on randomized experiments, and it often suggests that we can find out what works through testing narrow interventions and thereby bypass the messy policymaking process that plagues human societies, often characterized by ideology and corruption. As many critics of the evidence-based policy paradigm have pointed out, this movement is in line with broader attempts to present market-based interventions as *apolitical* (Drèze, 2020).

However, the way experiments are carried out often follows colonial practices of experimenting on people living in poverty with little regard for their dignity or consent. For example, one RCT in Nairobi, Kenya, involved disconnecting the water supply at randomly selected low-income rental properties to see if this would incentivize people to pay their water bills on time (Coville et al., 2023). This RCT did not involve informed consent of the subjects of the experiment (unless you agree with the researchers that signing up to the water company to begin with, which has a clause about the right to cut off the water supply in the case of failure to pay the bills, counts as consent to be part of an experiment), and it reproduced inequalities in access to water in Nairobi that were established during colonialism (Wilson et al., 2023). Hundreds of residents in low-income settlements in Nairobi were left without access to clean water for weeks, and in some cases months, but none of them knew they were a part of an RCT, and it was unclear how this experiment was making anyone better off. Although the study – rightly so – caused outrage among local activists and international researchers, the designers and authors of the RCT paper did not back down or apologize, rather they published an ethical statement defending their experiment. The paper has since been published in the highly ranked economics journal *The Review of Economics and Statistics.* In their appraisal of this study along with other recent RCTs, such as how a village in Kenya has become a setting of multiple overlapping RCTs often creating massive inequalities and changing the aspirations of people who have randomly been excluded from receiving treatments such as cash transfers, *The Economist* recently concluded that RCTs have problems, but "they may still be the best tool for solving poverty," thus reproducing the idea that RCTs are a kind of gold standard for gathering evidence and coming up with solutions (Kinstler, 2024).

Critically interrogating evidence-based policy from the perspective of a decolonization agenda would require an exploration of the forms of structural oppression faced by the communities in which the evidence is collected and where the policy is meant to be implemented. The communities where the policy is to be implemented would need to be involved in determining both the research questions and discussing the policy options, rather than these being determined by researchers based elsewhere. A decolonization agenda does not dispute the importance of evidence *per se*, but rather the assumption that researchers trained in Eurocentric knowledge systems are those best suited to determine policy options for communities across the world.

Health policy. Textbooks on health economics are concerned with the workings and failings of markets for the provision of healthcare, and the trade-offs between efficiency and equity in healthcare provision (McPake et al., 2020). Questions such as whether it is better to reduce deaths by 100 using public funds in a certain region, or to reduce deaths by 80 using the same public funds where the cost of reducing deaths is higher, are typical in economics (McPake et al., 2020). Using a cost–benefit framework to answer questions about health economics is quite limiting and leads to limited policy prescriptions. Even though health economists caution against using the techniques of economics uncritically, this necessarily means considering healthcare as a service and good health as a commodity that has a price. Global governance of health policy guided by these principles shapes access to medicine in highly unequal ways, as was evidenced most recently by the inequality in access to lifesaving COVID-19 vaccines and related drugs during the COVID-19 pandemic. The argument made is that intellectual property regimes are important to ensure that innovation that results in vaccines takes place at all, and that if intellectual property laws were waived, the revenues from vaccine production would not routinely be higher than its substantial costs. This is institutionalized in global health by the World Trade Organization's intellectual property regime and these rules are usually not waived in public health crises that lead to mass deaths. As a result, during the pandemic, the measures to prevent disease and death were available easily and rapidly in the countries of the center but scarce in peripheral countries. More generally, COVID-19 revealed that Eurocentric knowledge systems in local, national, and international health policy institutions were inadequate for shaping an adequate response to the pandemic, as responses failed to account for existing lines of oppression and therefore had highly unequal impacts on different groups (Büyüm et al., 2020). In addition, the global health system is less likely to create treatments and vaccines for diseases that mostly affect people in countries of the periphery. For instance, there was a global cholera vaccine shortage in 2022, as one out of the three producers of cholera vaccines wound down production given that it was not very profitable (Roth, 2022). Considering health policy from a decolonization agenda would, therefore, involve addressing and reversing the structural violence generated by legacies of colonialism and slavery, but also a knowledge shift that recognizes and values non-Eurocentric knowledge systems related to health.

Research has shown that histories of slavery, redlining, environmental racism, and imperialism underpin the design of global and public health systems, which in turn result in structural inequalities in terms of health outcomes (Büyüm et al., 2020; Sowemimo, 2023). For example, the Tuskegee syphilis study carried out by the United States Public Health Service between 1932 and 1972 has been widely recognized as racist, given its targeting of Black men to be given syphilis to observe the effects of the disease when untreated (Brandt, 1978). This context is extremely important to understand the lack of trust among Black communities in the United States toward public health measures, which contribute to worse health outcomes.

The role of the legacies of colonialism and the structures of capitalism in generating famines, disease and malnutrition in the periphery is often underappreciated, and therefore, health economics often only addresses the symptoms of ill health and malnutrition rather than the underlying forces causing it globally. While we know that more nutritious food can help improve nutritional outcomes, contemporary food systems advanced by the neoliberal order, which relies heavily on the penetration of ultra-processed food across the globe, does not make it easy for individuals, especially from marginalized groups, to make healthy food choices (Stevano et al., 2020). Therefore, understanding the production and distribution systems and the market mechanisms that prevent everyone from having sufficient nutritious food is also a matter for health policy.

–9–

Conclusion

Decolonization has become chic. It is à la mode to wear t-shirts with "decolonize" logos or attend Lululemon brand ambassadors' workshops on decolonizing gender. While these things will line corporations' pockets, they are unlikely to contribute to a decolonization agenda as we have defined it here. This is what Shringarpure (2020) has called *fake decolonization*. It cannot be avoided, because when something starts to gain as much traction as the decolonization agenda has in recent years, it will invariably be co-opted by corporations and entrepreneurs. It will be eagerly consumed by people who know something's not quite right and perhaps feel guilty about their privilege but are not fully aware of how structural power works. In a way, it is an encouraging sign that there are attempts to make an idea as powerful and disruptive as decolonization milquetoast for consumption in the popular zeitgeist. However, this co-optation is a distraction, and the work of challenging capitalist, patriarchal, racist, and colonial structures remains.

Decolonizing economics is necessarily a political and material process and is not possible by just working on curriculum and research. Calls for decolonization that are not political and that are disengaged from real struggles are misinformed and ineffective at best and harmful at worst. We saw this exposed very starkly in universities in the capitalist center in the wake of the beginning of the Israeli genocide on Palestinians after the October 7 Hamas-led attack on Israel, as universities went from being enthusiastic about efforts to decolonize university curricula to strictly policing any events related to the actual (de)colonization of Palestine.[1]

Economics shapes people's understanding of society and justifies policies that support the status quo (Amin, 2009 [1988]). Eurocentric economic theory has formed the ideological basis for a global polarizing project that has shaped capitalism and reinforced imperialism, as well as shaping economists' view of these processes. With the dominance of Eurocentrism in economics today, broad sections of our society are held hostage to a distorted understanding of the world. Despite the massive roadblocks that stand in the way of decolonization, recognizing the need to reject and challenge Eurocentrism to make way for something better is an important effort.

While decolonization is a material struggle, universities in general, and economics in particular, play an important role in shaping discourses around that struggle. We do not for a moment resist the idea that dispossession of land is a central aspect of colonialism and imperialism (as in Tuck and Yang, 2012), but we argue that decolonization cannot be easily reduced to only one specific and geographical articulation of the colonial and imperialist project. As universities brush such issues under the rug and systematically ignore the impact of colonization on indigenous land and life – and often also directly support imperialist projects – they serve to justify the status quo.

Decolonizing economics is an ongoing process. We make choices throughout our lives about how to teach, how and what to learn, who and what to read, which fights to pick. Choosing to engage in a decolonization project is also a choice. Many economists may not choose to do so, but at least let it be known that it is indeed a choice they make, whether consciously or unconsciously. Most economists will probably not read this book, or if they do, they will probably not make it this far, because the discipline is resistant to change and very sensitive to criticism. Some economists who do make it this far may be upset by our remarks and may be defensive about the discipline as well as their own work. But scientific rigor demands that this challenge is dealt with, even if it means discarding canonical frameworks. The challenge we present isn't motivated by an intention to undermine scholarship and teaching about economic issues; rather, it stems from our dedication to do better.

By writing this book, we hope to have made the options available to economists and students of economics clearer as we've drawn up assumptions and implications behind various theoretical, methodological, ideological, and pedagogical approaches to economics, to demonstrate what's at stake. We hope this book can serve as a platform for reflection and debate about how to achieve economic, social, and epistemic liberation.

Notes

Chapter 1: Introduction

1 We have made the choice in this book to use the binary of capitalist center and periphery, which was a categorization put forward by scholars in the periphery themselves to distinguish the capitalist center (the industrialized world: Europe, North America, Australia, New Zealand, and Japan, often referred to as the advanced countries, the developing world, the West, or the Global North) from the periphery (the global majority barring these few countries, often called the Third World, or the Global South). Any category is political. We have chosen to stick with center–periphery to denote the hierarchy that has been produced through capitalist expansion, colonialism, and imperialism. While there is no perfect form of categorization, we deem center–periphery preferable in this context to others because of the teleological connotations of the developed–developing binary, the misleading geographical connotations of the Global South–North binary, and the relative decline in use of the First/Third World category since the end of the Cold War (for a recent exposition of the political meanings of such categories, see Sud and Sánchez-Ancochea, 2022). This is not to say that categories such as Global South–North or First/Third World cannot also be used as progressive political categories (see, e.g., Ikejiaku, 2014; Wiegratz et al., 2023).

2 Rodrik is referring to the Sveriges Riksbank Prize in Economic Sciences in Memory of Alfred Nobel, which is not an official Nobel prize, although economists tend to refer to it as such. Nonetheless, it is considered among the most prestigious awards an economist can receive.

3 For discussion on the differences between mainstream and (late) neoclassical economics, see Dow (1997), Colander et al. (2004), Dequech (2007–8, 2012), and Lawson (2013).

4 See Christophers (2014) for an overview of the performativity studies literature – which puts forward claims about the economics field actively shaping economic markets – and the (largely Marxist) political economy literature – which sees markets as being shaped by material forces rather than economic theory – and how he reconciles the two literatures. Christophers (2014, p. 18) notes that even Marx himself saw close, reciprocal links between "the techno-calculative field of bourgeois economics and the lived milieu of capitalist political economy."

5 It is worth noting that the splitting off into disciplines cemented Eurocentrism, with some disciplines being more impacted than others (Bhambra and Holmwood, 2021; McKittrick, 2021). For example, anthropology is widely considered to be a child of imperialism (Gough, 1968), and the calls for the decolonization of sociology, politics, and geography have been widespread – as documented in the other books from the Polity Press series of which our book is a part (Meghji, 2020; Shilliam, 2021; Radcliffe, 2022; Bernard, 2023; Venkatesan, 2025).

6 It is worth emphasizing here that the material process of colonialism in the world has entailed various violent processes of dispossession, genocide, occupation, suppression of freedom, expropriation, and more. Here, we refer to a discursive colonization or an intellectual colonization of a disciplinary sphere. We use the word with caution so as not to downplay the violence that material colonization entails, much beyond any intellectual domain. However, in adopting this term of colonization within the intellectual domain of economics and social sciences, we also seek to unearth how the discursive colonization tends to legitimize material processes of colonization and oppression.

7 This idea has since been developed further by many scholars, including Hannah Arendt (1951), Michel Foucault (1976) and more recently by Kojo Koram (2022), Julian Go (2023) and Antony Loewenstein (2023) to explain various ways in which colonial and imperialist practices have returned to or impacted the former colonizers.

8 In India, for example, right-wing forces have been appropriating the decolonization agenda (A. Lewis and Lall, 2024). They misconstrue decolonization as a celebration of nativism and a distorted version of history to align it with a right-wing populist

agenda. It is also often used to justify various caste-based discriminatory practices and ostracization of religious minorities. Such appropriation poses a big threat to a decolonization agenda and needs to be, in our opinion, recognized and resisted.

Chapter 2: The Foundations of a Eurocentric Discipline

1 See also popular textbooks in economics such as Le Grand et al. (2008), Krugman and Wells (2005), and Mankiw (2008).

2 This argument has been dubbed the "Williams thesis," after Eric Williams' (1944) *Capitalism and slavery*. Williams argues that the Transatlantic Slave Trade shaped the development of capitalism, but note that he does not go so far as to claim that the triangular trade alone was responsible for financing British industrial capitalism (Bailey, 2014).

3 Mies draws this example for women's work in the lace-making industry in India in the 1980s, but this phenomenon resonates across various contexts and periods. For instance, in the subcontracted manufacturing sector in present-day India, out-contracted work often mirrors classic putting-out arrangements, predominantly undertaken by home-based women workers at very low wages (Kesar, 2024; Basole, 2016). In today's globalized landscape, such subcontracted work frequently exists at the bottom rungs of global value chains (Meagher, 2019).

4 For more on the Black Radical Tradition and racial capitalism, see Robinson (2000 [1983]), P. J. Hudson (2018), Burden-Stelly et al. (2020), Edwards (2020), Jenkins and Leroy (2021), Singh (2022) and Alexander (2023).

5 However, it is worth noting that there are some exceptions, as some, such as C. L. R. James, see race as secondary to class. Nonetheless, even James warned that "to neglect the racial factor as merely incidental is an error" (James, 1963 [1938], p. 283).

Chapter 3: Colonization of the Discipline: From Political Economy to Contemporary Economics

1 American Economic Association website: "What is economics? Understanding the discipline," available at: https://www.aeaweb.org/resources/students/what-is-economics.

2 Not to be confused with today's sub-discipline of political economy within mainstream economics, which is defined as the field of study that examines how politics affects the economy and how the economy affects politics. Politics is narrowly conceived as being related to political choices such

as those expressed by voters and interest groups and their impact on economic policy, or how the economic organization of firms and industries has an impact on political activity. Notably, as discussed by Frieden (2020, p. 7), in mainstream political economy, "[p]oliticians can be thought of as analogous to firms, with voters as consumers, or governments as monopoly providers of goods and services to constituent customers."

3 Note that the precise definitions of "marginalism" and "neoclassical economics" have been heavily debated. Here we simplify the debate for our purpose – to identify how economics has evolved and its relationship to Eurocentric features. For more about the debates about marginalism and neoclassical economics, see, for example, Aspromourgos (1986), Lawson (2013), and Zafirovski (1999).

4 For a critical and accessible history of general equilibrium theory, see Chappe (2016).

5 See Fajardo (2022) for a discussion of how Latin American theory also impacted thinking in the capitalist center.

6 Paul Baran and Paul Sweezy were based in the Economics departments of Stanford and Harvard, respectively.

7 The Walrasian equilibrium increasingly fell out of favor within mainstream economics because the basic tenets of the model – behavior based on self-interested exogenous preferences and complete and costless contracting – came under critical scrutiny (Bowles and Gintis, 2000). Marshall (1930), instead, advocated for empirically based assumptions concerning heterogeneous, yet regular, behavior and for the incorporation of incomplete markets, as such incorporating the particularities of human motivations and institutions into neoclassical equilibrium models. While Walrasian models are static equilibrium models based on individual rational agents, Marshallian models tend to take a partial equilibrium approach, emphasizing the use of representative agents (Madra, 2017). Nonetheless, both positions ascribe a constitutive role to the model of perfect competition as their ultimate point of reference.

8 See Hodgson (2009) for a detailed review.

9 See, for example, the widely used textbook by Mankiw (2020).

10 This factoid is based on discussions with researcher Divya Rabindrath.

Chapter 4: Development Economics: A Failed Attempt to Break from Colonial Roots

1 See Thornton (2023) for more examples, including a thorough exposition of the Pan-American Union, the proposal for an Inter-American Bank which was first floated in 1933, and the creation of the Inter-American Financial and Economic Committee in 1939.

2 For example, Arthur Lewis was one of President Kwame Nkrumah's advisers on Ghanaian development.

3 Note that considering alternative ways of understanding development does not mean necessarily celebrating the pre-modern, but rather considering other ways of conceiving of progress, economic equality, and political action (Nzegwu, 1995; Zein-Elabdin, 2009).

Chapter 5: Heterodox Economics and the Decolonization Agenda

1 In many countries in the periphery, traditions in heterodox economics are widely taught, especially at the postgraduate level, even if they are not identified as such. However, they are not taught as much at the undergraduate level; see, for example, De and Thomas (2018) for the Indian case.

2 By and large, the mainstream literature sees the original sin as caused not only by problems related to national policies and institutions, but also by international factors, including international transaction costs, network externalities, and global capital market imperfections, while the heterodox literature locates the source of the original sin in the currency hierarchy created through imperialism and uneven capitalist development (Eichengreen and Hausmann, 2005).

3 For some discussions of Marxism and Eurocentrism, see Lipietz (1982), Blaut (1999), Nilsen (2017), Pradella (2017), and M. N. Smith (2022).

4 Seventeen percent of heterodox economists who took part in the 2020–1 survey responded that they did not consider "challenging Eurocentrism that prevails in the field" to be of importance in the context of reforming economics teaching and pedagogy (Kvangraven and Kesar, 2023).

Chapter 6: Toward a Decolonization Agenda

1 For critiques, see Ince (2022a), Kabeer (2020), Koechlin (2019), and Bailey (2014) for each topic, respectively.

2 See, for example, Mamdani (2016) or Ndlovu-Gatsheni (2023)

on the post-colonial turn in African studies. While we do not have the space to go into it here, there are also many post-colonial scholars that resist the characterization of post-colonialism as a theoretical tradition primarily concerned with discourse at the expense of materialist approaches to political economy (e.g., Ahluwalia, 2001, 2010).

3 It may be helpful here to draw on the intersectional work of McCall (2005), who argues that there are three different kinds of approaches to intersectional research, namely anti-categorical, intra-categorical and inter-categorical. Which approach one might opt for will depend on whether we treat the categories as unstable or stable (Charusheela, 2013).

4 This argument is parallel to Charusheela's (2013) argument about the potential pitfalls of the use of *intersectionality* as a frame.

5 See also McKittrick's (2015) long-time engagement with Sylvia Winter, and her refusal to be "disciplined" into categories.

6 See El Nabolsy (2024) for a thorough exposition of the Dar es Salaam debates.

7 Perhaps unsurprisingly, such ideas did not go uncontested, and the scholars eventually became divided into the "radicals" who wanted the abolition of disciplines, "moderates" who supported transformation of the curriculum but who did not want to go so far as to abolish disciplines entirely, and the "conservatives" who supported the status quo (Mamdani, 2016, p. 74).

8 See Copley and Moraitis (2021) for an exposition of how analytically separating the state and the market leaves us unable to grasp the structures of the global capitalist political economy, even if we consider states and markets to be "mutually constituted."

9 Note that this chapter is not a literature review or critical assessment of all the different theoretical strands that could be helpful for the decolonization agenda, their respective potential, and limitations, as that is beyond the scope of this short book. For analyses and overviews of some important theoretical traditions that are relevant for the decolonization agenda, please consult the following: on racial capitalism and the Black Radical Tradition, see Williams (1944), Robinson (2000 [1983]), P. J. Hudson (2018), Burden-Stelly et al. (2020), Edwards (2020), Jenkins and Leroy (2021), Singh (2022), and Alexander (2023); on feminist political economy and social

reproduction theory, see Hull et al. (1982), Mies (1986), Minh-Ha (1987), Ferber and Nelson (1993), hooks (2000), Mohanty (2003), Barker and Kuiper (2003), Bergeron (2004), Kaul (2007), Charusheela (2013), T. Bhattacharya (2017), Tamale (2020), Barker et al. (2021), Ossome (2023), and Cantillon et al (2023); on critical race theory, see Crenshaw et al. (1995), Zuberi (2001), Delgado and Stefancic (2013), and Meghji (2021); on different views of post-colonial theory, see Spivak (1988), Bartolovich and Lazarus (2002), Kapoor (2002), Charusheela and Zein-Elabdin (2003), Charusheela (2004), Zein-Elabdin (2009), Ossome (2013), and Go (2016); on Marxist anti-colonial and/or anti-imperialist approaches to economics and Eurocentrism, see Rodney (1972), Amin (2009 [1988]), Sen and Marcuzzo (2017), Pradella (2017), Fraser (2019), Chibber (2020), Kvangraven (2021), Younis (2022), Adesina (2022), and Okoth (2023); for decolonial analysis, see Quijano (2007), Lugones (2010), and Ndlovu-Gatsheni and Ndlovu (2022); and for some critical engagements with decolonial theory, see Hull (2021), Lehmann (2022), Larsen (2022), and Naicker (2023). It goes without saying that this short list of references is non-exhaustive, and many brilliant overviews and scholars have been left out. This is meant as a starting point for further exploration by the reader rather than a full overview of relevant work.

10 See Canclini (1995), Chabal and Daloz (1999), Fafchamps (2004), and Zein-Elabdin (2009) for explanations of alternate forms of rationalities and alternative ways of understanding culture and economics, including through the idea of hybridity. We delve further into these issues in chapter 7.

11 See, for example, the work of the Nigerian anti-imperialist, humanist, and feminist activist Funmilayo Ransome-Kuti. In her 1947 article "We had equality till Britain came" she lays out the ways that colonialism led to marginalization of Nigerian women (Johnson-Odim, 1992).

12 See Kaul (2007) for more on how identity is conceived of in the mainstream, including discussions of critiques and implications.

13 For a summary of examples of the construction and deployment of multiple identities against multiple contested sites by feminist groups across the world, see Bergeron (2004). Bergeron also discusses how these examples can help us imagine and build a more transformative feminist vision that expands possible

forms of intervention and resistance beyond those offered in conventional nation-centered and economistic discourses.

14 The concept of intersectionality is generally dated back to Black feminist and legal scholar Kimberlé Crenshaw (1989), although as Crenshaw herself notes, it can be traced further back to the activism and work of the Combahee River Collective (1977). These ideas are often attributed to American Black feminist scholars, but they were developed in rich conversations with other minority feminist scholars both inside and outside the US, which may account for this concept's capacity to travel (Charusheela, 2013). Recognizing the collaborative space in which the concept has developed should of course not take away from the important role played by Black feminists in developing these sets of ideas.

15 For a short overview of political and methodological differences between different strands of racial capitalism, see Peter James Hudson's (2018) forum article in *Boston Review*.

16 Work in the Black Radical Tradition and by Third World Marxists can be helpful in this regard (see, e.g., Du Bois, 1935; Williams, 1944; Cox, 1948; James, 1963 [1938]; Cabral, 1972; Fanon, 2004 [1961]; Edwards, 2020), including work that also exposes the patriarchal dimension of racialized capitalism (A. Davis, 1981; Boyce-Davies, 2008; Gilmore, 2022).

17 For more on how categories are constructed and how to navigate political economy research with this in mind, see Omi and Winant (1994) and Brodkin (1998).

18 This relationship between global racialism and caste has long been studied by anti-caste Marxists (Omvedt, 1981; Teltumbde, 2018; More and More, 2020) but it has been severely neglected in the economics field and in studies of caste more generally.

Chapter 7: Exploring the Decolonization Agenda

1 For example, Ossome (2020) demonstrates how African feminism connects emancipatory economic questions to histories of slavery, colonialism, imperialism, and neoliberalization. All regions have their own histories that are relevant for grasping contemporary economic problems within a decolonization agenda.

2 See Fine (2000) for a critique of endogenous growth theory and Selwyn and Leyden (2021) for a critique of modern trade theory.

3 See Shaikh (2016) for a critique of Ricardian trade theory

and Lin and Chang (2009) for critiques of the widely used Hecksher–Ohlin model.

4 This point on rigidity of the wages in the center was later picked up by the neo-Marxist economist Samir Amin (1974) in his elaboration of unequal exchange.

5 There has been a revival of interest in dependency theory in recent years, as can be seen in two special issues, one in *Review of African Political Economy* and another in *Latin American Perspectives* (Kvangraven et al., 2021; Chilcote and Vasconcelos, 2022; Vasconcelos and Chilcote, 2022).

6 In the context of unequal exchange, the workers in the periphery are both exploited by local capitalist classes *and* receiving lower returns based on unequal trade relations (Amin, 1974; Bambirra, 1978; Marini, 1978; Hickel et al., 2021). However, there is debate about whether unequal exchange is the fundamental *cause* or rather a *symptom* of underdevelopment (Bettelheim, 1972) as well as about how to conceptualize exploitation and value transfers within a Marxist dependency tradition, where many radical non-Eurocentric scholars also reject theories of unequal exchange (Dussel, 2001; Kvangraven, 2023).

7 For further developments and interpretations, see Vernengo (2006) and Alami et al. (2023).

8 In the context of South Asia, in an Indian weekly journal magazine, *Economic and Political Weekly*.

9 The possibility of co-existence of multiple class structures in the periphery departs from traditional Marxist understandings that often assume the transition from a feudal mode of production to predominantly capitalist, where capital–labor is the most important social relation, as was the case in Europe. There is a wealth of recent scholarship on this co-existence of capitalist and non-capitalist structures (e.g., Fraser, 2016b; Arboleda et al., 2024), including by scholars exploring specific characteristics of capitalism in the capitalist center (Resnick and Wolff, 1987; Gibson-Graham, 2006).

10 Merchant capital is based on trading commodities – buying low and selling at a higher price – rather than the production of commodities. Merchant capital was dominant before capitalism, and in the center, merchant capital lost its previous independent role with the transition to capitalism and was reduced to serving industrial capital.

11 For a contemporary exploration of Sanyal's analysis, see the

work of Bhattacharya and Kesar (2020) and Kesar (2024) in the Indian context. This departure from an argument based on "capital's needs" also resonates with the argument advanced by the Quijano (1974) and Nun (2000) in a Latin American context, as they argue that the economy can be broadly viewed as comprising a dominant accumulation-driven hegemonic pole that controls the means of production, technology, and market in the economy, and a subordinate, subsistence-driven marginal pole which is considered afunctional to the hegemonic pole.

12 For a methodological critique, see Bhattacharjea (2006).

13 Given that Ubuntu is about how we as humans perceive ourselves and behave based on our connection to others, it has implications beyond how we understand individual rationalities to how we practice scholarship as well – a kind of scholarship that is in line with Ubuntu will be one that is humanizing, empowering, and collective. Such transformative scholarship may come at a price, however, in a system where promotion and tenure are based on individual rather than collective achievements (Mũgo, 2021).

14 The concept of systemic rationality is based on ideas shared by Snehashish Bhattacharya.

Chapter 8: What Is to Be Done?

1 The RAND Corporation is an American nonprofit global policy think tank, research institute, and consulting firm.

2 The Cowles Foundation (previously known as the Cowles Commission) is an influential economics research institute that was started by the US businessman Alfred Cowles, moved to the University of Chicago in 1939, and then to Yale University in 1955.

3 A new archive on the life and work of Emmanuel has recently been set up, which allows us to better understand how his experiences in the DRC and wider political work influenced his thinking. See https://unequalexchange.org/category/digital-archive/.

4 See Langdon (2013) for a discussion on how this was attempted in development studies courses in Canada.

5 See Chauí (2003) for the case of Brazil.

6 Details of the BDS movement in universities can be found at: https://bdsmovement.net/.

7 See, for example, Bayer and Rouse's (2016) work tracking how the relative absence of women and members of racial

and ethnic minority groups in the US and the UK begins at the undergraduate level and gets progressively worse as women and minorities drop off.

8 Universities located in the center are predominantly those who have agreements with multiple journal publication houses to release their staffs' research as open source. While this facilitates open access to knowledge, it exacerbates the bias against accessing scholarship from the universities in the periphery. Therefore, universities in the center should financially support open-source authorship agreements with their thinly resourced partner universities, or work toward reforming the publishing industry more generally.

Chapter 9: Conclusion

1 The policing of critique of Israel's colonization of Palestine in academia has a much longer history (e.g., Nadeau and Sears, 2010; Salaita, 2015; Ziadah, 2017), but it is only more recently that universities have co-opted the language of decolonization while at the same time remaining committed to settler colonialism.

References

Abreu, J.F. de and P. B. Haddad (2016) "Mapping the Brazilian cooperation with developing countries: A spatial analysis," in R. Efe, I. Curebal, G. Nyussupova and E. Atasoy (eds) *Recent Research in Interdisciplinary Sciences*. Sofia: St. Kliment Ohridski University Press.

Abu-Lughod, L. (1990) "Anthropology's Orient: The boundaries of theory on the Arab World," in H. Sharabi (ed.) *Theory, Politics and the Arab World: Critical Responses*. London: Routledge.

Acemoglu, D. and S. Johnson (2023) *Power and Progress: Our Thousand-Year Struggle over Technology and Prosperity*. London: Basic Books.

Acemoglu, D. and J. A. Robinson (2012) *Why Nations Fail: The Origins of Power, Prosperity and Poverty*. New York: Crown.

Acemoglu, D. and A. Wolitzky (2014) "Cycles of conflict: An economic model." *American Economic Review*, 104(4): 1350–67.

Acemoglu, D., S. Johnson and J. A. Robinson (2005) "Institutions as a fundamental cause of long-run growth," in P. Aghion and S. N. Durlauf (eds) *Handbook of Economic Growth, vol. 1A*. Amsterdam: Elsevier, pp. 385–472.

Adesina, J. O. (2022) "Variations in postcolonial imagination: Reflection on Senghor, Nyerere and Nkrumah." *Africa Development/Afrique et Développement*, 47(1), pp. 31–58.

Advani, A., E. Ash, A. Boltachka, D. Cai and I. Rasul (2024) "Race-related research in economics: Volume, content and publication incentives." Center for Law & Economics Working Paper Series, No. 08/2004.

Afshar, H. and S. Barrientos (eds) (1999) *Women, Globalization and Fragmentation in the Developing World*. New York: St. Martin's.

Agunsoye, A., T. Dassler, E. Fotopoulou and J. Mulberg (eds) (2024)

Heterodox Economics and Global Emergencies: Voices from around the World. London: Routledge.

Ahluwalia, P. (2001) *Politics and Post-Colonial Theory: African Inflections.* London: Routledge.

Ahluwalia, P. (2010) *Out of Africa: Post-Structuralism's Colonial Roots.* London: Routledge.

Aiginger, K. and D. Rodrik (2020) "Rebirth of industrial policy and an agenda for the twenty-first century." *Journal of Industry, Competition and Trade*, 20: 189–207.

Aigner, E., J. Greenspon and D. Rodrik (2024) "The global distribution of authorship in economics journals." NBER Working Paper No. 29435.

Ajl, M. (2021) "A people's Green New Deal: Obstacles and prospects." *Agrarian South: Journal of Political Economy*, 10(2): 371–90.

Akbulut, B., F. Adaman and Y. M. Madra (2015) "The decimation and displacement of development economics." *Development and Change*, 46(4): 733–61.

Ake, C. (1979) *Social Science as Imperialism: The Theory of Political Development.* Ibadan: Ibadan University Press.

Akerlof, G. A. and R. E. Kranton (2010) *Identity Economics: How Our Identities Shape Our Work, Wages, and Well-Being.* Princeton, NJ: Princeton University Press.

Al-Bulushi, Y. (2023). "Dar es Salaam on the frontline: Red and black internationalisms." *Third World Thematics: A TWQ Journal*, 8(1–3), 21–37.

Alami, I., C. Alves, B. Bonizzi, A. Kaltenbrunner, K. Kodddenbrock, I. H. Kvangraven and J. Powell (2023) "International financial subordination: A critical research agenda." *Review of International Political Economy*, 30(4): 1360–86.

Alatas, S. F. (1987) "Reflections on the idea of Islamic social science." *Comparative Civilizations Review*, 17(17): Art. 5.

Alavi, H. (1975) "India and the colonial mode of production." *Socialist Register*, 10(33/35): 1235–62.

Albelda, R. and Drago, R. (2013) *Unlevel Playing Fields: Understanding Wage Inequality and Discrimination*, 4th edn. Portsmouth: Dollar and Sense.

Alessandria, G., R. C. Johnson and K.-M. Yi (2023) "Perspectives on trade and structural transformation." *Oxford Development Studies*, 51(4): 455–75.

Alexander, N. (2023) *Against Racial Capitalism: Selected Writings.* London: Pluto Press.

Allen, R. C. (2011) *Global Economic History: A Very Short Introduction.* New York: Oxford University Press.

Alves, C. and I. H. Kvangraven (2020) "Changing the narrative: Economics after Covid-19." *Review of Agrarian Studies*, 10(1): 147–63.

Ambedkar, B. R. (2014) *Annihilation of Caste: The Annotated Critical Edition*. London: Verso.

American Economic Association (2024) "What is economics? Understanding the discipline." *AEA Resources for Students*, March 18. Available at: www.aeaweb.org/resources/students/what-is-economics.

Amin, S. (1972) "Underdevelopment and dependence in Black Africa – Origins and contemporary forms." *Journal of Modern African Studies*, 10(4): 105–20.

Amin, S. (1974) *Accumulation on a World Scale: A Critique of the Theory of Underdevelopment*. New York: Monthly Review Press.

Amin, S. (1982) "After the new international economic order: The future of international economic relations." *Journal of Contemporary Asia*, 12(4): 432–50.

Amin, S. (1984) "Self-reliance and the new international economic order," in H. Addo (ed.) *Transforming the World Economy? 9 Critical Essays on the New International Economic Order*. London: Hodder and Stoughton in association with the United Nations University.

Amin, S. (2009 [1988]) *Eurocentrism: Modernity, Religion, and Democracy: A Critique of Eurocentrism and Culturalism*, 2nd edn. Oxford: Pambazuka Press.

Amin, S. (2010) *Global History: A View from the South*. Dakar, Senegal: CODESRIA.

Amin, S. (2015) "From Bandung (1955) to 2015: Old and new challenges for the states, the nations and the peoples of Asia, Africa and Latin America." *International Critical Thought*, 5(4): 453–60.

Amsler, S. S. and C. Bolsmann (2012) "University ranking as social exclusion." *British Journal of Sociology of Education*, 33(2): 283–301.

Ancochea, D. S. (2004) "Building a successful heterodox graduate program in economics: An impossible task?" *New School Economic Review*, 1(1): 9–14.

Anghie, A. (2005) *Imperialism, Sovereignty and the Making of International Law*. Cambridge: Cambridge University Press.

Angrist, J. D. and J. Pischke (2010) "The credibility revolution in empirical economics: How better research design is taking the con out of econometrics." *Journal of Economic Perspectives*, 24(2): 3–30.

Angrist, J., P. Azoulay, G. Ellison, R. Hill and S. F. Lu (2020) "Inside job or deep impact? Extramural citations and the influence of economic scholarship." *Journal of Economic Literature*, 58(1): 3–52.

Angus, S. D., K. Atalay, J. Newton and D. Ubilava (2021) "Geographic diversity in economic publishing." *Journal of Economic Behavior & Organization*, 190: 255–62.

Anievas, A. and K. Nisancioglu (2015) *How The West Came to Rule: The Geopolitical Origins of Capitalism*. London: Pluto Press.

Ankarloo, D. (2002) "New Institutional Economics and economic history." *Capital & Class*, 26(3): 9–36.

Antunes de Oliveira, F. (2021) "Who are the super-exploited? Gender, race, and the intersectional potentialities of dependency theory," in A. Madariaga and S. Palestini (eds) *Dependent Capitalisms in Contemporary Latin America and Europe*. Cham, Switzerland: Palgrave Macmillan.

Arboleda, M., T. F. Purcell and P. Roblero (2024) "Fossil food: Landed property as a hidden abode of global warming." *Review of International Political Economy*, 31(1): 149–72.

Arendt, H. (1951) *The Origins of Totalitarianism*. Berlin: Schocken Books.

Arrighi, G., N. Aschoff and B. Scully (2010) "Accumulation by dispossession and its limits: The Southern Africa paradigm revisited." *Studies in Comparative International Development*, 45: 410–38.

Arrow, K. J. (1998) "What has economics to say about racial discrimination?" *Journal of Economic Perspectives*, 12(2): 91–100.

Arrow, K. J. (2007) "Getting to economic equilibrium: A problem and its history," in X. Deng and F. C. Graham (eds) *Internet and Network Economics*. Berlin, Heidelberg: Springer, pp. 1–2.

Arsel, M., A. Dasgupta and S. Storm (2021) "Introduction: The why and how of reclaiming Development Studies," in M. Arsel, A. Dasgupta and S. Storm (eds) *Reclaiming Development Studies: Essays for Ashwini Saith*. New York: Anthem Press.

Asher, S., P. Novosad and C. Rafkin (2024) "Intergenerational mobility in India: New measures and estimates across time and social groups." *American Economic Journal: Applied Economics*, 16(2): 66–98.

Asiyanbi, A. (2019) "Decolonising the environment: Race, rationalities and crises." Sheffield Institute for International Development blog, September 7.

Aspromourgos, T. (1986) "On the origins of the term 'neoclassical'." *Cambridge Journal of Economics*, 10(3): 265–70.

Assie-Lumumba, N-dri T. (2007) *Higher Education in Africa. Crises, Reforms and Transformation*. CODESRIA Working Paper Series. Available at: https://publication.codesria.org/index.php/pub/catalog /download/217/1258/4238?inline=1.

Auerbach, J. (2018) "What a new university in Africa is doing to decolonize social sciences," in S. de Jong, R. Icaza and O. U. Rutazibwa (eds) *Decolonization and Feminisms in Global Teaching and Learning*. New York: Routledge.

Auerbach, P. and P. Skott (2022) "Visions of the future – a socialist departure from gloom?" *PSL Quarterly Review*, 74(298): 155–77.

Austin, R. (2008) "Telling the real tale of the hunt: Toward a race conscious sociology of racial stratification," in T. Zuberi and E. Bonilla-Silva (eds) *White Logic, White Methods: Racism and Methodology*. Lanham, MD: Rowman & Littlefield.

Ayres, C. (1936) "Fifty years' development in ideas of human nature and motivation." *American Economic Review*, 26(1): 224–36.

Azad, R. and S. Chakraborty (2021) "Toward inverting environmental injustice in Delhi." *Economic and Labour Relations Review*, 32(2): 209–29.

Babb, S. (2001) *Managing Mexico: Economists from Nationalism to Neoliberalism*. Princeton, NJ: Princeton University Press.

Bacevic, J. (2019) "Knowing neoliberalism." *Social Epistemology*, 33(4): 380–92.

Bacharach, M. (2006) *Beyond Individual Choice: Teams and Frames in Game Theory*. Princeton, NJ: Princeton University Press.

Backhouse, R. E. (2010) *The Puzzle of Modern Economics: Science or Ideology?* Cambridge: Cambridge University Press.

Bailey, R. (1986) "Africa, the slave trade, and industrial capitalism in Europe and the United States: A historiographic review." *American History: A Bibliographic Review*, 2: 1–91.

Bailey, R. (2014) "Out of sight, out of mind: The struggle of African American intellectuals against the invisibility of the slave(ry) trade in world economic history," in T. D. Boston (ed.) *A Different Vision: Race and Public Policy*. New York: Routledge.

Bambirra, V. (1972) "Women's liberation and class struggle." *Review of Radical Political Economics*, 4(3): 75–84.

Bambirra, V. (1978) *Teoria de La Dependencia – um Anticritica*. Serie Popular Era. Mexico: Ediciones Era.

Banaji, J. (1972) "For a theory of colonial modes of production." *Economic and Political Weekly*, 7(52): 2498–502.

Banaji, J. (2010) *Theory as History: Essays on Modes of Production and Exploitation*. Leiden: Brill.

Banaji, J. (2020) *A Brief History of Commercial Capitalism*. Chicago, IL: Haymarket Books.

Banerjee, A. V. with A. H. Amsden, R. H. Bates, J. N. Bhagwati, A. Deaton and N. Stern (2007) *Making Aid Work*. Cambridge, MA: MIT Press.

Banerjee, A. V. and E. Duflo (2011) *Poor Economics: A Radical Rethinking of the Way to Fight Global Poverty*. New York: PublicAffairs.

Banerjee, A. V. and E. Duflo (2014) "Do firms want to borrow more? Testing credit constraints using a directed lending program." *Review of Economic Studies*, 81(2): 572–607.

Bangasser, P. E. (2000) "The ILO and the informal sector: An institutional history." Employment Paper Working Paper No. 2000/9. Available at: https://www.ilo.org/employment/Whatwedo/Publications/WCMS_142295/lang--en/index.htm.

Barker, D. K. and E. Kuiper (2003) *Toward a Feminist Philosophy of Economics*. New York: Routledge.

Barker, D. K., S. Bergeron and S. Feiner (eds) (2021) *Liberating Economics: Feminist Perspectives on Families, Work, and Globalization*. Ann Arbor, MI: University of Michigan Press.

Barrientos, S. (2019) *Gender and Work in Global Value Chains: Capturing the Gains?* Cambridge: Cambridge University Press.

Bartolovich, C. and N. Lazarus (eds) (2002) *Marxism, Modernity and Postcolonial Studies*. Cambridge: Cambridge University Press.

Basole, A. (2016) "Spare change for spare time? Homeworking women in Banaras," in S. Raju and S. Jatrana (eds) *Women Workers in Urban India*. Cambridge: Cambridge University Press.

Bassier, I. (2016) "UCT's economics curriculum is in crisis: Content of courses is not relevant to South Africa." *Ground Up*, March 9. Available at: https://groundup.org.za/article/ucts-economics-curriculum-crisis/.

Bassier, I. (2023) "Firms and inequality when unemployment is high." *Journal of Development Economics*, 161: 103029.

Basu, A. (1995) "Feminism and nationalism in India, 1917–1947," *Journal of Women's History*, 7(4): 95–107.

Baumol, W. (1995) "What's different about European economics?" *Kyklos*, 48(2): 187–92.

Bayer, A. (2021) "Diversifying economic quality: A wiki for instructors and departments," 2nd edn. Available at: https://works.swarthmore.edu/fac-economics/367.

Bayer, A. and C. E. Rouse (2016) "Diversity in the economics profession: A new attack on an old problem." *Journal of Economic Perspectives*, 30(4): 221–42.

Bayliss, K., B. Fine and E. Van Waeyenberge (2011) *The Political Economy of Development: The World Bank, Neoliberalism and Development Research*. London: Pluto Press.

Becchio, G. (2020) *A History of Feminist and Gender Economics*. Abingdon, Oxon: Routledge.

Becker, G. S. (1957) *The Economics of Discrimination*. Chicago, IL: University of Chicago Press.

Beckert, S. (2014) *Empire of Cotton: A Global History*. New York: Alfred A. Knopf.

Bédécarrats, F., I. Guérin and F. Roubaud (2017) "All that glitters is not gold: The political economy of randomized evaluations in development." *Development and Change*, 50(3): 735–62.

Benería, L. (1992) "Accounting for women's work: The progress of two decades." *World Development*, 20(11): 1547–60.

Berg, M. and P. Hudson (2023) *Slavery, Capitalism and the Industrial Revolution*. Hoboken, NJ: Polity Press.

Bergeron, S. (2004) *Fragments of Development: Nation, Gender and the Space of Modernity*. Ann Arbor, MI: University of Michigan Press.

Berman, E. P. (2022) *Thinking like an Economist*. Princeton, NJ: Princeton University Press.

Bernard, A. (2023) *Decolonizing Literature: An Introduction*. Cambridge: Polity Press.

Berndt, C. (2015) "Behavioural economics, experimentalism and the marketization of development." *Economy and Society*, 44(4): 567–91.

Besley, T. and R. Burgess (2004) "Can labor regulation hinder economic performance? Evidence from India." *Quarterly Journal of Economics*, 119(1): 91–134.

Bettelheim, C. (1972) "Theoretical comments," in A. Emmanuel, *Unequal Exchange: A Study of the Imperialism of Trade*. New York: Monthly Review Press, pp. 271–322.

Bhabha, H. K. (1983) "The other question: The stereotype and colonial discourse." *Screen*, 24(6): 18–36.

Bhabha, H. K. (1994) *The Location of Culture*. New York: Routledge.

Bhambra, G. K. (2014) *Connected Sociologies*. London: Bloomsbury Academic.

Bhambra, G. K. (2022) "For a reparatory social science." *Global Social Challenges Journal*, 1: 8–20.

Bhambra, G. K. and J. Holmwood (2021) *Colonialism and Modern Social Theory*. Cambridge: Polity Press.

Bhambra, G. K., D. Gebrial and K. Nisancioglu (2018) "Introduction: Decolonising the university?" in G. K. Bhambra, D. Gebrial and K. Nisancioglu (eds) *Decolonising the University*. London: Pluto Press.

Bhandar, B. (2018) *The Colonial Lives of Property: Land, Law, and Racial Regimes of Ownership*. Durham, NC: Duke University Press.

Bhattacharjea, A. (2006) "Labour market regulation and industrial

performance in India: A critical review of the empirical evidence."
Indian Journal of Labour Economics, 49(2): 211–32.

Bhattacharya, R., S. Bhattacharya and K. Gill (2017) "The Adivasi land
question in the neoliberal era," in A. P. D'Costa and A. Chakrabarty
(eds) *The Land Question in India: State, Dispossession, and
Capitalist Transition*. Oxford: Oxford University Press.

Bhattacharya, S. (2017) "Reproduction of noncapital: A Marxian
perspective on the informal economy in India," in T. Burczak, R.
Garnett Jr. and R. McIntyre (eds) *Knowledge, Class, and Economics*.
London: Routledge, pp. 346–58.

Bhattacharya, S. and S. Kesar (2020) "Precarity and development:
Production and labor processes in the informal economy in India."
Review of Radical Political Economics, 52(3): 387–408.

Bhattacharya, S. and S. Kesar (2024) "Development economics and the
colonial encounter: Informality, caste, and postcolonial capitalist
development in India." SOAS Working Paper Series.

Bhattacharya, S., S. Kesar and S. Mehra (2022) "Exclusion, surplus
population, and the labour question in postcolonial capitalism:
Future directions in political economy of development." *Review of
Political Economics*, 35(1): 145–73.

Bhattacharya, T. (2017) *Social Reproduction Theory: Remapping
Class, Recentering Oppression*. London: Pluto Press.

Bhattacharyya, G. (2018) *Rethinking Racial Capitalism – Questions of
Reproduction and Survival*. Lanham, MD: Rowman & Littlefield.

Bhopal, K. (2018) *White Privilege: The Myth of a Post-Racial Society*.
Bristol: Bristol University Press.

Bianchini, P., S. S. Ndongo and L. Zeilig (2024) *Revolutionary
Movements in Africa: An Untold Story*. London: Pluto Press.

Blaney, D. L. (2020) "Provincializing economics: Jevons, Marshall
and the colonial imaginaries of free trade." *Review of International
Political Economy*, 28(6): 1533–54.

Blaug, M. (2003) "The formalist revolution of the 1950s." *Journal of
the History of Economic Thought*, 25(2): 145–56.

Blaug, M. (2020) "The unintended effects of markets," in M. Blaug,
Encyclopedia Britannica, History and Theory: Economics. Available
at: https://www.britannica.com/money/economics/The-unintended
-effects-of-markets.

Blaut, J. M. (1993) *The Colonizer's Model of the World: Geographical
Diffusionism and Eurocentric History*. New York: Guilford Press.

Blaut, J. M. (1999) "Marxism and Eurocentric diffusionism," in R.M.
Chilcote (ed.) *The Political Economy of Imperialism*. Dordrecht:
Springer.

Bonefeld, W. (2014) *Critical Theory and the Critique of Political*

Economy: On Subversion and Negative Reason. London: Bloomsbury.

Bonilla-Silva, E. (2003) *Racism Without Racists: Color-Blind Racism and the Persistence of Racial Inequality in the United States.* Lanham, MD: Rowman & Littlefield.

Bonilla-Silva, E. and T. Zuberi (2008) "Toward a definition of white logic and white methods," in T. Zuberi and E. Bonilla-Silva (eds) *White Logic, White Methods – Racism and Methodology.* Lanham, MD: Rowman & Littlefield, pp. 3–27.

Boring, A. and S. Zignago (2018) "Economics: where are the women?" Available at: https://www.banque-france.fr/en/publications-and -statistics/publications/economics-where-are-women.

Boulding, K. (1969) "Economics as a moral science." *American Economic Review*, 59(1): 1–12.

Boutros-Ghali, B. (2006) "Reinventing UNCTAD." South Centre Research Paper No. 7. Available at: https://www.southcentre.int /wp-content/uploads/2013/05/RP7_Reinventing-UNCTAD_EN.pdf.

Bowles, S. (2003) *Microeconomics: Behavior, Institutions, and Evolution.* Princeton, NJ: Princeton University Press.

Bowles, S. and H. Gintis (2000) "Walrasian economics in retrospect." *Journal of Economics Perspectives*, 115(4): 1411–39.

Boyce-Davies, C. (2008). *Left of Karl Marx: The Political Life of Black Communist Claudia Jones.* Durham, NC: Duke University Press.

Brandt, A. M. (1978) "Racism and research: The case of the Tuskegee Syphilis study." *The Hastings Center Report*, 8(6): 21–9.

Braverman, I. (2023) *Settling Nature: The Conservation Regime in Palestine-Israel.* Minneapolis, MN: Minnesota University Press.

Breman, J. and M. Van der Linden (2014) "Informalizing the economy: The return of the social question at a global level." *Development and Change*, 45(5): 920–40.

Brenner, R. (1976) "Agrarian class structure and economic development in pre-industrial Europe." *Past & Present*, 70: 30–75.

Brites, M., F. Almeida and D. Guizzo (2022) "How do heterodox economists connect on social networks? A bibliometrical study of co-authorship in heterodox journals". Paper presented at 50th National Economics Conference of the Brazilian Association of Postgraduate Programmes in Economics (ANPEC), Natal/RN, December.

Brodkin, K. (1998) *How Jews Became White Folks and What That Says About Race in America.* New Brunswick, NJ: Rutgers University Press.

Brown, A. and D. A. Spencer (2014) "Understanding the Global Financial Crisis: Sociology, political economy and heterodox economics." *Sociology*, 48(5): 938–53.

Buckley, W. F. (1951) *God and Man at Yale: The Superstitions of Academic Freedom*. New York: Regnery Publishing.

Buck-Morss, S. (2009) *Hegel, Haiti, and Universal History*. Pittsburgh, PA: University of Pittsburgh Press.

Burden-Stelly, C., P. J. Hudson and J. Pierre (2020) "Racial capitalism, Black liberation, and South Africa editors." *The Black Agenda Report*, December 16. Available at: https://www.blackagendareport.com/racial-capitalism-black-liberation-and-south-africa.

Butler, J. (1990) *Gender Trouble: Feminism and the Subversion of Identity*. London: Routledge.

Büyüm, A. M., C. Kenney, A. Koris, L. Mkumba and T. Raveendran (2020) "Decolonising global health: if not now, when?" *BMJ Global Health*, 5(8): e003394.

Cabral, A. (1972) "Identity and dignity in the national liberation struggle." *Africa Today*, 19(4): 39–47.

Callari, A. (2004) "Economics as a colonial discourse," in S. Charusheela and E. Zein-Elabdin (eds) *Postcolonialism Meets Economics*. London: Routledge, pp. 113–29.

Campbell, A. (2019) "The principles of radical political economics." *American Review of Political Economy*, 14(1): 1–6.

Campling, L., M. Satoshi, J. Pattenden and B. Selwyn (2016) "Class dynamics of development: A methodological note." *Third World Quarterly*, 37(10): 1745–67.

Canclini, G. N. (1995) *Hybrid Cultures: Strategies for Entering and Leaving Modernity*. Minneapolis, MN: University of Minnesota Press.

Cantillon, S., O. Mackett and S. Stevano (2023) *Feminist Political Economy: A Global Perspective*. Newcastle upon Tyne: Agenda Publishing.

Caraballo, J. G. and X. Jiang (2016) "Value-added erosion in global value chains: an empirical assessment." *Journal of Economic Issues*, 50(1): 288–96.

Card, D. and A. B. Krueger (2000) "Minimum wages and employment: A case study of the fast-food industry in New Jersey and Pennsylvania: Reply." *American Economic Review*, 90(5): 1397–420.

Carrasco-Miró, G. (2022) "Decolonizing feminist economics: Interrogating the women's economic empowerment and gender equality development framework." *Social Politics: International Studies in Gender, State & Society*, 29(3): 771–89.

Carroll, J. and R. Manne (1992) *Shutdown: The Failure of Economic Rationalism and How to Rescue Australia*. Melbourne: Text Publishing Co.

Cartwright, N. (2011) "A philosopher's view of the long road from RCTs to effectiveness." *The Lancet*, 377(9775): 1400–1.

Carvalho, J. J. D. and J. Flórez-Flórez (2014) "The meeting of knowledges: A project for the decolonization of universities in Latin America." *Postcolonial Studies*, 17(2): 122–39.

Castelo, C. and M. G. Jerónimo (2017) *Casa dos estudantes do império: dinâmicas coloniais, conexões transnacionais*. Lisbon: Edições.

Césaire, A. (1950) *Discours sur le colonialisme*. Paris: Éditions Réclame.

Chabal, P. and J-P. Daloz (1999) *Africa Works: Disorder as Political Instrument*. Oxford: James Currey.

Chakrabarty, D. (2008) *Provincializing Europe: Postcolonial Thought and Historical Difference*. Princeton: Princeton University Press.

Chakravarty, P. and D. Ferreira da Silva (2012) "Accumulation, dispossession, and debt: The racial logic of global capitalism." *American Quarterly*, 64(3): 361–85.

Chandrachud, A. (2023) *These Seats are Reserved: Caste, Quotas, and the Constitution of India*. Delhi: Penguin Random House India.

Chandrasekhar, C. P. (2005a) "Alexander Gerschenkron and late industrialization," in J. K. Sundaram (ed.) *The Pioneers of Development Economics: Great Economists on Development*. New York: Zed Books.

Chandrasekhar, C. P. (2005b) "Financial liberalization, fragility and the socialization of risk: Can capital controls work?" *Social Scientist*, 33(3/4): 3–39.

Chang, H.-J. (2001) *Intellectual Property Rights and Economic Development: Historical Lessons and Emerging Issues*. Penang, Malaysia: Third World Network.

Chang, H.-J. (2002) *Kicking Away the Ladder: Development Strategy from a Historical Perspective*. New York: Anthem Press.

Chang, H.-J. (2014) *Economics: The User's Guide*. London: Penguin Books.

Chang, K. and L. H. M. Ling (2000) "Globalization and its intimate other: Filipina domestic workers in Hong Kong," in M. Marchand and A. S. Runyan (eds) *Gender and Global Restructuring: Sightings, Sites, and Resistances*. New York: Routledge.

Chappe, R. (2016) "General equilibrium theory: Sound and fury, signifying nothing?" Institute for New Economic Thinking, August 16. Available at: www.ineteconomics.org/perspectives/blog/general -equilibrium-theory-sound-and-fury-signifying-nothing.

Chari, S. (2024) *Apartheid Remains*. Durham, NC: Duke University Press.

Charusheela, S. (2000) "On history, love, and politics." *Rethinking Marxism*, 12(4): 45–61.

Charusheela, S. (2004) "Postcolonial thought, postmodernism and economics – Questions of ontology and ethics," in E. O. Zein-Elabdin and S. Charusheela (eds) *Postcolonialism Meets Economics*. London: Routledge, pp. 40–58.

Charusheela, S. (2005) *Structuralism and Individualism in Economic Analysis: The "Contractionary Devaluation Debate" in Development Economics*. New York: Routledge.

Charusheela, S. (2009) "Social analysis and the capabilities approach: A limit to Martha Nussbaum's universalist ethics." *Cambridge Journal of Economics*, 33(6): 1135–52.

Charusheela, S. (2010) "Engendering feudalism: Modes of production revisited." *Rethinking Marxism*, 22(3): 438–45.

Charusheela, S. (2013) "Intersectionality," in D. M. Figart and T. L. Warnecke (eds) *Handbook of Research on Gender and Economic Life*. Cheltenham: Edward Elgar Publishing.

Charusheela, S. and E. Zein-Elabdin (2003) "Feminism, post-colonial thought and economics," in M. A. Ferber and J. A. Nelson (eds) *Feminist Economics Today: Beyond Economic Man*. Chicago, IL: University of Chicago Press.

Chatterjee, P. (1986) *Nationalist Thought and the Colonial World: A Derivative Discourse?* London: Zed Books.

Chatterjee, P. (1993) *The Nation and its Fragments*. Princeton, NJ: Princeton University Press.

Chatterjee, P. (2008) "Democracy and economic transformation in India." *Economic and Political Weekly*, April 19.

Chauí, M. (2003) "A universidade pública sob nova perspectiva." *Revista Brasileira de Educação*, 24: 5–15.

Chelwa, G. (2021) "Does economics have an 'Africa problem'?" *Economy and Society*, 50(1): 78–99.

Chelwa, G., D. Hamilton and J. Stewart (2022) "Stratification economics: Core constructs and policy implications." *Journal of Economic Literature*, 60(2): 377–99.

Chen, Y. (2022) "How has ecological imperialism persisted? A Marxian critique of the Western climate consensus." *American Journal of Economics and Sociology*, 81(3): 473–501.

Chester, L. and T.-H. Jo (2022) *Heterodox Economics: Legacy and Prospects*. Bristol: World Economics Association.

Chilcote, R. H. and J. Salém Vasconcelos (2022) "Introduction: Whither development theory?" *Latin American Perspectives*, 49(1): 4–17.

Christensen, K. (2001) "'Thank God ... I thought for a moment you were going to confess to converting to socialism!': Gender and identity in Deirdre McCloskey's crossing." *Feminist Economics*, 7(2): 105–20.

Christophers, B. (2014) "From Marx to market and back again: Performing the economy." *Geoforum*, 57: 12–20.

Christophers, B. (2024) *The Price is Wrong: Why Capitalism Won't Save the Planet.* London: Verso.

Cini, L. (2019) "Disrupting the neoliberal university in South Africa: The #FeesMustFall movement in 2015." *Current Sociology*, 67(7): 942–59.

Coase, R. (1978) "Economics and contiguous disciplines." *Journal of Legal Studies*, 7(2): 201–11.

Cohn, S. (2021) "The implications of the triumph of neoclassical economics over Marxist economics in China." *Review of Radical Political Economics*, 53(2): 281–99.

Colander, D. (1995) "Marshallian general equilibrium analysis." *Eastern Economic Journal*, 21(3): 281–93.

Colander, D. (2009) "Moving beyond the rhetoric of pluralism: Suggestions for an 'inside-the-mainstream' heterodoxy," in R. F. Garnett, E. Olsen and M. Starr (eds) *Economic Pluralism*. London: Routledge, pp. 36–47.

Colander, D., R. Holt and B. Rosser Jr. (2004) "The changing face of mainstream economics." *Review of Political Economy*, 16(4): 485–99.

Combahee River Collective (1977) "The Combahee River Collective Statement." Available at: http://circuitous.org/scraps/combahee.html.

Commons, J. (1932) "Institutional economics: Comment." *American Economic Review*, 22(2): 264–8.

Cooke, B. (2003) "A new continuity with colonial administration: Participation in development management." *Third World Quarterly*, 24(1): 47–61.

Cooper, A. (2017 [1892]) *A Voice from the South: By a Black Woman of the South.* Chapel Hill, NC: University of North Carolina Press.

Copley, J. (2024) "Monetary sovereignty and the 'Invisible Leviathan': The politics of Marx's theory of money." *Global Political Economy*, 3(2): 229–49.

Copley, J. and A. Moraitis (2021) "Beyond the mutual constitution of states and markets: On the governance of alienation." *New Political Economy*, 26(3): 490–508.

CORE (2017) *The Economy 1.0.* www.core-econ.org/project/core-the-economy.

CORE (2023) *The Economy 2.0: Microeconomics.* Open access e-text https://core-econ.org/the-economy/.

Cornwall, A. (2007) "Buzzwords and fuzzwords: Deconstructing development discourse." *Development in Practice*, 17(4–5): 471–84.

Cornwall, A. (2018) "Beyond 'empowerment lite': Women's empowerment, neoliberal development and global justice." *Cadernos Pagu*, 52: e185202.

Coville, A., S. Galiani, P. Gertler and S. Yoshida (2023) "Financing municipal water and sanitation services in Nairobi's informal settlements." *The Review of Economics and Statistics*, https://doi.org/10.1162/rest_a_01379.

Cowen, M. P. and R. Shenton (1995) "The invention of development," in J. Crush (ed.) *Power of Development*. London: Routledge, pp. 27–43.

Cowen, M. P. and R. Shenton (1996) *Doctrines of Development*. New York: Routledge.

Cox, O. C. (1948) *Caste, Class and Race: A Study in Social Dynamics*. New York: Monthly Review Press.

Coyle, D. (2007) *The Soulful Science: What Economists Really Do and Why It Matters*. Princeton, NJ: Princeton University Press.

Crenshaw, K. (1989) "Demarginalizing the intersection of race and sex: A black feminist critique of antidiscrimination doctrine, feminist theory and antiracist politics." *The University of Chicago Legal Forum*, 1(8): 139–67.

Crenshaw, K. (1995) "Mapping the margins: Intersectionality, identity, politics, and violence against women of color," in K. Crenshaw, N. Gotanda, G. Peller and K. Thomas (eds) *Critical Race Theory: The Key Writings That Formed the Movement*. New York: New Press, pp. 357–83.

Crenshaw, K., N. Gotanda, G. Peller and K. Thomas (eds) (1995) *Critical Race Theory: The Key Writings That Formed the Movement*. New York: New Press.

Criado Perez, C. (2019) *Invisible Women: Data Bias in a World Designed for Men*. New York: Vintage Books.

Croom, N. N. (2017) "Promotion beyond tenure: Unpacking racism and sexism in the experiences of Black womyn professors." *The Review of Higher Education*, 40(4): 557–83.

Danby, C. (2004) "Contested states, transnational subjects: Toward a post Keynesianism without modernity," in E. O. Zein-Elabdin and S. Charusheela (eds) *Postcolonialism Meets Economics*. London, New York: Routledge.

Danby, C. (2009) "Post-Keynesianism without modernity." *Cambridge Journal of Economics*, 33(6): 1119–33.

Darity, W., Jr (1975a) "The numbers game and the profitability of the British trade in slaves." *Journal of Economic History*, 45(3): 693–703.

Darity, W. (1975b) "Economic theory and racial economic inequality." *The Review of Black Political Economy*, 5(3): 225–48.

Darity, W. A., D. Hamilton and J. B. Stewart (2015) "A tour de force in understanding intergroup inequality: An introduction to stratification economics." *The Review of Black Political Economy*, 42(1–2): 1–6.

Darity Jr, W. A., D. Hamilton, P. L. Mason, G. N. Price, A. Davila, M. T. Mora and S. K. Stockly (2020) "Stratification economics – A general theory of intergroup inequality," in A. Flynn, S. R. Holmberg, D. Warren and F. J. Wong (eds) *The Hidden Rules of Race: Barriers to an Inclusive Economy*, 2nd edn. Cambridge: Cambridge University Press, pp. 35–51.

Das, J., Q.-T. Do, K. Shaines and S. Srikant (2013) "US and them: The geography of academic research." *Journal of Development Economics*, 105: 112–30.

Das Gupta, C. (2016) *State and Capital in Independent India Institutions and Accumulations*. Cambridge: Cambridge University Press.

Davidson, P. (1981) "Post Keynesian economics, the public interest," in D. Bell and I. Kristol (eds) *The Crisis in Economic Theory*. New York: Basic Books, pp. 151–73.

Davis, A. (1981) *Women, Race and Class*. London: Random House.

Davis, J. B. (2003) *The Theory of the Individual in Economics*. London: Routledge.

Davis, K. (2008) "Intersectionality as a buzzword: A sociology of science perspective on what makes a feminist theory successful." *Feminist Theory*, 9(1): 67–85.

Davis, M. (2006) *Planet of Slums*. London: Verso.

De, R. and A. M. Thomas (2018) "Rethinking undergraduate economics education." *Economic & Political Weekly*, 53(3): 21–4.

De Neve, G. (2012) "Weaving for IKEA in South India: Subcontracting, labour markets and gender relations in a global value chain," in J. Assayag and C. Fuller (eds) *Globalizing India: Perspectives from Below*. Cambridge: Cambridge University Press.

de Paula, L. F., B. Fritz and D. M. Prates (2017) "Keynes at the periphery: Currency hierarchy and challenges for economic policy in emerging economies." *Journal of Post Keynesian Economics*, 40(2): 183–202.

de Rezende, F. C. (2009) "The nature of government finance in Brazil." *International Journal of Political Economy*, 38(1): 81–104.

de Soto, H. (2000) *The Mystery of Capital: Why Capitalism Triumphs in the West and Fails Everywhere Else*. New York: Basic Books.

de Sousa Santos, B. (2014) *Epistemologies of the South: Justice against Epistemicide*. Boulder, CO: Paradigm Publishers.

de Souza Leão, L. and G. Eyal (2019) "The rise of randomized controlled trials (RCTs) in international development in historical perspective." *Theory and Society*, 48: 383–418.

deGrassi, A. (2023) "Socionatures, space, and decolonisation: Amílcar Cabral's praxis of dialectics." *Antipode*, 55(5): 1560–86.

Delgado, R. and J. Stefancic (2013) *Critical Race Theory: The Cutting Edge*. Philadelphia, PA: Temple University Press.

DeMartino, G. F. (2011) *The Economist's Oath: On the Need for and Content of Professional Economic Ethics*. Oxford: Oxford University Press.

DeMartino, G. F. (2020) "The confounding problem of the counterfactual in economic explanation." *Review of Social Economy*, 80(2): 127–37.

Demery, L. (1994) "Structural adjustment: Its origins, rationale and achievements," in G. A. Cornia and G. K. Helleiner (eds) *From Adjustment to Development in Africa*. Basingstoke: Palgrave Macmillan, pp. 25–48.

Dengler, C. and L. M. Seebacher (2019) "What about the Global South? Towards a feminist decolonial degrowth approach." *Ecological Economics*, 157: 246–52.

Denning, M. (2010) "Wageless life." *New Left Review*, 66: 79–97.

Dennis, C. A. (2018) "Decolonising education: A pedagogic intervention," in G. K. Bhambra, D. Gebrial and K. Nisancioglu (eds) *Decolonising the University*. London: Pluto Press.

Deos, S. and E. Gerioni (2022) "Macroeconomic policy under a managed floating exchange rate regime: A critical appraisal of the International Currency Hierarchy literature." *Texto Para Discussão*, 428. Sao Paolo: Unicamp.

Deos, S., O. Bullio Mattos, F. Ultremare and A. R. Ribeiro de Mendonca (2021) "Modern money theory: Rise in the international scenario and recent debate in Brazil." *Brazilian Journal of Political Economy*, 41(2): 314–32.

Dequech, D. (2007–8) "Neoclassical, mainstream, orthodox, and heterodox economics." *Journal of Post Keynesian Economics*, 30(2): 279–302.

Dequech, D. (2012) "Post Keynesianism, heterodoxy and mainstream economics." *Review of Political Economy*, 24(2): 353–68.

Deshpande, A. (2002) "Assets versus autonomy? The changing face of the gender-caste overlap in India." *Feminist Economics*, 8(2): 19–35.

Deshpande, A. (2011) *The Grammar of Caste: Economic Discrimination in Contemporary India*. Oxford: Oxford University Press.

Dilawri, S. (2023) "The worldmaking of mobile vernacular capitalists: Tracing entanglements between race, caste and capital." *Millennium*, 52(1): 9–35.

D'Ippoliti, C. (2020) *Democratizing the Economics Debate: Pluralism and Research Evaluation*. London: Routledge.

D'Ippoliti, C. and A. Roncaglia (2015) "Heterodox economics and the history of economic thought," in T.-H. Jo and Z. Todorova (eds)

Advancing the Frontiers of Heterodox Economics: Essays in Honor of Frederic S. Lee. London: Routledge, pp. 21–38.

Dirks, N. B. (1992) *Colonialism and Culture*. Ann Arbor, MI: University of Michigan Press.

Dobb, M. (1972 [1946]) *Studies in the Development of Capitalism*. London: Routledge & Kegan Paul.

Dobusch, L. and J. Kapeller (2012) "Heterodox United vs. Mainstream City? Sketching a framework for interested pluralism in economics." *Journal of Economic Issues*, 46(4): 1035–58.

Donovan, K. P. (2018) "The rise of the Randomistas: On the experimental turn in international aid." *Economy and Society*, 47(1): 27–58.

Dorninger, C., A. Hornborg, D. J. Abson, H. von Wehrden, A. Schaffartzik, S. Giljum, J.-O. Engler, R. L. Feller, K. Hubacek and H. Wieland (2021) "Global patterns of ecologically unequal exchange: Implications for sustainability in the 21st century." *Ecological Economics*, 179: 106824.

dos Santos, T. (1970) "The structure of dependence." *The American Economic Review*, 60(2): 231–6.

Dow, S. C. (1990) "Beyond dualism." *Cambridge Journal of Economics*, 14: 143–57.

Dow, S. C. (1992) "Post Keynesian school," in D. Mair and A. Miller (eds) *Comparative Schools of Economic Thought*. Cheltenham: Edward Elgar.

Dow, S. C. (1997) "Mainstream economic methodology." *Cambridge Journal of Economics*, 21(1): 73–93.

Drèze, J. (2020) "Policy beyond evidence." *World Development*, 127, 104797.

Du Bois, W. E. B. (1935) *Black Reconstruction in America*. New York: Atheneum.

Du Bois, W. E. B. (1995 [1900]) "To the nations of the world," in D. L. Lewis (ed.) *W. E. B. Du Bois: A Reader*. New York: Henry Hold.

Du Bois, W. E. B. (1999 [1920]) "The souls of white folk," in *Darkwater: Voices within the Veil*. Mineola, NY: Dover.

Dube, A., S. Naidu and M. Reich (2007) "The economic effects of a citywide minimum wage." *ILR Review*, 60(4): 522–43.

Duflo, E. (2017) "The economist as plumber." *American Economic Review*, 107(5): 1–26.

Duflo, E., M. Kremer and J. Robinson (2008) "How high are rates of return to fertilizer? Evidence from field experiments in Kenya." *American Economic Review*, 98(2): 482–8.

Duncombe, J. and D. Marsden (1993) "Love and intimacy: The gender division of emotion and 'emotion work': A neglected aspect of sociological discussion of heterosexual relationships." *Sociology*, 27(2): 221–41.

Durand, C. and W. Milberg (2020) "Intellectual monopoly in global value chains." *Review of International Political Economy*, 27: 404–29.

Dussel, E. (1995) Eurocentrism and modernity (Introduction to the Frankfurt Lectures). In: J. Beverley, J. Oviedo and M. Aronna (eds) *The Postmodernism Debate in Latin America*. Durham, NC: Duke University Press, pp. 65–77.

Dussel, E. (2001) *Towards an Unknown Marx: A Commentary on the Manuscripts of 1861–63*. London: Routledge.

Dutt, D. (2021) "The political economy of the cost of foreign exchange intervention." Doctoral Dissertation, University of Massachusetts Amherst.

Eagleton, T. (2015) "The slow death of the university." *The Chronicle of Higher Education*, April 6.

Easton, D. (1991) "The division, integration, and transfer of knowledge," in D. Easton and C. Schelling (eds) *Divided Knowledge: Across Disciplines, Across Cultures*. Newbury Park, CA: Sage, pp. 7–36.

Economic and Political Weekly. 2021. "Rohith Vemula: Foregrounding caste oppression in Indian higher education institutions." *Economic and Political Weekly (Engage)*. Available at: https://www.epw.in /engage/article/rohith-vemula-foregrounding-caste-oppression.

Edwards, Z. (2020) "Applying the Black radical tradition: Class, race, and a new foundation for studies of development," in B. Eidlin and M. A. McCarthy (eds) *Rethinking Class and Social Difference*. Bingley: Emerald Publishing, pp. 155–83.

Eichengreen, B. (2019) *Globalizing Capital: A History of the International Monetary System*. Princeton, NJ: Princeton University Press.

Eichengreen, B. and R. Hausmann (eds) (2005) *Other People's Money: Debt Denomination and Financial Instability in Emerging Market Economies*. Chicago, IL: University of Chicago Press.

Ekbladh, D. (2010) *The Great American Mission: Modernization and the Construction of an American World Order*. Princeton, NJ: Princeton University Press.

El Nabolsy, Z. (2024) "Questions from the Dar es Salaam debates," in P. Bianchini, N. S. Sylla and L. Zeilig (eds) *Revolutionary Movements in Africa: An Untold Story*. London: Pluto Press.

Elson, D. and R. Pearson (1981) "'Nimble fingers make cheap workers': An analysis of women's employment in Third World export manufacturing." *Feminist Review*, 7: 87–107.

Emmanuel, A. (1972a) *Unequal Exchange: A Study of the Imperialism of Trade*. New York: Monthly Review Press.

Emmanuel, A. (1972b) "White-settler colonialism and the myth of investment imperialism." *New Left Review*, I(73): 35.

Engerman, S. L. (1972) "Slave trade and British capital formation in the eighteenth century: A comment on the William Thesis." *Journal of Business History*, 46: 430–43.

Erel, U., J. Haritaworn, E. G. Rodriguez and C. Klesse (2011) "On the depoliticisation of intersectionality talk: Conceptualising multiple oppressions in critical sexuality studies," in Y. Taylor, S. Hines and M. E. Casey (eds) *Theorizing Intersectionality and Sexuality*. New York: Palgrave Macmillan, pp. 56–77.

Escobar, A. (1989) "The professionalization and institutionalization of 'development' in Colombia in the early post World War II period." *Educational Development*, 9(2): 139–54.

Escobar, A. (1995) *Encountering Development: The Making and Unmaking of the Third World*. Princeton, NJ: Princeton University Press.

Everson, T. (2022) "A look into student divestment campaigns at US universities." *DU Clario*, February 7.

Fafchamps, M. (2004) *Market Institutions in Sub-Saharan Africa: Theory and Evidence*. Cambridge, MA: MIT Press.

Fajardo, M. (2022) *The World That Latin America Created: The United Nations Economic Commission for Latin America in the Development Era*. Boston, MA: Harvard University Press.

Falola, T. (2001) *Nationalism and African Intellectuals*. Rochester, NY: University of Rochester Press.

Fanon, F. (2004 [1961]) *Wretched of the Earth*. New York: Grove Press.

Farber, H. S., D. Herbst, I. Kuziemko and S. Naidu (2021) "Unions and inequality over the twentieth century: New evidence from survey data." *The Quarterly Journal of Economics*, 136(3): 1325–85.

Federici, S. (2004) *Caliban and the Witch*. New York: Autonomedia.

Felipe, J. and S. T. Fullwiler (2022) "How 'monetization' really works – Examples from three Asian nations' responses to Covid-19." *Review of Political Economy*, 34(3): 397–419.

Féliz, M. (2014) "Neo-developmentalism, accumulation by dispossession and international rent – Argentina, 2003–2013." *International Critical Thought*, 4(4): 499–509.

Ferber, M. A. and J. A. Nelson (eds) (1993) *Beyond Economic Man: Feminist Theory and Economics*. Chicago, IL: University of Chicago Press.

Ferguson, J. (1990) *The Anti-Politics Machine: "Development," Depoliticization, and Bureaucratic Power in Lesotho*. Cambridge: Cambridge University Press.

Ferguson, S. (2016) "Intersectionality and social-reproduction feminisms: Toward an integrative ontology," *Historical Materialism*, 24(2): 38–60.

Fernandez, B. (2018) "Dispossession and the depletion of social reproduction." *Antipode*, 50: 142–63.

Figart, D. M. (2005) "Gender as more than a dummy variable: Feminist approaches to discrimination." *Review of Social Economy*, 63(3): 509–36.

Fine, B. (1978) "On the origins of capitalist development." *New Left Review*, I/109, 88–95.

Fine, B. (2000) "Endogenous growth theory: A critical assessment." *Cambridge Journal of Economics*, 24(2): 245–65.

Fine, B. (2006) *The New Development Economics: Post Washington Consensus Neoliberal Thinking*. London: Zed Books.

Fine, B. and D. Milonakis (2009) *From Economics Imperialism to Freakonomics: The Shifting Boundaries between Economics and other Social Sciences*. London: Routledge.

Fischer, A. M. (2018) *Poverty as Ideology: Rescuing Social Justice from Global Development Agendas*. London: Bloomsbury Publishing.

Fleetwood, S. (2017) "The critical realist conception of open and closed systems." *Journal of Economic Methodology*, 24(1): 41–68.

Fogel, R. and S. L. Engerman (1974) *Time on the Cross: The Economics of American Negro Slavery*. Boston, MA: Little, Brown and Co.

Folbre, N. (1986) Hearts and spades: Paradigms of household economics. *World Development*, 14(2): 245–55.

Folbre, N. (2012) "Valuing domestic product." *New York Times*, May 28.

Folbre, N. and J. Nelson (2000) "For love or money – Or both?" *Journal of Economic Perspectives*, 14(4): 123–40.

Foley, D. (2006) *Adam's Fallacy*. Boston, MA: Harvard University Press.

Fontana, M., F. Montobbio and P. Racca (2019) "Topics and geographical diffusion of knowledge in top economic journals." *Economic Inquiry*, 57(4): 1771–97.

Fourcade, M. (2009) *Economists and Societies: Discipline and Profession in the United States, Britain, and France, 1890s to 1990s*. Princeton, NJ: Princeton University Press.

Fourcade, M., E. Ollion and Y. Algan (2015) "The superiority of economists." *Revista de Economía Institucional*, 17(33): 13–43.

Foucault, M. (1976) "Society must be defended." Lecture Series.

Franczak, M. (2017) "'Asia' at Bretton Woods: India, China, and Australasia in comparative perspective," in G. Scott-Smith and J. S. Rofe (eds) *Global Perspectives on the Bretton Woods Conference and the Post-War World Order*. Cham, Switzerland: Palgrave Macmillan, pp. 111–27.

Frank, A. G. (1966) "The development of underdevelopment." *Monthly Review*, 18(4): 17.

Frank, A. G. (1967) *Capitalism and Underdevelopment in Latin America: Historical Studies of Chile and Brazil*. New York: Monthly Review Press.

Fraser, N. (2016a) "Contradictions of capital and care." *New Left Review*, 100(99): 99–117.

Fraser, N. (2016b) "Expropriation and exploitation in racialized capitalism: A reply to Michael Dawson." *Critical Historical Studies*, 3(1): 163–78.

Fraser, N. (2017) "Behind Marx's hidden abode: For an expanded conception of capitalism," in C. Lafont and P. Deutscher (eds) *Critical Theory in Critical Times: Transforming the Global Political and Economic Order*. New York: Columbia University Press, pp. 141–59.

Fraser, N. (2019) "Is capitalism necessarily racist?," Politics Letters, May 20. Available at: http://quarterly.politicsslashletters.org/is-capitalism-necessarily-racist/.

Freeman, R. B., D. Xie, H. Zhang and H. Zhou (2024) "High and rising institutional concentration of award-winning economists." NBER Conference Paper. Available at: https://conference.nber.org/conf_papers/f204525.pdf.

Freire, P. (1970) *Pedagogy of the Oppressed*. London: Bloomsbury Academic.

Frieden, J. (2020) "The political economy of economic policy." *Finance and Development*, June 20, pp. 1–9.

Friedman, M. (1962) *Capitalism and Freedom*. Chicago, IL: University of Chicago Press.

Fukuda-Parr, S., J. Heintz and S. Seguino (2015) *Critical Perspectives on Financial and Economic Crises: Heterodox Macroeconomics Meets Feminist Economics*. New York: Routledge.

Furtado, C. (1964) *Development and Underdevelopment*. Berkeley, CA: University of California Press.

Furtado, C. (1970) *Economic Development of Latin America: A Survey from Colonial Times to the Cuban Revolution*. Cambridge: Cambridge University Press.

Furtado, C. (1974) *The Myth of Economic Development and the Future of the Third World*. Cambridge: Cambridge University Press.

Gadha, M. B., F. Kaboub, K. Koddenbrock, I. Mahmoud and N. S. Sylla (2021) *Economic and Monetary Sovereignty in 21st Century Africa*. London: Pluto Press.

Galbraith, J. K. (1998) *The Affluent Society*. Boston, MA: Houghton Mifflin Harcourt.

Galeano, E. (1973) *Open Veins of Latin America*. London: Latin America Bureau.

Galí, J. and M. Gertler (2007) "Macroeconomic modeling for monetary policy evaluation." *Journal of Economic Perspectives*, 21(4): 25–45.

Galí, J., F. Smets and R. Wouters (2012) "Unemployment in an estimated New Keynesian model." *NBER Macroeconomics Annual*, 26(1): 329–60.

Gallas, A. (2018) "Introduction: The proliferation of precarious labour in academia." *Global Labour Journal*, 9(1): 69–75.

Gani, J. K. and J. Marshall (2022) "The impact of colonialism on policy and knowledge production in International Relations." *International Affairs*, 98(1): 5–22.

Gates, D. and P. Steane (2007) "Historical origins and development of economic rationalism." *Journal of Management History*, 13(4): 330–58.

Geda, A. (2011) "African economies and relevant economic analysis: A heterodox approach to economic research in Africa." *CODESRIA Bulletin* 03-04.

Geda, A., L. W. Senbet and W. Simbanegavi (2018) "The illusive quest for structural transformation in Africa: Will China make a difference?" *Journal of African Economies*, 27(1): 4–14.

Gerschenkron, A. (1962) *Economic Backwardness in Historical Perspective*. Cambridge, MA: Belknap Press of Harvard University Press.

Getachew, A. (2019) *Worldmaking After Empire: The Rise and Fall of Self-Determination*. Princeton, NJ: Princeton University Press.

Ghosh, J. (2009) *Never Done and Poorly Paid: Women's Work in Globalizing India*. New Delhi: Women Unlimited.

Ghosh, J. (2021) *Informal Women Workers in the Global South: Policies and Practices for the Formalisation of Women's Employment in Developing Economies*. London: Routledge.

Gibson-Graham, J. K. (1993) "Waiting for the revolution, or How to smash capitalism while working at home in your spare time." *Rethinking Marxism*, 6(2): 10–24.

Gibson-Graham, J. K. (1996) *The End of Capitalism (as We Knew It): A Feminist Critique of Political Economy*. Oxford: Blackwell.

Gibson-Graham, J. K. (2006) *A Postcapitalist Politics*. Minneapolis, MN: University of Minnesota Press.

Gilmore, R. W. (2011) "What is to be done?" *American Quarterly*, 63(2): 245–65.

Gilmore, R. W. (2022) *Abolition Geography: Essays Towards Liberation*. London: Verso.

Gimene, M., D. N. Conceição and A. de Melo Modenesi (2022) "Limits to the exercise of monetary sovereignty in peripheral countries." *Cadernos de Finanças Públicas*, 22(2).

Giraud, Y. (2014) "Negotiating the 'middle of the road' position: Paul Samuelson, MIT, and the politics of textbook writing," in E. R. Weintraub (ed.) *MIT and the Transformation of American Economics*. Durham, NC: Duke University Press, pp. 134–52.

Giroux, H. A. (2014) *Neoliberalism's War on Higher Education*. Chicago, IL: Haymarket Books.

Go, J. (2013) "For a postcolonial sociology." *Theory and Society*, 42(1): 25–55.

Go, J. (2016) *Postcolonial Thought and Social Theory*. Oxford: Oxford University Press.

Go, J. (2023) *Policing Empires: Militarization, Race, and the Imperial Boomerang in Britain and the US*. Oxford: Oxford University Press.

Gomez Betancourt, R. and C. Orozco Espinel (2018) "The invisible ones: Women at CEPAL (1948–2017)," in K. Madden and R. W. Dimand (eds) *The Routledge Handbook of the History of Women's Economic Thought*. New York: Routledge.

Gonzalez Casanova, P. (1965) "Internal colonialism and national development." *Studies in Comparative International Development*, 1(4): 27–37.

Goodacre, H. (2018) *The Economic Thought of William Petty: Exploring the Colonialist Roots of Economics*. London: Routledge.

Goodwin, C. (1998) "The patrons of economics in a time of transformation," in M. S. Morgan and M. Rutherford (eds) *From Interwar Pluralism to Postwar Neoclassicism*. Durham, NC: Duke University Press, pp. 53–81.

Gopal, P. (2021) "On decolonisation and the university." *Textual Practice*, 35(6): 873–99.

Gordon, L. R. and J. A. Gordon (2006) *Not Only the Master's Tools: African American Studies in Theory and Practice*. Boulder, CO: Paradigm.

Gornitzka, Å., S. Kyvik and I. M. Larsen (1998) "The bureaucratisation of universities." *Minerva*, 36(1): 21–47.

Gough, K. (1968) "Anthropology and imperialism." *Monthly Review*, April, 12–27.

Graeber, D. (2011) *Debt: The First 5000 Years*. Brooklyn, NY: Melville House.

Grande, S. (2004) *Red Pedagogy: Native American Social and Political Thought*. Boulder, CO: Rowman & Littlefield.

Grewal, I. and C. Kaplan (1994) *Scattered Hegemonies: Postmodernity and Transnational Feminist Practices.* Minneapolis, MN: University of Minnesota Press.

Grinberg, N. (2018) "Institutions and capitalist development: A critique of the new institutional economics." *Science & Society*, 82(2): 203–33.

Grosfoguel, R. (2007) "The epistemic decolonial turn: Beyond political-economy paradigms." *Cultural Studies*, 21(2–3): 211–23.

Guizzo, D. (2020) "Why does the history of economic thought neglect Post-Keynesian economics?" *Review of Keynesian Economics*, 8(1): 119–37.

Guizzo, D., A. Mearman and S. Berger (2021) "'TAMA' economics under siege in Brazil: The threats of curriculum governance reform." *Review of International Political Economy*, 28(1): 258–81.

Gupta, C. (2010) "Feminine, criminal or manly? Imaging Dalit masculinities in colonial North India." *Indian Economic Social History Review*, 47(3): 309–42.

Habib, I. (2017) "Towards a political economy of colonialism." *Social Scientist*, 45(3/4): 9–15.

Hamouchene, H. (2023) *Dismantling Green Colonialism: Energy and Climate Justice in the Arab Region.* London: Pluto Press.

Harding, S. (1992) "Rethinking standpoint epistemology: What is 'strong objectivity'?" *The Centennial Review*, 36(3): 437–70.

Harding, S. (1995) "Can feminist thought make economics more objective?" *Feminist Economics*, 1(1): 7–32.

Harding, S. (1997) "Comment on Hekman's 'Truth and method: Feminist standpoint theory revisited': Whose standpoint needs the regimes of truth and reality?" *Signs: Journal of Women in Culture and Society*, 22(2): 382–91.

Hartley, D. (2006) "The instrumentalization of the expressive in education," in A. Moore (ed.) *Schooling, Society and Curriculum.* London: Routledge.

Hartsock, N. (2006) "Globalization and primitive accumulation: The contributions of David Harvey's dialectical Marxism," in N. Castree and D. Gregory (eds) *David Harvey: A Critical Reader.* Oxford: Blackwell Publishing, pp. 167–90.

Harvey, D. (2003) *The New Imperialism.* Oxford: Oxford University Press.

Haupert, M. (2017) "The impact of cliometrics on economics and history." *Revue d'économie politique*, 6(127): 1059–81.

Heckman, J. J. and S. Moktan (2020) "Publishing and promotion in economics: The tyranny of the top five." *Journal of Economic Literature*, 58(2): 419–70.

Helleiner, E. (2014) *Forgotten Foundations of Bretton Woods:*

International Development and the Making of the Postwar Order. Ithaca, NY: Cornell University Press.

Helleiner, E. (2018) "Sun Yat-Sen as a pioneer of international development." *History of Political Economy*, 50(S1): 76–93.

Helleiner, E. (2021) *The Neomercantilists: A Global Intellectual History.* Ithaca, NY: Cornell University Press.

Hewitson, G. J. (1999) *Feminist Economics: Interrogating the Masculinity of Rational Economic Man.* Northampton, MA: Edward Elgar.

Hickel, J., D. Sullivan and H. Zoomkawala (2021) "Plunder in the post-colonial era: Quantifying drain from the Global South through unequal exchange, 1960–2018." *New Political Economy*, 26(6): 1030–47.

Hirschman, A. O. (1961) *The Strategy of Economic Development.* New Haven, CT: Yale University Press.

Hirschman, A. O. (1970) *Exit, Voice, and Loyalty: Responses to Decline in Firms, Organizations, and States.* Cambridge, MA: Harvard University Press.

Hirschman, A. O. (1981) *Essays in Trespassing: Economics to Politics and Beyond.* Cambridge: Cambridge University Press.

Hirschman, D. and E. P. Berman (2014) "Do economists make policies? On the political effects of economics." *Socio-economic Review*, 12(4): 779–811.

Hobson, J. M. (2004) *The Eastern Origins of Western Civilisation.* Cambridge: Cambridge University Press.

Hobson, J. M. (2012) *The Eurocentric Conception of World Politics: Western International Theory, 1760–2010.* Cambridge: Cambridge University Press.

Hodgson, G. M. (2009) "Institutional economics into the twenty-first century." *Studi e Note Di Economia*, 14(1): 3–26.

Hoffman, N. (2020) "Involuntary experiments in former colonies: The case for a moratorium." *World Development*, 127: 104805.

Hong, K. (2008) "Professionalization and the spread of marginalist economics in the United States." *The Kyoto Economic Review*, 77(2): 127–55.

hooks, b. (1994) *Teaching to Transgress: Education as the Practice of Freedom.* New York: Routledge.

hooks, b. (2000) *Where We Stand: Class Matters.* New York: Routledge.

Hostettler, N. (2012) *Eurocentrism: A Marxian Critical Realist Critique.* London: Routledge.

Hountondji, P. J. (1990) "Scientific Dependence in Africa Today." *Research in African Literatures*, 21(3): 5–15.

Hountondji, P. J. (ed.) (1997) *Endogenous Knowledge: Research Trails.* Dakar, Senegal: Codesria.

Howey, R. S. (1989) *The Rise of the Marginal Utility School, 1870–1889*. New York: Columbia University Press.

Huber, M. T. (2022) *Climate Change as Class War: Building Socialism on a Warming Planet*. London: Verso.

Hudec, R. E. (1987) *Developing Countries in the GATT Legal System*. London: Trade Policy Research Center.

Hudson, M. (2003) *Super Imperialism: The Origins and Fundamentals of US World Dominance*. London: Pluto Press.

Hudson, P. J. (2018) "Racial capitalism and the dark proletariat." *Boston Review*, February 20.

Hull, G. (2021) "Some pitfalls of decolonial theory." *The Thinker: A Pan African Quarterly for Thought Leaders*, 89(4): 63–74.

Hull, G. T., P. B. Scott, and B. Smith (eds) (1982) *All the Women Are White, All the Blacks Are Men, But Some of Us Are Brave*. Old Westbury, NY: The Feminist Press.

Hunter, M. (2002) "Rethinking epistemology, methodology, and racism: Or, is White sociology really dead?" *Race and Society*, 5(2): 119–38.

Ikejiaku, B. (2014) "International law is Western made global law: The perception of Third-World category." *African Journal of Legal Studies*, 6(2–3): 337–56.

Ilaiah, K. (1990) "SCs and STs: Systemic exploitation." *Economic and Political Weekly*, 25(51): 2771–4.

ILO (International Labour Organization) (2022) *World Employment and Social Outlook – Trends 2022*. Geneva: International Labour Office.

Inayatullah, N. and D. L. Blaney (2015) "A problem with levels: How to engage a diverse IPE." *Contexto Internacional*, 37: 889–911.

Ince, O. U. (2018) *Colonial Capitalism and the Dilemmas of Liberalism*. Oxford: Oxford University Press.

Ince, O. U. (2022a) "Saving capitalism from empire: Uses of colonial history in new institutional economics." *International Relations*, https://doi.org/10.1177/00471178221104699.

Ince, O. U. (2022b) "Deprovincializing racial capitalism: John Crawfurd and settler colonialism in India." *American Political Science Review*, 116(1): 144–60.

Inikori, J. (1976) "Measuring the Atlantic slave trade: An assessment of Curtin and Anstey." *Journal of African History*, 17: 197–223.

Inikori, J. (1981) "Market structure and the profits of the British African trade in the late eighteenth century." *Journal of Economic History*, 41: 745–76.

Inikori, J. (2020) "Atlantic slavery and the rise of the capitalist global economy." *Current Anthropology*, 61(S22): S159–S171.

Irwin, R. (2018) *Ibn Khaldun: An Intellectual Biography*. Princeton, NJ: Princeton University Press.

Işıkara, G. (2023) "Capitalism, economics, and externalities: What are externalities external to?" *Capitalism Nature Socialism*, 34(2): 40–56.

Jaffé, W. (ed.) (1965) *Correspondence of Leon Walras and Related Papers, vol. III*. Amsterdam: North-Holland.

James, C. L. R. (1963 [1938]) *The Black Jacobins: Toussaint L'Ouverture and the San Domingo Revolution*. New York: Vintage Books.

Jayawardena, K. (1986) *Feminism and Nationalism in the Third World*. London: Zed Books.

Jenkins, D. and J. Leroy (2021) *Histories of Racial Capitalism*. New York: Columbia University Press.

Jennings, M. (2005) "A short history of failure? Development processes over the course of the twentieth century," in A. S. Huque and H. Zafarullah (eds) *International Development Governance*. New York: Marcel Dekker, pp. 599–610.

Jevons, S. W. (2012) *Theory of Political Economy*. San Bernardino, CA: Forgotten Books.

Jo, T.-H., L. Chester and C. D'Ippoliti (2017) *The Routledge Handbook of Heterodox Economics: Theorizing, Analyzing, and Transforming Capitalism*. London: Routledge.

Jodhka, S. S. (2017) *Caste in Contemporary India*. Delhi: Routledge India.

Johnson-Odim, C. (1992) "On behalf of women and the nation: Funmilayo Ransome-Kuti and the struggles for Nigerian independence," in C. Johnson-Odim and M. Strobel (eds) *Expanding the Boundaries of Women's History: Essays on Women in the Third World*. Bloomington, IN: Indiana University Press.

Joireman, S. F. (2008) "The mystery of capital formation in sub-Saharan Africa: Women, property rights and customary law." *World Development*, 36(7): 1233–46.

Kabeer, N. (2020) "Women's empowerment and economic development: A feminist critique of storytelling practices in 'Randomista' economics." *Feminist Economics*, 26(2): 1–26.

Kalecki, M. (1943) "Political aspects of full employment." *The Political Quarterly*, 14(4): 322–30.

Kamola, I. A. (2019) *Making the World Global: US Universities and the Production of the Global Imaginary*. Durham, NC: Duke University Press.

Kapoor, I. (2002) "Capitalism, culture, agency: Dependency versus postcolonial theory." *Third World Quarterly*, 23(4): 647–64.

Kassem, S. (2023) *Work and Alienation in the Platform Economy:*

Amazon and the Power of Organization. Bristol: Bristol University Press.

Katz, C. (2023) *Dependency Theory After Fifty Years: The Continuing Relevance of Latin American Critical Thought*. Chicago, IL: Haymarket Books.

Kaul, N. (2007) *Imagining Economics Otherwise – Encounters with Identity/Difference*. New York: Routledge.

Kay, C. (1989) *Latin American Theories of Development and Underdevelopment*. London: Routledge.

Kay, C. (2009) "The Latin American Structuralist School," in R. Kitchin and N. Thrift (eds) *International Encyclopaedia of Human Geography*. Amsterdam: Elsevier.

Kay, C. (2020) "Theotonio Dos Santos (1936–2018): The revolutionary intellectual who pioneered dependency theory." *Development and Change*, 51(2): 599–630.

Kay, G. (1975) *Development and Underdevelopment: A Marxist Analysis*. London: Palgrave Macmillan.

Kayatekin, S. A. (2009) "Between political economy and postcolonial theory: first encounters." *Cambridge Journal of Economics*, 33(6): 1113–18.

Keeanga-Yamahtta, T. (2016) *From# BlackLivesMatter to Black Liberation*. Chicago, IL: Haymarket Books.

Keita, L. (2020) "Eurocentrism and the contemporary social sciences." *Africa Development*, 45(2): 17–38.

Kelton, S. (2020) *The Deficit Myth: Modern Monetary Theory and the Birth of the People's Economy*. New York: PublicAffairs.

Kentikelenis, A. E., T. H. Stubbs and L. P. King (2016) "IMF conditionality and development policy space, 1985–2014." *Review of International Political Economy*, 23(4): 543–82.

Kesar, S. (2024) "Subcontracting linkages in India's informal economy." *Development and Change*, 55(1): 38–75.

Kesar, S. and S. Bhattacharya (2020) "Dualism and structural transformation: The informal manufacturing sector in India." *European Journal of Development Research*, 32: 560–86.

Kesar, S. and I. H. Kvangraven (2024) *Decolonizing Economic Development: Investigating the INGOs Sector*. London: Bond.

Kesar, S., S. Bhattacharya and L. Banerjee (2022) "Contradictions and crisis in the world of work: Informality, precarity and the pandemic," *Development and Change*, 53(6): 1254–82.

Khan, M. H. (2012) "Beyond good governance: An agenda for developmental governance," in J. K. Sundaram and A. Chowdhury (eds) *Is Good Governance Good for Development?* London: Bloomsbury Academic.

Khan, M. (2021) "The indebted among the 'free': Producing Indian labour through the layers of racial capitalism," in D. Jenkins and J. Leroy (eds) *Histories of Racial Capitalism*. New York: Columbia University Press.

Khan, T., K. Dickson and M. Sondarjee (2023) *White Saviorism in International Development: Theories, Practices and Lived Experiences*. Quebec: Daraji Press.

Khudori, D., D. A. Arimbi and I. Bazié (2022) *Bandung-Belgrade-Havana in Global History and Perspective: The Deployment of Bandung Constellation towards a Global Future*. Jawa Timur, Indonesia: Penerbit Airlangga University Press.

Kiely, R. (1999) "The last refuge of the noble savage? A critical assessment of post-development theory." *European Journal of Development Research*, 11(1): 30–55.

Kimambo, I. (2008) *In Search of Relevance: A History of the University of Dar-es-Salaam*. Dares-Salaam, Tanzania: Dar-es-Salaam University Press.

Kinstler, L. (2024) "How poor Kenyans became economists' guinea pigs." *The Economist*, March 1.

Klaes, M. and E.-M. Sent (2005) "A conceptual history of the emergence of bounded rationality." *History of Political Economy*, 37(1): 27–59.

Klamer, A. (2007) *Speaking of Economics: How to Get in the Conversation*. London: Routledge.

Knafo, S., S. J. Dutta, R. Lane and S. Wyn-Jones (2019) "The managerial lineages of neoliberalism." *New Political Economy*, 24(2): 235–51.

Koddenbrock, K. and N. S. Sylla (2019) "Towards a political economy of monetary dependency: The case of the CFA franc in West Africa." MaxPo Discussion Paper No. 19/2.

Koddenbrock, K., I. H. Kvangraven and N. S. Sylla (2022) "Beyond financialisation: the *longue durée* of finance and production in the Global South." *Cambridge Journal of Economics*, 46(4): 703–33.

Koechlin, T. (2018) "The sound of silence: Capitalism, 'choice,' and racial inequality." *Challenge*, 61: 435–49.

Koechlin, T. (2019) "Whitewashing capitalism: Mainstream economics' resounding silence on race and racism." *Review of Radical Political Economics*, 51(4): 562–71.

Konadu-Agyemang, K. (ed.) (2018) *IMF and World Bank Sponsored Structural Adjustment Programs in Africa: Ghana's Experience, 1983–1999*. London: Routledge.

Koram, K. (2022) *Uncommon Wealth: Britain and the Aftermath of Empire*. London: John Murray.

Kothari, U. (2019) "From colonialism administration to development studies: A postcolonial critique of the history of development studies," in U. Kothari (ed.) *A Radical History of Development Studies: Individuals, Institutions and Ideologies*. London: Zed Books, pp. 47–66.

Krueger, A. (2004) "Meant well, tried little, failed much: Policy reforms in emerging market economies." Remarks by Anne O. Krueger, Acting Managing Director, IMF, March 23.

Krugman, P. and R. Wells (2005) *Economics*. New York: Worth Publishers.

KS, J. and B. Fine (2006) *The New Development Economics: After the Washington Consensus*. New York: Zed Books.

Kuhn, T. (1962) *The Structure of Scientific Revolutions*. Chicago, IL: University of Chicago Press.

Kuiper, E. (2022) *A Herstory of Economics*. Cambridge: Polity Press.

Kurz, H. D. (2009) "Ricardian vice," in W. A. Darity (ed.) *International Encyclopedia of the Social Sciences*, 2nd edn. Detroit, MI: Macmillan Reference USA, pp. 241–3.

Kurz, H. D. (2017) "Is there a 'Ricardian Vice'? And what is its relationship with economic policy ad'vice'?" *Journal of Evolutionary Economics*, 27: 91–114.

Kvangraven, I. H. (2020) "Nobel rebels in disguise: The rise and rule of the Randomistas." *Review of Political Economy*, 32(3): 305–41.

Kvangraven, I. H. (2021) "Beyond the stereotype: Restating the relevance of the dependency research programme." *Development and Change*, 52(1): 76–112.

Kvangraven, I. H. (2023) "Dependency theory: Strengths, weaknesses, and its relevance today," in E. S. Reinert and I. H. Kvangraven (eds) *A Modern Guide to Uneven Economic Development*. Cheltenham, UK: Edward Elgar, pp. 147–70.

Kvangraven, I. H. and C. Alves (2019) "Heterodox Economics as a Positive Project: Revisiting the Debate." ESRC GPID Research Network Working Paper 19.

Kvangraven, I. H. and S. Kesar (2023) "Standing in the way of rigor? Economics' meeting with the decolonizing agenda." *Review of International Political Economy*, 30(5): 1723–48.

Kvangraven, I. H. and M. D. Styve (2024) "The hierarchies of global finance: An anti-disciplinary research agenda." *Review of Political Economy*, 36(2): 504–27.

Kvangraven, I. H., M. D. Styve and U. Kufakurinani (2021) "Samir Amin and beyond: The enduring relevance of Amin's approach to political economy." *Review of African Political Economy*, 48(167): 1–7.

Lakatos, I. (1978) *The Methodology of Scientific Research Programmes: Philosophical Papers Volume 1*. Cambridge: Cambridge University Press.

Landes, D. S. (2006) "Why Europe and the West? Why not China?" *Journal of Economic Perspectives*, 20(2): 3–22.

Landy, D., R. Lentin and C. McCarthy (2020) *Enforcing Silence: Academic Freedom, Palestine and the Criticism of Israel*. London: Bloomsbury.

Langdon, J. (2013) "Decolonising development studies: Reflections on critical pedagogies in action." *Canadian Journal of Development Studies*, 34(3): 384–99.

Larsen, N. (2022) "The jargon of decoloniality." *Catalyst: A Journal of Theory & Strategy*, 6(2).

Lavoie, M. (2000) "A post Keynesian view of interest parity theorems." *Journal of Post Keynesian Economics*, 23(1): 163–79.

Lawson, T. (2006) "The nature of heterodox economics." *Cambridge Journal of Economics*, 30(4): 483–505.

Lawson, T. (2013) "What is this 'school' called neoclassical economics?" *Cambridge Journal of Economics*, 37(5): 947–83.

Lazarus, N. (2011) "What postcolonial theory doesn't say." *Race and Class*, 53: 3–27.

Lazear, E. P. (2000) "Economics imperialism." *Quarterly Journal of Economics*, 115(1): 99–146.

Le Grand, J., C. Propper and S. Smith (2008) *The Economics of Social Problems*. Basingstoke: Palgrave Macmillan.

Lee, C. J. (2019) *Making a World after Empire: The Bandung Moment and Its Political Afterlives*. Athens, OH: Ohio University Press.

Lee, F. S. (2009) *A History of Heterodox Economics: Challenging the Mainstream in the Twentieth Century*. London: Routledge.

Lee, F. S. and B. C. Cronin (2010) "Research quality rankings of heterodox economic journals in a contested discipline." *American Journal of Economics and Sociology*, 69(5): 1409–52.

Lee, F. S. and T.-H. Jo (2018) *Microeconomic Theory: A Heterodox Approach*. London: Routledge.

Leech, G. (2012) *Capitalism: A Structural Genocide*. London: Zed Books.

Lehmann, D. (2022) *After the Decolonial*. Cambridge: Polity Press.

Leibowitz, M. (2003) *Beyond Capital*. Basingstoke, UK: Palgrave.

Lenin, V. (1902) *What Is to Be Done? Burning Questions of Our Movement*. Stuttgart: J. H. W. Dietz.

Lerner, A. P. (1972) "The economics and politics of consumer sovereignty." *American Economic Review*, 62(1–2): 258–66.

Lewis, A. and M. Lall (2024) "From decolonisation to authoritarianism: the co-option of the decolonial agenda in higher education by right-wing nationalist elites in Russia and India." *Higher Education*, 87: 1471–88.

Lewis, T. E. (2020) "Education for potentiality (against instrumentality)." *Policy Futures in Education*, 18(7): 878–91.

Lewis, W. A. (1954) "Economic development with unlimited supplies of labour." *The Manchester School*, 22(2): 139–91.

Li, T. M. (2010) "To make live or let die? Rural dispossession and the protection of surplus populations." *Antipode*, 41(s1): 66–93.

Lin, J. (2011) "New structural economics: A framework for rethinking development." *The World Bank Research Observer*, 26(2): 193–221.

Lin, J. and H.-J. Chang (2009) "Should industrial policy in developing countries conform to comparative advantage or defy it? A debate between Justin Lin and Ha-Joon Chang." *Development Policy Review*, 27(5): 483–502.

Lipietz, A. (1982) "Marx or Rostow?" *New Left Review*, 48(132).

List, F. (1841) *The National System of Political Economy*. New York: Augustus M. Kelly.

Locker-Biletzki, A. (2018) "Rethinking settler colonialism: A Marxist critique of Gershon Shafir." *Rethinking Marxism*, 30(3): 441–61.

Loewenstein, A. (2023) *The Palestine Laboratory: How Israel Exports the Technology of Occupation Around the World*. London: Verso.

Loomba, A. (2009) "Race and the possibilities of comparative critique." *New Literary History*, 40(3): 501–22.

Love, J. L. (1980) "Raúl Prebisch and the origins of the doctrine of unequal exchange." *Latin American Research Review*, 15(3): 45–72.

Lugones, M. (2010) "Toward a decolonial feminism." *Hypatia*, 25(4): 742–59.

Lukka, P. (2020) "Repairing harm caused: What could a reparations approach mean for the IMF and World Bank?" Bretton Woods Project, October 6.

Macekura, S. and E. Manela (eds) (2018) *The Development Century: A Global History*. Cambridge: Cambridge University Press.

Madden, K. and R. W. Dimand (2018) *Routledge Handbook of the History of Women's Economic Thought*. New York: Routledge.

Madra, Y. (2017) *Late Neoclassical Economics: The Restoration of Theoretical Humanism in Contemporary Economic Theory*. London: Routledge.

Majumdar, N. (2021) *The World in a Grain of Sand: Postcolonial Literature and Radical Universalism*. London: Verso Books.

Maldonado-Torres, N., R. Vizcaino, J. Wallace and J. E. A. We (2018) "Decolonising philosophy," in G. K. Bhambra, D. Gebrial and K. Nişancıoğlu (eds) *Decolonising the University*. London: Pluto, pp. 64–89.

Mamdani, M. (1996) *Citizen and Subject: Contemporary Africa and the Legacy of Late Colonialism*. Princeton, NJ: Princeton University Press.

Mamdani, M. (2007) *Scholars in the Marketplace: The Dilemmas of Neo-Liberal Reform at Makerere University, 1989–2005*. Kampala: Fountain Publisher.

Mamdani, M. (2016) "Between the public intellectual and the scholar: Decolonization and some post-independence initiatives in African higher education." *Inter-Asia Cultural Studies*, 17(1): 68–83.

Mankiw, N. G. (2008) *Principles of Economics*, 6th edn. Mason, OH: South-Western Cengage Learning.

Mankiw, N. G. (2020) *Principles of Economics*, 9th edn. Boston, MA: Cengage.

Marglin, S. A. (1974) "What do bosses do? The origins and functions of hierarchy in capitalist production." *Review of Radical Political Economics*, 6(2): 60–112.

Margulis, M. E. (2017) *The Global Political Economy of Raúl Prebisch*. New York: Routledge.

Marini, R. M. (1978) "Las Razones Del Neodesarollismo (Respuesta a F. H. Cardoso y J. Serra) [The reasons for neo-developmentalism (A reply to F. H. Cardoso and J. Serra)]." *Revista Mexicana de Sociologia*, 40(E): 57–106.

Marini, R. M. (2011 [1973]) "Dialética da dependencia," in J. P. Stedile and R. Traspadini (eds) *Ruy Mauro Marini – vida e obra*. São Paulo: Expressao Popular. Translated as: Marini, R.M. (2022) *Dialectics of Dependency*. New York: Monthly Review Press.

Marshall, A. (1930) *Principles of Economics*, 8th edn. London: Macmillan.

Marx, K. (1977 [1867]) *Capital: A Critique of Political Economy, vol. 1*. New York: Vintage Books.

May, A. M., M. McGarvey and D. Kucera (2018) "Gender and European economic policy: A survey of the views of European economists on the contemporary economic policy." *International Review of Social Sciences*, 71(1): 162–83.

Mayer, T. (1992) *Truth versus Precision in Economics*. Cheltenham, UK: Edward Elgar.

Mbiti, J. S. (1990) *African Religions and Philosophy*, 2nd edn. Oxford: Heinemann.

McCall, L. (2005) "The complexity of intersectionality." *Signs: Journals of Women in Culture and Society*, 30(3): 1771–800.

McCloskey, D. N. (1985) *The Rhetoric of Economics*. Madison, WI: University of Wisconsin Press.

McClure, J. (2021) "Connected global intellectual history and the decolonisation of the curriculum," *History Compass*, 19(1): e12645.

McDowell, D. (2017) *Brother, Can You Spare a Billion? The United States, The IMF, and the International Lender of Last Resort.* Oxford: Oxford University Press.

McGee, T. (1973) "Peasants in the cities: a paradox, a paradox, a most ingenious paradox." *Human Organization*, 32(2): 135–42.

McGoey, L. (2017) "The elusive rentier rich: Piketty's data battles and the power of absent evidence." *Science, Technology, & Human Values*, 42(2): 257–79.

McKenzie, F. (2020) *GATT and Global Order in the Postwar Era.* Cambridge: Cambridge University Press.

McKittrick, K. (2015) *Sylvia Wynter: On Being Human as Praxis.* Durham, NC: Duke University Press.

McKittrick, K. (2021) *Dear Science and Other Stories.* Durham, NC: Duke University Press.

McPake, B., C. Normand, S. Smith and A. Nolan (2020) *Health Economics: An International Perspective.* London: Routledge.

McVety, A. (2018) "Wealth and nations: The origins of international development assistance," in S. J. Macekura and E. Manela (eds) *The Development Century: A Global History.* Cambridge: Cambridge University Press, pp. 21–39.

Meagher, K. (2019) "Working in chains: African informal workers and global value chains." *Agrarian South: Journal of Political Economy*, 8(1–2): 64–92.

Mearman, A. (2011) "Who do heterodox economists think they are?" *American Journal of Economics and Sociology*, 70(2): 480–510.

Mearman, A., D. Guizzo and S. Berger (2018a) "Whither political economy? Evaluating the CORE project as a response to calls for change in economics teaching." *Review of Political Economy*, 30(2): 241–59.

Mearman, A., D. Guizzo and S. Berger (2018b) "Is UK economics teaching changing? Evaluating the new subject benchmark statement." *Review of Social Economy*, 76(3): 377–96.

Mearman, A., S. Berger and D. Guizzo (2019) *What is Heterodox Economics? Conversations with Leading Economists.* London: Routledge.

Meek, R. (1976) *Social Science and the Ignoble Savage.* Cambridge: Cambridge University Press.

Meghji, A. (2021) *Decolonizing Sociology: An Introduction.* Cambridge: Polity Press.

Meier, G. M. (1974) *Problems of Cooperation for Development.* London: Oxford University Press.

Melamed, J. (2015) "Racial capitalism." *Critical Ethnic Studies*, 1(1): 76–85.

Menkiti, I. A. (1984) "Person and community in African traditional thought," in R. A. Wright (ed.) *African Philosophy: An Introduction*, 3rd edn. New York: University Press of America, pp. 171–81.

Mentan, T. (2015) *Decolonizing Democracy from Western Cognitive Imperialism*. Bamenda: Langaa Research & Publishing CIG.

Meyer, B. (2002) "Extraordinary stories: Disability, queerness and feminism." *NORA: Nordic Journal of Feminist and Gender Research*, 10(3): 168–73.

Mies, M. (1982) *Lace Makers of Narsapur: Indian Housewives Produce for the World Market*. London: Zed Books.

Mies, M. (1986) *Patriarchy and Accumulation on a World Scale: Women in the International Division of Labour*. London: Zed Books.

Milanovic, B. (2012) "Global inequality: From class to location, from proletarians to migrants." *Global Policy*, 3(2): 125–34.

Milonakis, D. and B. Fine (2009) *From Political Economy to Economics: Method, the Social and the Historical in the Evolution of Economic Theory*. New York: Routledge.

Minh-Ha, T. T. (1987) *Difference: A Special Third World Women's Issue*, 25(1).

Minsky, H. (1986) *Stabilizing an Unstable Economy*. New York: McGraw-Hill Professional.

Mirowski, P. (1984) "Physics and the 'marginalist revolution.'" *Cambridge Journal of Economics*, 8: 361–79.

Mirowski, P. (2002) *Machine Dreams: Economics Becomes a Cyborg Science*. New York: Cambridge University Press.

Mitchell, T. (2005) "The work of economics: How a discipline makes its world." *European Journal of Sociology/Archives Européennes de Sociologie*, 46(2): 297–320.

Mitchell, T. (2007) "The properties of markets," in D. MacKenzie, F. Muniesa and L. Siu (eds) *Do Economists Make Markets? On the Performativity of Economics*. Princeton, NJ: Princeton University Press, pp. 244–75.

Mkandawire, T. (2005) "Maladjusted African economies and globalisation." *Africa Development*, 30: 1–33.

Mkandawire, T. (2010) "On tax efforts and colonial heritage in Africa." *Journal of Development Studies*, 46(10): 1647–69.

Mkandawire, T. (2011) *Running While Others Walk: Knowledge and The Challenge of Africa's Development*. London: London School of Economics and Political Science.

Mkandawire, T. (2014) "The spread of economic doctrine and policy-making in postcolonial Africa." *African Studies Review*, 57(1): 171–98.

Mkandawire, T. (2020) "Colonial legacies and social welfare regimes in Africa: An empirical exercise," in K. Hujo (ed.) *The Politics of Domestic Resource Mobilization for Social Development*. Cham, Switzerland: Springer, pp. 139–72.

Moghadam, V. (1989) "Against Eurocentrism and nativism: A review essay on Samir Amin's Eurocentrism and other texts," *Socialism and Democracy*, 5(2): 81–104.

Mohanty, C. T. (1991) "Cartographies of struggle: Third World women and the politics of feminism," in C. Mohanty, D. Russo and M. Torres (eds) *Third World Women and the Politics of Feminism*. Bloomington, IN: Indiana University Press.

Mohanty, C. T. (2003) *Feminism without Borders: Decolonizing Theory, Practicing Solidarity*. Durham, NC: Duke University Press.

Mokyr, J. (2004) *The Gifts of Athena: Historical Origins of the Knowledge Economy*. Princeton, NJ: Princeton University Press.

Moore J. W. (2022) "Anthropocene, capitalocene and the flight from world history: Dialectical universalism and the geographies of class power in world-ecological perspective, 1492–2021." *Nordia Geographical Publications*, 51(2): 1–24.

More, R. B. and S. More (2020) *Memoirs of a Dalit Communist: The Many Worlds of R. B. More*. New Delhi: LeftWord Books.

Morrison, T. (2001) "How can values be taught in the university?" *Michigan Quarterly Review*, 40(2): 273–8.

Mueller, J. (2011) "The IMF, neoliberalism and hegemony." *Global Society*, 25(3): 377–402.

Mũgo, M. G. (2021) *The Imperative of Utu/Ubuntu in Africana Scholarship*. Quebec: Daraja Press.

Muller, S. M. (2021) *The Incentivised University: Scientific Revolutions, Policies, Consequences*. Cham, Switzerland: Springer.

Munck, R. (2002) *Globalisation and Labour: The New "Great Transformation."* London: Zed Books.

Munck, R. (2013) "The precariat: A view from the South." *Third World Quarterly*, 34(5): 747–62.

Musthaq, F. (2021) "Dependency in a financialised global economy." *Review of African Political Economy*, 48(167): 15–31.

Myrdal, G. (2017 [1932]) *The Political Element in the Development of Economic Theory*. London: Routledge.

Nadeau, M.-J. and A. Sears (2010) "The Palestine test: Countering the silencing campaign." *Studies in Political Economy*, 85(1): 7–33.

Naicker, V. (2023) "The problem of epistemological critique in contemporary decolonial theory." *Social Dynamics*, 49(2): 220–41.

Naidu, S. (2016) "Domestic labour and female labour force participation: Adding a piece to the puzzle." *Economic and Political Weekly*, 51(44/45): 101–8.

Naoroji, D. (1901) *Poverty and Un-British Rule in India.* London: S. Sonnenschein.

Naritomi, J., S. Sequeira, J. Weigel and D. Weinhold (2020) "RCTs as an opportunity to promote interdisciplinary, inclusive, and diverse quantitative development research." *World Development,* 127: 104832.

Narsey, W. (2016) *British Imperialism and the Making of Colonial Currency Systems.* Basingstoke: Palgrave Macmillan.

Nasong'o, S. and E. Ikpe (2024) *Beyond Disciplines: African Perspectives on Theory and Method.* Dakar: CODESRIA.

Ndlovu-Gatsheni, S. J. (2018) *Epistemic Freedom in Africa – Deprovincialization and Decolonization.* New York: Routledge.

Ndlovu-Gatsheni, S. J. (2023) "Intellectual imperialism and decolonisation in African studies." *Third World Quarterly,* https://doi.org/10.1080/01436597.2023.2211520.

Ndlovu-Gatsheni, S. J. and M. Ndlovu (eds) (2022) *Marxism and Decolonization in the 21st Century – Living Theories and True Ideas.* New York: Routledge.

Negi, A. (2017) "Assessing the 'multilateral' nature of the 1944 Bretton Woods Conference: An analysis of Indian participation," in G. Scott-Smith and J. S. Rofe (eds) *Global Perspectives on the Bretton Woods Conference and the Post-War World Order.* Cham, Switzerland: Palgrave Macmillan, pp. 129–48.

Nelson, J. A. (1995) "Feminism and economics." *Journal of Economic Perspectives,* 9(2): 131–48.

Neubeck, K. and N. Cazenave (2001) *Welfare Racism: Playing the Race Card against America's Poor.* New York: Routledge.

Nilsen, A. G. (2017) "Development beyond Eurocentrism," in H. Veltmeyer and P. Bowles (eds) *The Essential Guide to Critical Development Studies.* London: Routledge.

Nkrumah, K. (1963) *Africa Must Unite.* London: Heinemann.

Nkrumah, K. (1970 [1965]) *Neocolonialism: The Last Stage of Imperialism.* London: PANAF.

Nobel Prize Outreach (2021) "Prize announcement." Available at: https://www.nobelprize.org/prizes/economic-sciences/2021/prize-announcement.

North, D. C. (1991) "Institutions." *Journal of Economic Perspectives,* 5(1): 97–112.

Nun, J. (2000) "The end of work and the 'Marginal Mass' thesis." *Latin American Perspectives,* 27(1): 6–32.

Nussbaum, M. (2003) "Capabilities as fundamental entitlements: Sen and social justice." *Feminist Economics,* 9 (2–3): 33–59.

Nyamu-Musembi, C. (2007) "De Soto and land relations in rural

Africa: Breathing life into dead theories about property rights." *Third World Quarterly*, 28(8): 1457–78.

Nyerere, J. K. (1977) "The plea of the poor: New economic order needed for the world community." *New Directions*, 4(4): 8.

Nyerere, J. K. (1980) "Unity for a new order." *The Black Scholar*, 11(5), *Africa: The New Societies*: 55–63.

Nzegwu, N. (1995) "Recovering Igbo traditions: A case for indigenous women's organizations in development," in M. C. Nussbaum and J. Glover (eds) *Women, Culture, and Development*. Oxford: Clarendon Press.

Oakley, A. (1972) *Sex, Gender and Society*. London: Temple Smith.

Ogle, V. (2014) "State rights against private capital: The 'New International Economic Order' and the struggle over aid, trade, and foreign investment, 1962–1981." *Humanity: An International Journal of Human Rights, Humanitarianism, and Development*, 5(2): 211–34.

Ohnsorge, F. and S. Yu (eds) (2022) *The Long Shadow of Informality*. Washington: The World Bank.

O'Kane, C. (2020) "Capital, the state, and economic policy: Bringing open Marxist critical political economy back into contemporary heterodox economics." *Review of Radical Political Economics*, 52(4), 684–92.

Okoth, K. O. (2023) *Red Africa: Reclaiming Revolutionary Black Politics*. London: Verso.

Olukoshi, A. (2006) "African scholars and African studies." *Development in Practice*, 16(6): 533–44.

Omi, M. and H. Winant (1994) *Racial Formation in the United States: From the 1960s to the 1990s*. New York: Routledge.

Omvedt, G. (1981) "Capitalist agriculture and rural classes." *Economic and Political Weekly*, 16(2).

O'Rourke, L. A. (2019) "The strategic logic of covert regime change: US-backed regime change campaigns during the Cold War." *Security Studies*, 29: 92–127.

Ortiz, I. and M. Cummings (2022) *End Austerity: A Global Report on Budget Cuts and Harmful Social Reforms in 2022*. Public Services International.

Ossome, L. (2013) "Postcolonial discourses of queer activism and class in Africa," in H. Abbas and S. Ekine (eds) *Queer African Reader*. Oxford: Pambazuka Press, pp. 32–47.

Ossome, L. (2020) "African feminism," in R. Rabaka (ed.) *Routledge Handbook of Pan-Africanism*. London: Routledge.

Ossome, L. (2021) "Land in transition: From social reproduction of labour power to social reproduction of power." *Journal of Contemporary African Studies*, 39(4): 550–64.

Ossome, L. (2023) "Gender and uneven development," in E. S. Reinert and I. H. Kvangraven (eds) *A Modern Guide to Uneven Economic Development*. Cheltenham: Edward Elgar Publishing, pp. 135–46.

Oteiza, E. (1978) "Introduction," in Institute of Development Studies, *Bibliography of Selected Latin American Publications on Development*. Vol. 13 of Occasional Guides, Institute of Development Studies, University of Sussex.

Ouma, S. (2021) "Challenging the orthodoxy: Race, racism and the reconfiguration of economics." *Developing Economics*, July 11. Available at: https://developingeconomics.org/2021/07/11/challenging-the-orthodoxy-race-racism-and-the-reconfiguration-of-economics/.

Padmore, G. (1936) *How Britain Rules Africa*. New York: Wishart Books.

Pailey, R. N. (2020) "De-centering the white gaze of development." *Development and Change*, 51(3): 729–45.

Palermo, G. (2007) "The ontology of economic power in capitalism: mainstream economics and Marx." *Cambridge Journal of Economics*, 31(4): 539–61.

Pappé, I. (2006) *The Ethnic Cleansing of Palestine*. Oxford: Oneworld.

Parashar, S. (2017) "Feminism and postcolonialism: (En)gendering encounters." *Postcolonial Studies*, 19(4): 371–7.

Parrish, J. B. (1967) "Rise of economics as an academic discipline: The formative years to 1900." *Southern Economic Journal*, 34(1): 1–16.

Patnaik, P. (1997) *Accumulation and Stability Under Capitalism*. Oxford: Oxford University Press.

Patnaik, P. (2009) *The Value of Money*. New York: Columbia University Press.

Patnaik, P. (2022) "Social sciences and the colonised mind." IDEAS, January 24. Available at: https://www.networkideas.org/tag/decolonization-of-the-mind/.

Patnaik, P. and U. Patnaik (2021) *Capital and Imperialism: Theory, History, and the Present*. New York: Monthly Review Press.

Patnaik, U. (1990) *Agrarian Relations and Accumulation – The Mode of Production Debate in India*. Bombay: Oxford University Press.

Patnaik, U. (2018) "India's global trade and Britain's international dominance," in S. Sen and M. C. Marcuzzo (eds) *The Changing Face of Imperialism: Colonialism to Contemporary Capitalism*. Oxford: Routledge, pp. 201–25.

Patnaik, U. (2022) "On political economy and its fallacies: Why critiques and rethinking matter." *Agrarian South: Journal of Political Economy*, 11(3): 333–51.

Patnaik, U. and S. Moyo (2011) *The Agrarian Question in the*

Neoliberal Era: Primitive Accumulation and the Peasantry. Dar es Salaam: Pambazuka Press, an imprint of Fahamu, and the Mwalimu Nyerere Chair in Pan-African Studies, University of Dar es Salaam.

Perelman, M. (2000) *The Invention of Capitalism: Classical Political Economy and the Secret History of Primitive Accumulation*. Durham, NC: Duke University Press.

Perez, F. (2018) "Solidarity vs similarity: The political economy of currency unions," in G. A. Epstein (ed.) *The Political Economy of International Finance in an Age of Inequality: Soft Currencies, Hard Landings*. Cheltenham, UK: Edward Elgar, pp. 213–32.

Perez, F. (2023) "Liberating African money: Joseph Tchundjang Pouemi's Theory of Financial Repression." Unpublished manuscript.

Perry, K. K. (2023) "(Un)Just transitions and Black dispossession: The disposability of Caribbean 'refugees' and the political economy of climate justice." *Politics*, 43(2): 169–85.

Phelps, E. S. (1972) "The statistical theory of racism and sexism." *The American Economic Review*, 62(4): 659–61.

Pierre, J. (2012) *The Predicament of Blackness: Postcolonial Ghana and the Politics of Race*. Chicago, IL: University of Chicago Press.

Pietsch, T. (2013) *Empire of Scholars – Universities, Networks and the British Academic World 1850–1939*. Manchester: Manchester University Press.

Pigeaud, F. and N. S. Sylla (2021) *Africa's Last Colonial Currency*. London: Pluto Press.

Piketty, T. (2020) *Capital and Ideology*. Boston, MA: Harvard University Press.

Polanyi, K. (1944) *The Great Transformation: The Political and Economic Origins of Our Time*. New York: Farrar & Rinehart.

Pomeranz, K. L. (2000) *The Great Divergence: Europe, China, and the Making of the Modern World Economy*. Princeton, NJ: Princeton University Press.

Pouemi, J. T. (2000 [1980]) *Monnaie, servitude et liberté: La répression monétaire de l'Afrique*. Paris: Menaibuc.

Powell, J. (2013) *Subordinate Financialisation: A Study of Mexico and its Non-Financial Corporations*. PhD dissertation, SOAS, University of London.

Pradella, L. (2014) "New developmentalism and the origins of methodological nationalism." *Competition & Change*, 18(2): 180–93.

Pradella, L. (2017) "Marx and the Global South: Connecting history and value theory." *Sociology*, 51(1): 146–61.

Prebisch, R. (1950) *The Economic Development of Latin America and Its Principal Problems*. New York: United Nations.

Protin, P. (2014 [1863]) *Les Économistes Appréciés, Ou Nécessité de la Protection*. Paris: Hachette-Livre.

Quijano, A. (1974) "The marginal pole of the economy and the marginalized labour force." *Economy and Society*, 3(4): 393–428.

Quijano, A. (2007) "Coloniality and modernity/rationality." *Cultural Studies*, 21(2): 168–78.

Radcliffe, S. (2022) *Decolonizing Geography: An Introduction*. Cambridge: Polity Press.

Raj, J. (2022) *Plantation Crisis: Ruptures of Dalit Life in the Indian Tea Belt*. London: UCL Press.

Rakowski, C. A. (1994) *Contrapunto: The Informal Sector Debate in Latin America*. Albany, NY: State University of New York Press.

Ramose, M. (1999) *African Philosophy through Ubuntu*. Harare, Zimbabwe: Mond Books.

Ranis, G. and F. Stewart (1999) "V-Goods and the role of the urban informal sector in development." *Economic Development and Cultural Change*, 47(2): 259–88.

Rao, V. and M. Woolcock (2007) "The disciplinary monopoly in development research at the World Bank." *Global Governance*, 13(4): 479–84.

Reddy, S. (2012) "Randomise this! On poor economics." *Review of Agrarian Studies*, 2(2): 60–73.

Reich, M., D. M. Gordon and R. C. Edwards (1973) "A theory of labor market segmentation." *The American Economic Review*, 63(2): 359–65.

Reinert, E. S. and I. H. Kvangraven (2023) "Introduction: uneven development – addressing causes versus treating symptoms," in E. Reinert and I. H. Kvangraven (eds) *A Modern Guide to Uneven Economic Development*. Cheltenham, UK: Edward Elgar.

Reinert, E. and F. Reinert (2018) "33 economic bestsellers published before 1750." *European Journal of the History of Economic Thought*, 25: 1206–63.

Reinert, E. S., J. Ghosh and R. Kattel (2016) *Handbook of Alternative Theories of Economic Development*. Northampton, MA: Edward Elgar.

Reinsberg, B., T. Stubbs, A. Kentikelenis and L. King (2019) "The political economy of labor market deregulation during IMF interventions." *International Interactions*, 45(3): 532–59.

Reis, N. and F. Antunes de Oliveira (2023) "Peripheral financialization and the transformation of dependency: A view from Latin America." *Review of International Political Economy*, 30(2): 511–34.

Renton, D. (2024) "British universities are repressing free speech on Palestine." *Jacobin*, January 1.

Resnick, D. (2016) "Strong democracy, weak state: The political economy of Ghana's stalled structural transformation." IFPRI Discussion Paper 01574. Washington, D.C.: International Food Policy Research Institute.

Resnick, S. and R. Wolff (1987) *Knowledge and Class*. Chicago, IL: University of Chicago Press.

Resnick, S. and R. Wolff (2006) *New Departures in Marxian Theory*. London: Routledge.

Resnick, S. and R. Wolff (2010) "The economic crisis: A Marxian interpretation." *Rethinking Marxism*, 22(2): 170–86.

Reyes, V. and K. A. C. Johnson (2020) "Teaching the veil: Race, ethnicity, and gender in classical theory courses." *Sociology of Race and Ethnicity*, 6(4): 562–7.

Ribeiro, D. (1969) *A Universidade Necessária*. Rio de Janeiro: Paz ae Terra.

Rist, G. (1997) *The History of Development: From Western Origins to Global Faith*. New York: Zed Books.

Robbins, L. (1932) *An Essay on the Nature and Significance of Economic Science*. London: Macmillan.

Robinson, C. (2000 [1983]) *Black Marxism: The Making of the Black Radical Tradition*. Totowa, NJ: Zed Books.

Rodney, W. (1972) *How Europe Underdeveloped Africa*. London: Bogle-L'Ouverture Publications.

Rodrik, D. (2021) "Economics has another diversity problem." *Project Syndicate*, August 7.

Rodrik, D., M. McMillan and C. Sepúlveda (2013) "Overview: Structural change, fundamentals, and growth," in M. McMillan, D. Rodrik and C. Sepúlveda (eds) *Structural Change, Fundamentals, and Growth: A Framework for Case Studies*. Washington, DC: World Bank, pp. 1–38.

Roediger, D. (2017) *Class, Race and Marxism*. London: Verso.

Rollock, N. (2019) *Staying Power: The Career Experiences and Strategies of UK Black Female Professors*. London: University and College Union.

Rosenstein-Rodan, P. (1944) "The international development of economically backward areas." *International Affairs*, 20(2): 157–65.

Rostow, W. (1959) "The stages of economic growth." *The Economic History Review*, 12(1): 1–16.

Roth, C. (2022) "Why is the world experiencing a cholera vaccine shortage?" DW, November 4. Available at: https://www.dw.com /en/why-is-the-world-experiencing-a-cholera-vaccine-shortage /a-63639495.

Rowbotham, S. and S. Mitter (eds) (1994) *Dignity and Daily Bread:*

New Forms of Economic Organizing among Poor Women in the Third World and the First. New York: Routledge.

Ruccio, D. F. and L. H. Simon (1986) "Methodological aspects of a Marxian approach to development: An analysis of the modes of production school." *World Development,* 14(2): 211–22.

Runyan, A. S. (1999) "Women in the neoliberal 'frame'," in M. K. Meyer and E. Prügl (eds) *Gender Politics in Global Governance.* Lanham, MD: Rowman and Littlefield, pp. 210–20.

Ruwanpura, K. (2008) "Multiple identities, multiple discrimination: a critical review." *Feminist Economics,* 14(3): 77–105.

Sabaratnam, M. (2017) "Decolonising the curriculum: What's all the fuss about?" SOAS blog, January 18.

Sachs, W. (1992) *The Development Dictionary: A Guide to Knowledge as Power.* London: Zed Books.

Sahasrabuddhe, A. (2019) "Drawing the line: The politics of federal currency swaps in the global financial crisis." *Review of International Political Economy,* 26(3): 461–89.

Said, E. (1979) *Orientalism.* New York: Vintage Books.

Said, E. (1993) *Culture and Imperialism.* New York: Chatto & Windus.

Salaita, S. (2015) *Uncivil Rites: Palestine and the Limits of Academic Freedom.* Chicago, IL: Haymarket Books.

Salaita, S. (2024) "So you're a professor? Here's what you can do to oppose genocide." Steve Salaita's website, January 7.

Samuelson, P. A. and W. A. Barnett (2007) *Inside the Economist's Mind: Conversations with Eminent Economists.* Malden, MA: Blackwell Publishing.

Sanyal, K. (2007) *Rethinking Capitalist Development: Primitive Accumulation, Governmentality and Post-Colonial Capitalism.* New Delhi: Routledge.

Sarkar, B. K. (1932) *Studies in Applied Economics.* Kolkata, India: N. C. Paul.

Schmitt, C. (2020) *From Colonialism to International Aid – External Actors and Social Protection in the Global South.* Cham, Switzerland: Palgrave Macmillan.

Schrecker, E. (2002) *The Age of McCarthyism: A Brief History with Documents.* New York: Palgrave.

Schultz, T. W. (1961) "Investment in human capital." *The American Economic Review,* 51(1): 1–17.

Schumpeter, J. (1954) *History of Economic Analysis.* London: Allen & Unwin.

Scott, C. (1995) *Gender and Development: Rethinking Modernization and Dependency Theory.* Boulder, CO: Lynne Rienner.

Sealey-Huggins, L. (2017) "'1.5°C to stay alive': Climate change, imperialism and justice for the Caribbean." *Third World Quarterly*, 38(11): 2444–63.

Selwyn, B. and D. Leyden (2021) "Oligopoly-driven development: The World Bank's trading for development in the age of global value chains in perspective." *Competition & Change*, 26(2): 174–96.

Sen, A. (1983) "Poor, relatively speaking." *Oxford Economic Papers*, 35(2): 153–69.

Sen, A. (1992) "Objectivity and position." The Lindley Lecture, The University of Kansas.

Sen, S. (2019) "On the evolution of heterodox economic thinking in India," in A. Sinha and A. M. Thomas (eds) *Pluralistic Economics and Its History*. New York: Routledge, pp. 256–68.

Sen, S. and C. Marcuzzo (2017) *The Changing Face of Imperialism Colonialism to Contemporary Capitalism*. London: Routledge.

Shahjahan, R., G. B. Ramirez, and V. de Oliveira Andreotti (2017) "Attempting to imagine the unimaginable: A decolonial reading of global university rankings." *Comparative Education Review*, 61(S1): S51–S73.

Shaikh, A. (2016) *Capitalism: Competition, Conflict, Crises*. Oxford: Oxford University Press.

Sharma, S. (2020) "JNU violence: Indian university's radical history has long scared country's rulers." University of Keele Faculty News, January, 13.

Shie, V. H. and C. D. Meer (2010) "The rise of knowledge in dependency theory: The experience of India and Taiwan?" *Review of Radical Political Economics*, 42(1), 81–99.

Shilliam, R. (2021) *Decolonizing Politics: An Introduction*. Cambridge: Polity Press.

Shringarpure, B. (2020) "Notes on fake decolonization." Africa Is A Country, December 18.

Simon, H. (1957) *Models of Man: Social and Rational*. New York: John Wiley.

Singer, H. (1950) "The distribution of gains between investing and borrowing countries." *American Economic Review, Papers and Proceedings*, 40: 473–85.

Singh, N. P. (2022) "Black Marxism and the antinomies of racial capitalism," in C. Lye and C. Nealon (eds) *After Marx: Literature, Theory, and Value in the Twenty-first Century*. Cambridge: Cambridge University Press, pp. 23–39.

Six, C. (2018) "Challenging the grammar of difference: Benoy Kumar Sarkar, global mobility and anti-imperialism around the First World

War." *European Review of History: Revue européenne d'histoire*, 25(3–4): 431–49.

Smith, A. (1776) *An Inquiry into the Nature and Causes of the Wealth of Nations*. London: W. Strahan and T. Cadell.

Smith, L. T. (1999) *Decolonizing Methodologies: Research and Indigenous Peoples*. London: Bloomsbury.

Smith, M. N. (2022) "The limits of postcolonial critique of Marxism: A defense of radical universalism," in S. Ndlovu-Gatsheni (ed.) *Marxism and Decolonization in the 21st Century: Living Theories and True Ideas*. Abingdon, Oxon: Routledge.

Smith, M. N. and C.-A. Lester (2023) "From 'dependency' to 'decoloniality'? The enduring relevance of materialist political economy and the problems of a 'decolonial' alternative." *Social Dynamics*, 49(2): 196–219.

Solberg, W. U. and R. W. Tomilson (1997) "Academic McCarthyism and Keynesian economics: The Bowen controversy at the University of Illinois." *History of Political Economy*, 29: 55–81.

Sowemimo, A. (2023) *Divided: Racism, Medicine and Why We Need to Decolonise Healthcare*. London: Profile Books.

Spivak, G. (1988) "Can the subaltern speak?" in C. Nelson and L. Grossberg (eds) *Marxism and the Interpretation of Culture*. Basingstoke: Macmillan Education, pp. 271–313.

Spriggs, W. (2020) "Is now a teachable moment for economists? An open letter to economists from Bill Spriggs." Department of Economics, Howard University.

Standing, G. (2011) *The Precariat: The New Dangerous Class*. London: Bloomsbury Academic.

Stansbury, A. and L. H. Summers (2020) "The declining worker power hypothesis: An explanation for the recent evolution of the American economy." NBER Working Paper No. 27193.

Stavenhagen, R. (1971) "Cómo descolonizar las ciencias sociale?" in R. Stavenhagen, *Sociología y Subdesarrollo*. Mexico City: Editorial Nuestro Tempo.

Stein, H. (1995) "Institutional theories and structural adjustment in Africa," in J. Harriss, J. Hunter and C. Lewis (eds) *The New Institutional Economics and Third World Development*. London: Routledge.

Stein, H. (2021) "Institutionalizing neoclassical economics in Africa: Instruments, ideology and implications." *Economy and Society*, 50(1): 120–47.

Steinmetz, G. (2014) "British sociology in the metropole and the colonies, 1940s–60s," in J. Holmwood and J. Scott (eds) *The Palgrave Handbook of Sociology in Britain*. Basingstoke: Palgrave, pp. 302–37.

Stevano, S. (2020) "Small development questions are important, but they require big answers." *World Development* 127: 104826.

Stevano, S., D. Johnston and E. Codjoe (2020) "The urban food question in the context of inequality and dietary change: A study of schoolchildren in Accra." *Journal of Development Studies*, 56(6): 1177–89.

Stigler, G. J. (1972) "The adoption of the marginal utility theory." *History of Political Economy*, 4(2): 571–86.

Stiglitz, J. (1973) "Approaches to the economics of discrimination." *The American Economic Review*, 63(2): 287–95.

Stiglitz, J. (2001) "Information and the change in the paradigm in economics." Nobel Prize Lecture. Available at: https://www.nobelprize.org/uploads/2018/06/stiglitz-lecture.pdf.

Straussman, D. (1993) "Not a free market: The rhetoric of disciplinary authority in economics," in M. A. Ferber and J. A. Nelson (eds) *Beyond Economic Man: Feminist Theory and Economics.* Chicago, IL: University of Chicago Press.

Styve, M. D. and P. R. Gilbert (2023) "'The hole in the ground that cannot be moved': Political risk as a racial vernacular of extractive industry development." *The Extractive Industries and Society*, 13: 101100.

Sud, N. and D. Sánchez-Ancochea (2022) "Southern discomfort: Interrogating the category of the Global South." *Development and Change*, 53(6): 1123–50.

Sukarieh, M. (2023) "The Zionist lobby's threat to academic freedom in UK universities." *Mondoweiss*, December 22.

Sun, Y.-s. (2021 [1923]) *The International Development of China: A Project to Assist the Readjustment of Post-Bellum Industries.* Singapore: Springer.

Sunkel, O. (1969) "National development policy and external dependence in Latin America." *Journal of Development Studies*, 6(1): 23–48.

Sutch, R. (2018) "The economics of African American slavery: The cliometrics debate." NBER Working Paper No. 25197.

Suwandi, I., R. Jamil Jonna and J. B. Foster (2019) "Global commodity chains and the New Imperialism." *Living Wages North and South: Essays on True Democracy and Capitalism*, May, pp. 1–22.

Sweezy, P. M. and M. Dobb (1950) "The transition from feudalism to capitalism." *Science & Society*, 14(2): 134–67.

Sylla, N. S. (2020a) "What does MMT have to offer developing nations?" *Brave New Europe*, February 27.

Sylla, N. S. (2020b) "Moving forward to African monetary integration." *Africa Development/Afrique et Développement*, 45(2): 39–58.

Sylla, N. S. (2023) "Imperialism and Global South's debt: Insights from modern money theory, ecological economics and dependency theory," in N. S. Sylla (ed.) *Imperialism and the Political Economy of Global South's Debt*. Bingley: Emerald.

Sylla, N. S. (2024) "Modern monetary theory as an analytical framework and a policy lens: An African perspective," in Y. Nersisyan and L. R. Wray (eds) *The Elgar Companion to Modern Money Theory*. Cheltenham: Edward Elgar Publishing, pp. 314–28.

Syrquin, M. (1988) "Patterns of structural change," in H. Chenery and T. N. Srinivasan (eds) *Handbook of Development Economics*. New York: Elsevier, pp. 203–73.

Tabak, F. and M. A. Crichlow (2000) *Informalization: Process and Structure*. Baltimore, MD: Johns Hopkins University Press.

Tagat, A., M. Parekh, A. Priya, J. N. Hafiz, A. Kumar, S. Pal, A. Apum, A. Sharma, T. Chandra and R. Shah (2021) "Diversity and representation in economics in India." Rethinking Economics India Network – Monk Prayogshala – Bahujan Economists Policy Brief.

Táíwò, O. (2022) *Against Decolonisation: Taking African Agency Seriously*. London: Hurst.

Tamale, S. (2020) *Decolonization and Afro-Feminism*. Quebec: Daraja Press.

Tauheed, L. F. (2008) "Black political economy in the 21st century: Exploring the interface of economics and Black Studies: Addressing the challenge of Harold Cruse." *Journal of Black Studies*, 38(5): 692–730.

Tavares, M. da C. (1985) "The resumption of North American hegemony." *Brazilian Journal of Political Economy*, 5(2): 157–67.

Tavasci, D. and L. Ventimiglia (2018) *Teaching the History of Economic Thought: Integrating Historical Perspectives into Modern Economics*. Northampton, MA: Edward Elgar.

Taylor, Y., S. Hines and M. E. Casey (eds) (2011) *Theorizing Intersectionality and Sexuality*. New York: Palgrave Macmillan.

Tejeda, C., M. Espinoza and K. Gutierrez (2003) "Toward a decolonizing pedagogy: Social justice reconsidered," in P. Trifonas (ed.) *Pedagogies of Difference: Rethinking Education for Social Justice*. New York: RoutledgeFalmer, pp. 10–40.

Teltumbde, A. (2010a) "Globalization and caste." *Voice of Dalit*, 3(2): 101–38.

Teltumbde, A. (2010b) *The Persistence of Caste: The Khairlanji Murders and India's Hidden Apartheid*. Delhi: Navayana.

Teltumbde, A. (2018) *Republic of Caste*. Delhi: Navayana.

Thaler, R. and C. Sunstein (2008) *Nudge: Improving Decision about Health, Wealth and Happiness*. London: Penguin.

The Economist (2018) "Tyranny of the few." Available at: https://www

.economist.com/finance-and-economics/2018/10/06/economists
-care-about-where-they-publish-to-the-cost-of-the-profession.

Thiong'o, N. w. (1986) *Decolonizing the Mind: The Politics of Language in African Literature*. Oxford: James Currey.

Thompson, E. P. (1963) *The Making of the English Working Class*. London: Victor Gollancz.

Thornton, C. (2023) "Developmentalism as internationalism: Toward a global historical sociology of the origins of the development project." *Sociology of Development*, 9(1): 33–55.

Tilley, L. and R. Shilliam (2018) "Raced markets: An introduction." *New Political Economy*, 23(5): 534–43.

Tomba, M. (2015) "1793: The neglected legacy of insurgent universality." *History of the Present: A Journal of Critical History*, 5(2): 109–36.

Tontoh, E. A. (2022) "The triple day thesis: Theorising motherhood as a capability and a capability suppressor within Martha Nussbaum's feminist philosophical capability theory." *Journal of Human Development and Capabilities*, 23(4): 593–610.

Toporowski, J. (2021) "Is economics always politics?" *Royal Economics Society Newsletter*, 193, 18.

Toye, R. (2003) "Developing multilateralism: The Havana Charter and the fight for the International Trade Organization, 1947–1948." *International History Review*, 25(2): 282–305.

Trouillot, M.-R. (1995) *Silencing the Past: Power and the Production of History*. Boston, MA: Beacon Press.

Tuck, E. and K. W. Yang (2012) "Decolonization is not a metaphor." *Tabula Rasa*, 38: 61–111.

UNICEF (2021) "COVID-19 and the looming debt crisis: Protecting and transforming social spending for inclusive recoveries." Innocenti Research Report, no. 01. Florence: UNICEF Office of Research – Innocenti.

Vasconcelos, S. and R. H. Chilcote (2022) "Reassessing development and dependency in Latin American case studies." *Latin American Perspectives*, 49(2): 3–7.

Vasudevan, R. (2009) "From the gold standard to the floating dollar standard: An appraisal in the light of Marx's theory of money." *Review of Radical Political Economics*, 41(4): 473–91.

Venkatesan, S. (2025) *Decolonizing Anthropology*. Cambridge: Polity Press.

Vernengo, M. (2006) "Technology, finance, and dependency: Latin American radical political economy in retrospect." *Review of Radical Political Economics*, 38(4): 551–68.

Vernengo, M. and E. P. Caldentey (2020) "Modern money theory

(MMT) in the tropics: Functional finance in developing countries." *Challenge*, 63(6): 332–48.

Visser, M. and S. Ferrer (2015) *Farm Workers' Living and Working Conditions in South Africa: Key Trends, Emergent Issues, and Underlying and Structural Problems*. Pretoria: International Labour Organization.

Wallerstein, I. (1996) *Open the Social Sciences – Report of the Gulbenkian Commission on the Restructuring of the Social Sciences*. Stanford, CA: Stanford University Press.

Walras, L. (1954) *Elements of Pure Economics*. London: Allen and Unwin.

Waring, M. (1990) *If Women Counted: A New Feminist Economics*. San Francisco, CA: HarperCollins.

Warren, B. (1980) *Imperialism: The Pioneer of Capitalism*. New York: New Left Books.

Wasserfall, R. R. (1997) "Reflexivity, feminism, and difference," in R. Hertz (ed.) *Reflexivity and Voice*. Thousand Oaks, CA: Sage Publications, pp. 150–68.

Watson, M. (2018) "Crusoe, Friday and the raced market frame of orthodox economics textbooks." *New Political Economy*, 23(5): 544–59.

Weber, M. (1971 [1904]) *The Protestant Ethic and the Spirit of Capitalism*, 11th edn. London: Unwin.

Weintraub, E. R. (ed.) (2014) *MIT and the Transformation of American Economics*. Durham, NC: Duke University Press.

Weintraub, E. R. (2017) "McCarthyism and the mathematization of economics." *Journal of the History of Economic Thought*, 39(4): 571–97.

Wheiler, K. (1991) "Freire and a feminist pedagogy of difference." *Harvard Educational Review*, 61(4): 449–74.

Wiegratz, J., P. Behuria, C. Laskaridis, L. L. Pheko, B. Radley and S. Stevano (2023) "Common challenges for all? A critical engagement with the emerging vision for post-pandemic development studies." *Development and Change*, 54(5): 921–53.

Wilder, C. S. (2013) *Ebony and Ivy: Race, Slavery, and the Troubled History of America's Universities*. New York: Bloomsbury.

Williams, E. (1944) *Capitalism and Slavery*. Chapel Hill, NC: University of North Carolina Press.

Wilson, A. and C. Buchholz (2020) "Abolition will not be randomized." Developing Economics blog, June 15. Available at: https://developingeconomics.org/2020/06/15/abolition-will-not-be-randomized/.

Wilson, A., F. Kasina, I. Nduta and J. A. Akallah (2023) "When economists shut off your water." Developing Economics blog, December 11. Available at: https://developingeconomics.org/2023/12/11/when -economists-shut-off-your-water/.

Wilson, J. (2022) "The insurgent universal: Between Eurocentric universalism and the pluriverse." *Nordia Geographical Publications*, 51(2): 153–62.

Wolff, R. D. and S. A. Resnick (2012) *Contending Economic Theories: Neoclassical, Keynesian, and Marxian.* Cambridge, MA: MIT Press.

Wolff, R. D., S. A. Resnick and Y. Madra (2012) "Late neo-classical theory," in R. D. Wolff and S. A. Resnick (eds) *Contending Economic Theories: Neoclassical, Keynesian, and Marxian.* Cambridge, MA: MIT Press, pp. 251–310.

Wolpe, H. (1972) "Capitalism and cheap labour-power in South Africa: From segregation to apartheid." *Economy and Society*, 1(4): 425–56.

Wolpe, H. (1975) "The theory of internal colonization: The South African case." Collected Seminar Papers. Institute of Commonwealth Studies, 18, pp. 105–20.

Wood, C. (2003) "Economic marginalia: Postcolonial readings of unpaid domestic labor and developments," in D. Barker and E. Kuiper (eds) *Toward a Feminist Philosophy of Economics.* New York: Routledge, pp. 304–20.

Wood, E. M. (2000) "Capitalism or enlightenment?" *History of Political Thought*, 21(3): 405–26.

Wood, E. M. (2002) *The Origins of Capitalism: A Longer View.* London: Verso.

Wootton, B. (1938) *Lament for Economics.* London: George Allen.

Wu, A. H. (2017) *Gender Stereotyping in Academia: Evidence from Economics Job Market Rumors Forum.* Undergraduate thesis, UC Berkeley.

Wu, A. H. (2020) "Gender bias among professionals: An identity-based interpretation." *Review of Economics and Statistics*, 102(5): 867–80.

Wynter, S. (2003) "Unsettling the coloniality of being/power/truth/ freedom: Towards the human, after man, its overrepresentation – An argument." *CR: The New Centennial Review*, 3(3): 257–337.

Yassir, S. (2024) "It is suffocating: A top liberal university is under attack in India." *New York Times*, February 10. Available at: https:// www.nytimes.com/2024/02/10/world/asia/india-bjp-jnu.html.

Younis, M. (2022) *On the Scale of the World: The Formation of Black Anticolonial Thought.* Oakland, CA: University of California Press.

Zacchia, G. (2021) "What does it take to be top women economists? An analysis using rankings in RePEc." *Review of Political Economy*, 33(2): 170–93.

Zafirovski, M. (1999) "What is really rational choice? Beyond the utilitarian concept of rationality," *Current Sociology*, 47(1): 47–113.

Zein-Elabdin, E. O. (2009) "Economics, postcolonial theory and the problem of culture: Institutional analysis and hybridity." *Cambridge Journal of Economics*, 33(6): 1153–67.

Zein-Elabdin, E. O. (2011) "Postcoloniality and development: Development as a colonial discourse," in L. Keita (ed.) *Philosophy and African Development: Theory and Practice*. Dakar, Senegal: CODESRIA, pp. 215–30.

Zein-Elabdin, E. O. and S. Charusheela (2004) *Postcolonialism Meets Economics*. New York: Routledge.

Zeleza, P. T. (2006) "The troubled encounter between postcolonialism and African history." *Journal of the Canadian Historical Association*, 17(2): 98–136.

Zeleza, P. T. (2009) "African studies and universities since independence: The challenges of epistemic and institutional decolonization." *Transition*, 101: 110–27.

Ziadah, R. (2017) "Disciplining dissent: Multicultural policy and the silencing of Arab-Canadians." *Race & Class*, 58(4): 7–22.

Zuberi, T. (2001) *Thicker than Blood: How Racial Statistics Lie*. Minneapolis, MN: University of Minnesota Press.

Zuberi, T. and E. Bonilla-Silva (2008) *White Logic, White Methods – Racism and Methodology*. Lanham, MD: Rowman & Littlefield.

Index

discrimination, 28–9, 204
diversity, 30
private property rights, 11
scholarship on, 189
Castro, Fidel, 101
center–periphery binary, 142,
    216 n.1
  capitalism, 119–20, 121,
    130–1, 163–4
  climate change, 207
  dependency theory, 166–7
  development economics,
    84–6, 94, 95–6, 99–100
  Eurocentrism, 17–18, 130
  finance, 169
  heterodox economics,
    119–22, 126
  institutions, 71–2
  journals, 29–30
  modernization theory, 95
  rationality, 71–2
  RCTs, 99
  structural transformation,
    170–1
  technology, 168–9
  trade relations, 165–6
  traditional–modern binary,
    147–8
  UNCTAD, 101
  unequal exchange, 193–4
  wage differences, 167–8
  see also hierarchies;
    periphery
CEPAL (UN Economic
    Commission for Latin
    America and the
    Caribbean), 92–3, 166
Chakravarty, D., 126
Charusheela, S., 138
Chile, 90, 101, 164, 166
China, 46, 50, 88, 90, 93
choice, 62, 83
Christophers B., 217 n.4
civilizing mission, 86, 87

class, 60, 61, 68, 143, 144,
    167–8, 179–80
  bourgeoisie, 96
  capitalist, 10, 19, 25, 171
  financialized dependence,
    169
  Nigeria, 181
  race, 54
  struggle, 18
  see also working class, the
climate change, 206–8
cliometrics, 55–6, 114–16
Coase, Ronald, 70
CODESRIA (Council for the
    Development of Social
    Science Research in
    Africa), 93
cognitive imperialism, 138
Colander, D. et al., 20
Cold War, the, 65–6, 100–1,
    193
Collier, John, 87
Colombia, 91
colonial fixed exchange rate
    systems, 113
colonial hierarchies, 144–50
colonialism/colonization, 12,
    16–20, 23, 101, 147–8,
    217 n.6
  capitalism, 43, 47–9, 130,
    148, 164
  civilizing mission, 86, 87
  development economics,
    86–8, 96–100, 103
  dichotomy of, 155–6
  dispossession, 121
  hegemony, 71–2
  heterodox economics, 119
  institutions, 206
  Petty, William, 87–8
  universities, 196–7, 206
  see also decolonization
color line, the, 155–6
commodification, 183, 198